Home Fix-It 101

Home Fix-It 101

The Anyone-Can-Do-It Guide to Home Repair

Al Carrell and Kelly Carrell

TAYLOR TRADE PUBLISHING
Lanham • New York • Oxford

This Taylor Trade Publishing paperback edition of *Home Fix It 101* is an original publication. It is published by arrangement with the authors.

Published by Taylor Trade Publishing
An imprint of the Rowman & Littlefield Publishing Group
4501 Forbes Boulevard, Suite 200
Lanham, Maryland 20706

Distributed by National Book Network

Library of Congress Cataloging-in-Publication Data

Carrell, Al.
    Home fix-it 101 : the anyone-can-do-it guide to home repair / Al Carrell and Kelly Carrell.
        p. cm.
    ISBN 0-87833-310-X (pbk. : alk. paper)
    1. Dwellings—Maintenance and repair—Amateurs' manuals. I. Carrell, Kelly. II. Title.
    TH4817.3 .C3627 2003
    643'.7—dc21   2003005016

∞™ The paper used in this publication meets the minimum requirements of
American National Standard for Information Sciences—Permanence of
Paper for Printed Library Materials, ANSI/NISO Z39.48–1992.
Manufactured in the United States of America.

Contents

Contents

Introduction

A Course to Help You Earn a Degree in D-I-Y

The aim of this co-ed book is to take the all-thumbs freshman, teach him or her the basics, and then lead them into more advanced chores.

Each project will have easy to understand step-by-step instructions, including a list of tools and materials needed. Illustrations will help make things go even easier.

The skill level required is beginner or freshman, unless otherwise indicated.

Throughout the book, there will be "Teacher's Tips," helpful hints to make the job go smoother.

Like any class, we'll assign homework. This will be in the form of inspections to make from time to time.

If you have questions, but are afraid to raise your hand in class, feel free to contact us at our web site, www.thesuperhandyman.com. It's a fun place to visit and has lots of good information.

As you will see from the table of contents, we've covered just about every facet of your home that can give you cause for trouble. As you use your newfound knowledge, you'll not only be saving money but you'll also gain a new feeling of self-reliance, knowing that when something goes wrong, you can do it yourself!

Enjoy!

Maintenance 101

1

THE EASIEST FIX-IT PROJECT IS ONE THAT DOESN'T HAVE TO BE DONE!

We know what you're thinking: *How can there be a fix-it project that doesn't have to be done?* The lesson for today is "Maintenance." Properly maintaining the various parts of you home will nearly always extend the life of all those components, as well as make your life a lot easier.

Also, taking care of the small things in time will probably prevent them from becoming big disasters in the not-so-distant future.

MAINTENANCE BY THE CALENDAR

The seasoned homeowner knows that as the season changes, certain things should be done. This chapter gives a rundown on steps to take. In fact, it will be a good idea to have an actual calendar in front of you as you read the text for this lesson. Jot down on that calendar the maintenance steps that apply to your home. When it is time for graduation, you'll have your work for the next year already scheduled.

Let's get busy!

SPRING BREAK

Your freshman year of home maintenance could be full of repairs to damage done by Jack Frost. By doing the right things throughout the school year, you will probably be able to do away with many of these steps in future years. Here's your homework:

1. Take a caulking tour around your house to find any failed caulking. (See page 164.)
2. Examine concrete items such as walks, drives, and patios to see if Jack Frost has caused damage. (See page 203.)
3. Get your lawn and garden tools ready to attack the landscape.
4. Consult your local nursery expert for advice on feeding and irrigating your lawn and garden.
5. Get or perform a preseason check up on your air conditioning system. (See chapter 17.)
6. If the cold weather is gone, clean out the fireplace. Move firewood away from the house.
7. Remove covers from crawl space vents.
8. It may be a good time to paint the exterior of the house. Just be sure when you paint that there's not a rainstorm around the corner.
9. Speaking of rain, go outside during the next April shower and check around the perimeter of your home looking for places where water puddles up. (See chapter 7.)
10. Make certain your gutters are not leaking and that there is no blockage to dam up the flow. Any standing water becomes a breeding ground for mosquitoes.

SUMMER SCHOOL

Here are a few hot maintenance ideas for the good old summertime to help your home play it cool:

1. Turn off pilot lights for furnaces.
2. Check the outside air conditioning compressor/condenser unit to be sure nothing blocks the flow of air across the fins. Look for vines, grass clippings, pet hair, or weeds. Also, bent fins on the outside unit should be combed to straighten them out. More on this in chapter 17.
3. Get the outdoor grill ready for heating the hot dogs and burning the burgers!
4. Each month during the cooling season clean, or replace the air conditioning filter.
5. Check for sweating pipes in the basement or crawl space.

> **BE A TEACHER'S PET!**
>
> You can get extra credit for interior painting, and summertime is good for this because you can open windows. Painting is not only good maintenance to keep your home more livable but also can make it more loveable. (See chapter 15.)

AUTUMN

Part of the fall lineup is getting ready for winter, but before we get into that, here's your schedule for the fall semester:

1. Check the roof for loose shingles, leaks, and flashing woes.
2. YEAH TEAM! While you're up there, be sure the TV antenna is o.k. so you can catch all thirty-seven football games each weekend.
3. When you rake up all those autumn leaves, consider starting a compost heap.
4. Inspect the mortar joints in the fireplace.
5. Take a look at all doors and windows for any flaws in weather stripping and caulking.
6. Before heating season, give or have a pro perform an annual checkup to ensure safety and efficiency. Is the ductwork in the attic or basement completely sealed? If not, you can be losing big bucks!
7. Properly clean and store your lawn and garden tools, with particular attention to the mower and other power tools.
8. If any outdoor light bulbs are burned out, change them now before it's too cold.

> **TEACHER'S TRICK**
>
> If you don't like heights, use your binoculars to check the roof!

> **TEACHER'S TIP**
>
> Why not put new bulbs in all outdoor sockets? Sure beats doing it on the coldest day of the year.

WINTER

Here are steps that will make you and your family feel warm all over:

1. Protect all outside hydrants against freezing. See "Freeze Protection" in chapter 4.
2. Bring in houseplants that might die from frostbite.
3. Clean the heating system's thermostat. (See page 145.)
4. Make sure the home has ample humidity so furniture doesn't dry out and crack. Proper humidity also makes us humans feel warmer.

> **A BIOLOGY LESSON**
>
> Often when plants are brought inside, there'll be a lizard or a bug hidden in the pot. This is a surprise you may not want, so look for the pests before you move 'em in.

NOT SEASONAL BUT VITAL

Here are some things you should do every year:

1. Trip each circuit breaker switch manually and then push it back to the "ON" position. (See page 35 for details.)
2. Replace the batteries in your smoke alarm twice a year. The same day we change our clocks for daylight savings time makes it easier to remember.
3. Run a gallon of vinegar through the short wash cycle of your automatic dishwasher. This rids the appliance of minerals from water.
4. The same goes for the clothes washer.
5. Drain the water heater tank. (See page 122.) Once a year is about right for most homes, but if you have very hard water it may require draining more often.

NOW, IF YOU CAN ONLY REMEMBER WHERE YOU KEEP THE CALENDAR!

Tools 101

TOOL ADAGES FROM THE OLD SCHOOL!

"A workman is only as good as his tools!"

"A novice with the right tool can achieve success while a pro with the wrong tool may fail."

Our basic list of tools is not very long. It is intended to let you be prepared for the everyday disasters that can happen around the house . . . and usually do. These "supplies" that you buy for the freshman year can last through graduation and beyond, IF you buy quality tools and IF you take proper care of them. Quality tools also perform better. Often the price difference between a good tool and a cheapie is only a matter of pennies. We've known of some tools from the bargain bin to not even last through the first project.

THE BASIC LIST

HAMMER—Our choice for an all-around hammer for home use is a 16-oz. curved-claw nail hammer. But we recommend you take a few practice swings to find the weight best for you. Avoid getting a hammer that's too small, or you may not ever be able to drive a nail.

You also have a choice of handles. A wooden handle absorbs shock but can be broken. Steel and fiberglass are both almost damage-proof and have shock absorbing grips of rubber or plastic, so they might be a better choice.

SCREWDRIVERS—You should buy sets of both slotted and Phillips screwdrivers to handle the two most popular types of screws. If you don't use the right type or the right size, you'll probably botch up the screw head, and maybe the whole job.

> **WARNING**
>
> The screwdriver is not an ice pick, pry bar, chisel, or punch. Use it only to drive or remove screws . . . and maybe to pick your teeth.

PLIERS—This gripping tool has many uses. It can tighten or loosen bolts, but not as well as a proper wrench. Many can cut wire, but not as well as a wire cutter. Get a medium size slip-joint pliers. Even though this is a single tool, it's called a "pair of pliers." Go figure!

ADJUSTABLE WRENCH—The adjustable open-end wrench takes the place of a lot of different sized wrenches.

STAPLER—This single tool takes care of lots of tacking and hammering chores. Get a stapler that will handle several sizes of staples. One new model drives both staples and brads.

SAW—Our recommendation for someone who'll have only one handsaw is to go for a 26-inch crosscut saw. Most sawing is across the grain, but this type of saw will also "rip," which is cutting with the grain. There are several short crosscut saws that are easier for the freshman to handle and do a great job. At some point, you may want to cut metal. Buy a hacksaw at that time.

PLUMBER'S FRIEND—This plunger, or force cup, is a must for every household. Many old toilets and drains get clogged. Some new toilets don't flush well. This tool can save you big bucks.

UTILITY KNIFE—Get a utility knife that stores extra replaceable blades in a compartment in the handle of the tool. It is also safer to get one that retracts the blade when not in use.

LEVEL—Even a cheap level will help level appliances and aid in installing shelves.

MEASURING DEVICE—Even a yardstick will help. But we suggest you get the type that is retractable and has a clip to wear on your belt. It makes you look more like an upper classman.

TOOLBOX—It's a good idea to keep all of your hand tools together, and a toolbox makes them handy. A large bucket will also work as long as it has a handle. Later on, when you spring for the real thing, the bucket will have lots of other uses.

SOME THINGS OTHER THAN ACTUAL TOOLS YOU'LL WANT TO HAVE

GLUE—Get a tube of all-purpose glue and a bottle of white glue.

SANDPAPER—A small assortment pack will do.

TAPE—The ever-popular duct tape is a must. It wouldn't hurt to add a roll each of masking tape and electrician's tape.

LUBRICANTS—A small can of machine oil and a spray lube will silence most household squeaks.

DOO-DADS—Get an assortment pack each of screws, nuts and bolts, and nails. It may include the exact fastener you need . . . but probably not.

FLASHLIGHT—Bad things happen at night and often in unlit places like the basement or attic. Have a special flashlight dedicated to the toolbox. Otherwise, when you need it, it will be in the car or in a drawer.

HOW ABOUT POWER TO THE PEOPLE?

Yes, I know we didn't mention any power tools. For the basic list, you can get by without a power tool. However, the first one to buy would be a power drill. This is not a big-ticket item, and we suggest you get a 3/8" model that has variable speeds and is reversible. Also get an assortment set of drill bits.

DID WE FORGET PAINTING TOOLS?

No, but we suggest you wait until you are actually ready to paint. No sense in having extra stuff around to trip over for no telling how long. Right?

TOOL CARE

In grade school we learned about the three "R's." In tool care we learn about the three "M's." Moisture, Mysterious disappearance, and Marring.

Moisture causes rust, so you should store your tools in a dry place, protected from the elements. If you have high humidity in your shop, garage, or wherever you keep the tools, they'll eventually start to rust. Dehumidifiers, either electric or chemical can lower the moisture content in the air. A light coat of oil will protect a seldom-used tool. Get additional protection by wrapping the tools in foil or Saran wrap. A desiccant can control humidity within a tool chest.

Mysterious disappearance happens because we loan tools to neighbors who forget to return them. Sometimes we leave a tool out and it walks off. Paint tools a bright color, and they will be easier to spot.

However, the most common reason for disappearance is that tools are often stolen. Keep all your tools in a securely locked area. Use an electric etching tool to put your name and driver's license number or other ID on each tool.

Marring can occur in storage when points, teeth, or cutting edges are not protected. Storing lots of tools together in a drawer can result in damage. Usually, hanging tools from shop or garage walls is the best way to prevent their damaging each other.

Eventually, you'll need to expand into your very own workshop. You'll find some good ideas on this topic in chapter 21, as well as some safety advice on using the tools in a safe manner. It's more fun that way!

TOOL RENTAL

In many cases, it makes sense to rent tools that maybe you can't afford to buy or may only use once. Scaffolding is one such situation—storing scaffolding often presents a challenge. If your project is a major carpentry effort, rather than wear out your arm, head for a tool rental place for a nailer or other heavy-duty *weapons of mass construction!*

THE SUPER SAGE SAYS, "A tool and his project are soon started!"

Home Emergencies 101

3

Mother Nature sometimes comes calling with a chip on her shoulder. Floods, hurricanes, tornadoes, high winds, earthquakes, blizzards, lightning, and ice storms can all happen.

But these natural disasters aren't the only emergencies we might face. The burst water supply hose for the washing machine can cause just as much damage as when the creek overflows. The fire from an electrical short burns just as hot as a direct strike from a bolt of lightning. Home emergencies can happen at any moment, often when you least expect them.

So our aim in this course will not be about tracking hurricanes, boarding up windows, or sand bagging the river. Folks who live where these acts of nature happen usually know about all the preparations needed to fight back.

We'll concentrate mostly on home happenings and how to act fast to stop the cause of the emergency. Then we'll look at how to minimize the damage.

There are a few things you can do in advance to fight these problems:

1. Locate the shut-off valves for the water supply, the natural gas, and the breaker or fuse box for electricity. Once you've found them, be sure you know how to operate them and that they are actually operable. Then make sure all responsible family members know what you know. If you need a wrench to turn the valves, put one in a plastic baggie and keep it at the site of the valve.

2. Keep in mind that there are shut-off valves for the water supply under each sink and toilet and usually for each outside hydrant.

3. Make a list of emergency phone numbers that not only has police, fire department, and medical help, but also includes tradesman and other repair people. Don't forget your insurance agent.
4. Have proper fire extinguishers in working order and in the areas where a fire might start. Inspect these regularly.
5. Install smoke alarms in all the right places and test them every month.
6. Establish an escape plan in case of fire and have a fire drill so everyone knows where to go. If yours is a two-story house, provide safety ladders that hang out from a windowsill on the top floor.

The main villains in home emergencies are flooding, fire, natural gas leaks, and blackouts. Here's our game plan:

FLOODING

1. Stop the source of water. If it's from a burst hose or a sink riser, use the individual shut-off valve. If the water is from inside a wall, use the main shut-off. If it's from an act of nature, try to plug up entryways, like under doors or around windows. If it's a roof leak, see if you can plug the hole from within the attic.
2. Remember that water and electricity don't mix. Don't go into a flooded basement if the breaker box is down there. Call the electric power company.
3. Move furniture and rugs to higher ground, if possible.
4. Use a floor squeegee, sponges, a wet/dry vacuum, or whatever is available to remove the water as quickly as possible.
5. Dry out the wet areas using fans and open windows.

> **REMEMBER**
> Almost everything in your home can be replaced. People cannot! THE LESSON: Don't try to save any treasures until you and all the family are safe.

FIRES

1. Obviously, the first act is to get everyone out of the house at the first sign of smoke or fire. Have a designated spot for the family to gather. This way, nobody goes back into a burning building to save someone who escaped on the other side of the house.
2. Don't stop to phone 911 if there's the least doubt you can do so safely. Get out and then use a neighbor's phone.
3. The most common kitchen fire is a grease fire. If the fire is in a skillet, turn off the heat and put the lid on, and the fire will go out from lack of oxygen. Never

pour water on a grease or oil fire, as this may cause spreading. Never try to carry a burning skillet outside. It's liable to either splatter on you or ignite something else.

4. An oven fire will usually burn itself out if you cut off the heat and keep the door closed.

5. Grass fires or trash burning that gets out of control can usually be best handled with water from a garden hose.

6. If your clothing is on fire, don't panic and run. Lie down and roll over and over to put out the fire. Better still, wrap your body in a blanket while rolling.

GAS LEAK

At the first whiff of natural gas:

1. Get everyone out of the house. DO NOT hesitate for even a second.

2. DO NOT flip on any electrical switch. It might cause a spark that could cause an explosion.

3. DO NOT use your phone. It could cause the same spark problem. Make the call from a cellular phone outside or from a neighbor's phone.

4. Once all are out, if the meter is outside, you can turn the gas off. Most meters have a rectangular valve handle. When moved a quarter turn, so that it's perpendicular to the pipe, the gas is off.

5. DO NOT turn the gas back on until the leak has been taken care of and the house is completely aired out.

BLACKOUTS

Usually, a power outage is just an inconvenience. But stumbling and groping around in a pitch-black house can be dangerous.

The first thing to do is determine whether it's "us or them." Is the blackout just in your home or throughout the neighborhood? If you look out and see bright lights shining from the neighbors' homes, the problem is most likely just your house.

Q: You suggested having fire extinguishers, but ignored fighting the fire. What gives?

A: Certainly you should try to put the fire out. BUT ONLY if you are sure you can still get out if your efforts fail. A rapidly spreading fire can suddenly trap you.

Q: Are all fire extinguishers created equal?

A: No. There are three basic classes of fires: Class A has burning solids like wood or paper, Class B has burning liquids like grease or oil, and Class C fires burn from live electrical circuits. Get an extinguisher classed for the fire likely to be at hand. There are also units classified as ABC, which means they fight all types of fires.

No matter what the cause, you'll be a lot better off if you put together a small blackout kit. Include a few candles, matches, a flashlight, and a battery powered radio. Also, have additional flashlights stashed around your home in strategic places. . . like next to the electric entry box, and at the top and bottom of stairways.

If you establish that the blackout involves more than just your home, report the problem to the utility company. Next, remember what appliances and lights were on when the blackout occurred and turn them all off, except for a light that would let you know when power has been restored. The battery powered radio will keep you company but also may have information regarding the outage.

If the problem is just in your house, you most likely have a blown fuse or tripped circuit breaker switch. Usually the problem will affect only a single circuit. Inspect the entry box, and you should spot the fuse that is blown or the tripped breaker. With a blown plug-type fuse, the glass will be blackened or the metal element will have developed a gap. A tripped breaker will actually cause the switch to flip over to the "off" position. Before restoring power, turn off all the gadgets and lights that were on. Otherwise, if a circuit is overloaded it may go out again.

"Now, class, what is the missing piece of the puzzle here? Let's see a show of hands. If you wondered how the replacement fuse suddenly appeared, that's the mystery! Those students who have a system that uses fuses will have thought ahead and have a back-up supply for all the different sizes."

REMEMBER
Always Play It Safe When Dealing with Electricity.
See page 35 for Safety at the Entry Box!

Plumbing 101

4

A survey of homeowners shows that among the most feared and hated of all systems in a house is the plumbing. We've always felt this was because so much of the stuff involved is hidden behind walls, under counters, buried underground, and sometimes even encased in concrete. Therefore, plumbing is often deemed as being very mysterious.

Also, solving a plumbing problem is perceived to be rather messy. Let's face it, Class . . . it can turn really yucky!

Our lesson today is hopefully going to help remove most of the mystery and much of the mess.

To make a long story short—actually, plumbing is pretty simple. There are just two components: incoming and outgoing. "Incoming" is the water supply that provides water for drinking, cooking, bathing, water balloon fights, clothes washing, and other daily activities. "Outgoing" is the drain system. Never the twain shall meet.

INCOMING

THE DRIPPING FAUCET

One tiny drip every few seconds may seem insignificant, but in a year's time it can waste thousands of gallons of water, a precious commodity. To many of us, money is also a precious commodity and these thousands of gallons of water wasted means you're pouring a couple of hundred bucks down the drain every year.

The most common reason for the drip is a failed part inside. This problem part is usually a washer or an O-ring. The skill level for this repair is "Freshman." The cost for repair parts runs from less than a dollar to a few bucks, depending on the type of faucet.

First, let's talk about the faucet that drips from the spout. Here's what you do:

> **TEACHER'S TIP**
>
> When using a wrench or pliers on chrome, pad the metal with a rag or tape to avoid bite marks from the tools.

1. Turn off the water supply, usually with stop valves under the sink (figure 4-1). If there are two separate faucets and only one is leaking, just shut off the valve on the leaking side. If you don't have shut off valves under the sink, go to the main shut off as detailed in Emergencies on page 9.
2. Remove the handle. Often the handle will be held in place by a hidden screw. This may be under a decorative plate (figure 4-2) that can be pried off with a tiny screwdriver. Sometimes the handle will be attached by a small setscrew on the back (figure 4-3). Under the handle, there will be a nut from which the stem sticks out. Turn this nut counterclockwise.
3. With the nut removed, you may need to replace the handle temporarily to back the stem out.
4. At the bottom of the stem will be the washer, usually held on by a brass screw (figure 4-4). Some washers resemble a tiny diaphragm and others have prongs that snap into place in the screw hole. Take the old part in to the retailer for an exact replacement.

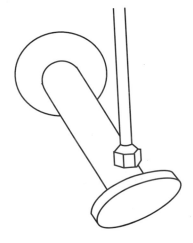

figure 4-1

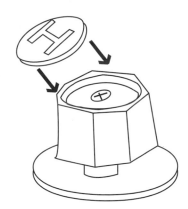

figure 4-2

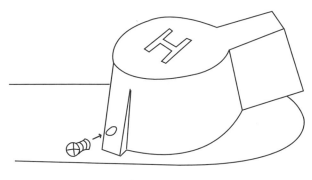

figure 4-3

figure 4-4

5. Now put everything back in place, restore the water supply, and you should have solved the drip problem.

Sometimes after performing this chore you start to pat yourself on the back, then you see that the faucet still drips. This is usually because of a botched up seat. Shut off the water supply and remove the stem again. Look down into the body of the faucet. You should see a brass collar with a hole in it. This is called a "seat." The hole is usually hexagonal, but can be square. If the brass is badly scarred, the washer can't compress and seal itself against the collar; thus, the drip is still with us.

There are two ways to solve this problem. One is to replace the seat. You'll need a very inexpensive tool called a seat wrench (figure 4-5). This makes removal and replacement a piece of cake. You just poke the tool into the hole until it engages and then turn counterclockwise. The second way is to grind the seat off so it's smooth again. This is done with a seat-dressing tool (figure 4-6), also inexpensive.

figure 4-5

What about the newer single handled faucets? This repair is also very simple:

1. Shut off both hot and cold water supply valves.
2. Remove the handle, usually held on by a setscrew on the back.
3. Unscrew the cap under the handle.

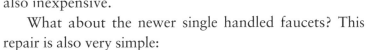

figure 4-6

4. Now you should be able to lift out the cartridge or whatever type mechanism operates the faucet. Since there are so many different types, I hope you saved the owner's manual.

5. If you know the make and model of the faucet, you can get a repair kit with all the replaceable parts, along with really good instructions on replacement. To be sure you get the right kit, take the mechanism into the parts place.

THE DRIPPING FAUCET HANDLE

The faucet oozes water out from under the handle when the water is running. You can solve this easily:

1. Take a wrench to the packing nut under the handle and make sure it's tight.
2. Remember, right is tight, so turn right or clockwise. If that's not the problem, it's the packing. Packing is located under the packing nut (figure 4-7).
3. Shut off both hot and cold water supply.
4. Remove the packing nut using a wrench and turning counterclockwise.

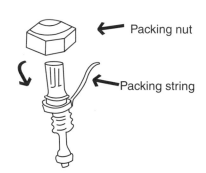

Packing nut

Packing string

figure 4-7

5. Remove and replace packing, which may be a solid piece (figure 4-8), an O-ring, or self-forming, a string of packing that resembles burned spaghetti. This stuff is tightly wrapped around the stem under the nut (see figure 4-7).

THE AERATOR

Sink and basin faucets usually have a small device on the end of the spout called an aerator. Inside are perforated discs and screens that mix air with the water to lessen the force of the water and reduce splashing. Any time that you have shut off the water supply to work on the faucet, you should clean the

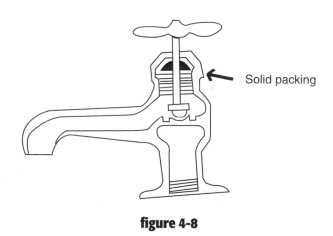

Solid packing

figure 4-8

aerator. Restoring the water supply often will send minute particles through the pipes to be caught by the aerator.

If you notice a drop in water pressure at only one faucet, cleaning the aerator at that faucet may solve the problem. Here's how:

Step 1. Unscrew the aerator by turning it counterclockwise.

Step 2. Keep track of the sequence of all the little parts.

Step 3. Tap the parts sharply against a hard surface to loosen the particles. Then use a brush or wire to remove stubborn crud. Soaking the parts in hot vinegar will dissolve mineral deposits.

> **TEACHER'S TIP**
>
> Before using pliers on the aerator, wrap a wide rubber band tightly around it. This could give you enough of a grip for hand removal.

SHOWER AND TUB DRIPS

The same principle, but often the handles come out from the wall and tiles were added after the plumbing was put in place. This prevents an ordinary wrench from getting in to remove the nut. A deep-set socket wrench (figure 4-9) of the proper size will work.

Deep set socket wrench

figure 4-9

THE MARATHON TOILET (Continuously Running)

The sound of a babbling brook is soothing and very pleasant. That same sound, from a running toilet, however, can drive you bonkers.

The toilet that won't shut off wastes a lot more water than a dripping faucet. Before we talk about solving the problem, it would be good for you to know how a toilet works. Look at the tank diagram (figure 4-10) as we carry you through a flush cycle.

1. Push the handle down.
2. That action raises the trip lever.

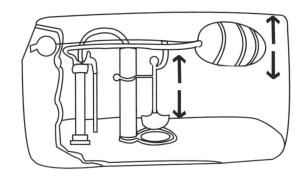

figure 4-10

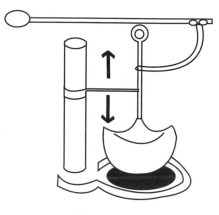

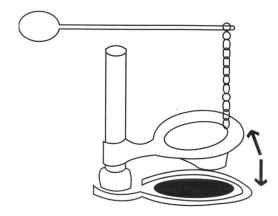

figure 4-11   **figure 4-12**

3. This pulls up the lift wires or chain.

4. Which in turn raises the tank ball (figure 4-11), or flapper (figure 4-12), opening the drain hole in the bottom of the tank.

5. The water rushes into the bowl to flush.

6. With the water in the tank gone, the float ball no longer floats and as it drops, it opens the water valve (its plumbing name, and we're not making this up, is ballcock assembly), back over on the left side of the tank.

7. Fresh water refills the tank and buoys the float ball upward until it shuts the valve off at the proper level.

Just knowing how the thing works will make it easier to solve all toilet troubles. So let's stop the constantly running toilet. Here's how:

1. Remove the tank lid and carefully place it flat on the floor and out of the way.

2. If the water is going out the overflow tube, lift up on the float arm. If the running water stops, it means the water level is too high. This means the ball is positioned wrong.

3. Using both hands, gently bend down the float arm until the water level is shut off before it gets higher than the overflow tube.

If this cure doesn't work, the problem could be in the water inlet valve. Not quite so easy, but not too bad. Probably in the Sophomore skill level. Here we go:

> **FACT**
>
> I know what you're thinking ...that was too easy! But it is the most common cause for the running toilet!

1. Turn off the water supply to the tank, using the shut off valve under the tank.
2. Look at figure 4-13, a typical metal water inlet valve. Remove the two thumbscrews.
3. This allows you to remove the flat rod going through the slot. Lift up on the slot that is at the top of the valve plunger unit. Check the washer and/or O-rings and replace any that are bad.

> **Q:** "What if the water isn't going out over the over-flow tube?"
> **A:** That was next up in my lesson plan.

You can still have a running toilet if water is seeping out around the tank ball or flapper. Here are the reasons this can happen:

1. The tank ball, or flapper, which acts as a stopper to close the drain hole in the bottom of the tank, may not be dropping straight into the hole.
2. If you have a tank ball:
   A. The lift wires travel through a guide (figure 4-15). The guide could have moved out of alignment. Move the guide back into alignment.
   B. A burr or mineral deposits could prevent the tank ball from dropping all the way down. Steel wool can remove a burr. Put the wires in hot vinegar to dissolve mineral deposits.
3. If you have a flapper:
   A. The chain may not have enough slack to allow the flapper to drop all the way down. Adjust the chain to make it longer or move the chain to another hole in the float arm.

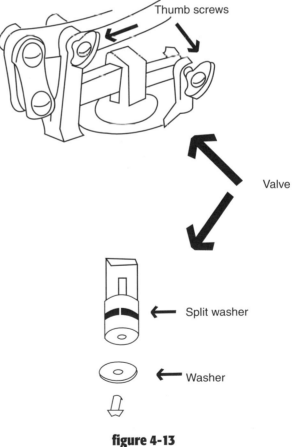

Thumb screws

Valve

Split washer

Washer

figure 4-13

B. The flapper may need to be realigned. Some are held in place by a ring around the overflow tube and can be turned by hand.

4. With either type:

A. Old age may have set in and these stoppers are disintegrating. Replacement of either the flapper or the tank ball is easy and inexpensive.

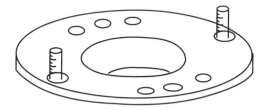

figure 4-14

B. The drain hole may have a build up of lime and scale, so the stopper is not to blame. To remove these deposits, turn off the water supply and use wet/dry sandpaper to smooth the lip of the opening. If you can't get it smooth enough, buy a Flusher Fixer Kit which includes a metal ring that is glued in place over the drain hole with waterproof adhesive. A flapper is attached to the ring. This is an easy and inexpensive solution.

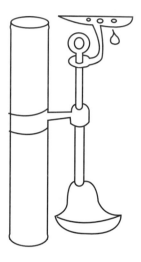

THE TOILET LEAKS AROUND THE BASE
(Skill Level: "Senior")

figure 4-15

This problem should be taken care of immediately. Not only will the water damage the floor, in some cases rotting it out completely, it can also ruin the floor covering. But the worst thing is that this could allow sewer gas to come into your home.

In most cases, the culprit is the wax or putty seal that seats the toilet to the flange. To replace the faulty seal, you must take up the toilet. The idea of doing this strikes terror in the hearts of many. Actually, it's not that big a deal. Here are the steps:

> **TEACHER'S TIP**
>
> Pouring a bucket of water into the bowl will cause the toilet to flush. Since the tank is empty, no new water comes into the bowl so you don't have much left to bail out.

1. Shut off the water supply.

2. Flush to empty the tank and then bail out the water in the bowl.

3. Disconnect the water supply tube.

4. Most toilets today are one piece, but if yours has a separate tank attached to the wall, you can remove the bolts holding the tank to the wall.

5. The bowl is attached to the flange at the floor by a pair of bolts, each of which are hidden by a cap (figure 4-16). These caps usually just pry up but some are screwed in place.

6. With the caps gone, remove the nuts and washers and the toilet can be lifted straight up.

7. Scrape away all remains of the putty seal or wax ring.

8. Our preference is to use a wax ring for replacement because it's much less messy than plumber's putty.

9. We prefer to turn the toilet upside down and install the wax ring (figure 4-17).

10. Carefully turn the bowl right side up and place it onto the threaded studs sticking up from the flange. When it's in place, twist the bowl slightly while pushing down to seal the wax ring.

11. Employ a level to be sure the bowl is level, using shims if needed.

12. In reinstalling the nuts, DO NOT OVER TIGHTEN! The porcelain has been known to crack.

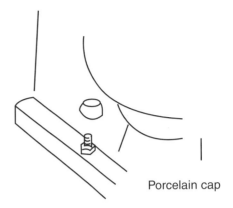

Porcelain cap

figure 4-16

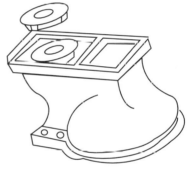

figure 4-17

OTHER TOILET TROUBLES

THE PHANTOM FLUSH

Sometimes the toilet will flush without anyone having flushed it. This usually happens when your toilet has a FluidMaster brand refill valve. This unit replaces water in the tank with the flow running full tilt, so it's easily heard. What has happened in most cases is the water in the tank is seeping out around the flapper, and when the level gets down to a certain level, the valve replaces the missing water. Check back on page 17 for solving this problem.

THE SINGING OR GROANING TOILET

This happens with a conventional valve toilet and occurs as the toilet is almost refilled after a flush. It's a sign the valve has some sort of restriction. Shut off the water supply under the tank and check for a damaged washer or O-ring. Also look for mineral deposits and remove any you see.

Now that you know how to remove and reinstall a toilet, putting a new toilet in place is not that different. Before buying the new unit, measure from the center of the closet flange to the wall, not to the baseboard. Toilets are "forever" so get a good one, even if it costs a little extra.

REPLACING A TOILET SEAT

Nowadays, the toilet seat is a decorator item. They come in a variety of colors. They are even available in your old school colors with a picture of the mascot on the lid. Some are padded. Some are heated. Just remove the two bolts holding the old seat on and put the new one in its place.

Sound easy? It is, except often the nuts holding the old one in place are stubborn to remove. Try penetrating oil. Sometimes you must use a hacksaw to remove the bolts. You'll be sawing through the bolt just above the surface of the bowl. Smear petroleum jelly on the saw blade and place a strip of tape on the bowl to protect it. Take your time and you'll get the old one off without a scratch.

PIPE LEAKS

We've already talked about emergency pipe leaks and the quick action that should be taken. Now let's talk about how to patch, repair, or replace various types of water supply lines. In all cases, it is best to shut off the water supply.

If you're fortunate enough to have access to the pipes in a crawl space or basement, you can easily turn the disaster into another triumph.

A MUST FOR SUCCESS

Get the correct size sleeve for the diameter of the pipe involved.

Different Pipe Materials Use Different Leak Repair Methods

1. Galvanized iron pipe—A device called a pipe sleeve clamp (figure 4-18) works well to stop a leak. The gadget involves a rubber patch and two sleeve parts held together by nuts and bolts. When properly tightened, the pressure against the pad stops the leak. This method can also be used on copper pipe.

2. MAKE YOUR OWN PATCH—Use a worm gear hose clamp to apply pressure to a section of old auto inner tube as shown in figure 4-19.

3. Epoxy glue may be a temporary patch that can last forever! There is a plumber's epoxy putty that you mix by kneading between your hands. It works best if all the pipe surfaces are dry and when the adhesive is given adequate time to set up.

4. Copper pipe—If a copper pipe joint has come loose, copper can be resoldered. See how to sweat solder copper starting on page 24.

5. Threaded pipe is usually made of galvanized steel. The best patch may be to remove the damaged area, using a hacksaw and wrench. Then replace the section with two shorter threaded pipes plus a device called a "union," as shown in figure 4-20. The total combined length of the replacement, including the union, should be the same as the old pipe. So, do the math!

Installing the union requires using two wrenches. One tightens the ring nut while the other holds the exposed union nut. (If this sounds strange, you'll easily understand it once you have the union in hand.)

PVC plastic pipe isn't acceptable for potable water in a few local plumbing codes. Where it is OK, it's great. PVC can handle cold water and CPVC can be used for hot and cold. It is lightweight, inexpensive, and easy to use. It is easily cut with a hacksaw but there are PVC pipe cutters that are better. Burrs are easily removed with a pocketknife. Joining the pipe with fittings is done with a solvent and

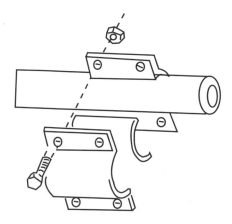

Pipe sleeve

figure 4-18

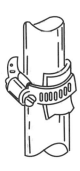

figure 4-19

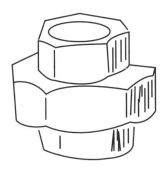

Union fitting

figure 4-20

adhesive that are brushed on (the brush is usually included with the lid of these two products).

Plastic pipe can be joined to any other type of pipe because there are transition fittings.

Most homeowner's policies cover the leaking problem, including repairs. However, don't let them come in and tear into your foundation. A better repair is to install new pipe in tunnels under the slab. If this is acceptable under the code, pressure your insurance company to do it this way. They will resist because it's more costly than the old jackhammer way—but the jackhammer method can damage the slab, and that could mean bigger problems!

> **Q:** What about a leak under a slab? Wouldn't that require a jackhammer?
> **A:** That's a bummer but maybe not as bad as it sounds.

THE PIPES, THE PIPES, THEY ARE A CALLING

If you get very deeply into plumbing repair, you may get involved with pipes. The materials used include copper, plastic, galvanized steel, and cast iron. The type you have in your home is probably governed by what your local plumbing codes find acceptable, so we won't cover all pipes known to man.

COPPER—One that is most prominent in water supply lines is copper, which comes in two varieties: rigid and flexible tubing. Our favorite way to join rigid copper pipe to the many fittings is a process called "sweat soldering." The tools and materials you need include copper pipe, fittings of the same diameter, paste flux, a roll of solid core wire solder, emery cloth, and a propane torch. All of these things are available at your hardware store or home center. Here are the basic steps:

> **CAUTION**
> Don't just read this and then tackle an actual plumbing job. Get the tools and materials and practice, practice, practice before you use the process for real! Then you're ready for the real thing!

1. A straight cut at the end of copper pipe gets the best fit. A tube cutter (figure 4-21.) gives the best results. A hacksaw would be our second choice.

Tube cutter

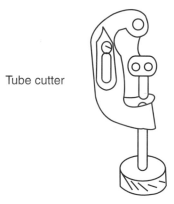

figure 4-21

2. After cutting, remove any burrs. Most tube cutters have a pointed blade that deburrs the cut.

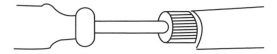

Wire brush cleans
inside copper pipe

figure 4-22

The surfaces of both the pipe and fitting must be shiny clean. A strip of emery cloth works well for outside. A special wire brush (figure 4-22) is best for inside a fitting, but you can wrap the emery cloth around a finger. After polishing, don't touch the surfaces.

3. Coat these surfaces with a paste type flux.
4. Make sure the parts fit.
5. Now comes the fun part. Light your propane torch. Play the flame over the fitting but don't bring the solder into the act until the metal is hot. Then you still don't play the flame on the solder but when you touch the tip of the solder against the joint, the solder will melt and be sucked into the joint by capillary action. This happens even if the joint is positioned so the solder would have to travel upward. It is almost like magic!

THAT'S IT! SWEAT SOLDERING IS NO SWEAT!

TEACHER'S TIP

In an actual plumbing situation, you may still have water in the pipes. This moisture can turn to steam and make for a weak joint. Roll a piece of bread into a tight blob that you can push into the pipe. This acts as a dam and keeps the water away from your work. Then when the work is complete and the water supply is restored, the water will dissolve the bread and the particles will come out at the nearest faucet.

FREEZE PROTECTION

As we all know, water freezes when the temperature goes down to 32° F. There are those that say, "So what! It will eventually melt." Au contraire. Frozen pipes often lead to burst pipes that can lead to floods, which lead to thousands of dollars in damage to other parts of your home.

Here are some ways to prevent freezing:

1. Wrap all exposed pipes. Pipe wrap is not all that expensive and is easy to apply if pipes are accessible. If there's a sudden freeze and no wrap is available, wrap several layers of newspaper around the pipes and secure with duct tape.
2. Running water is slower to freeze, so turn on faucets to a slight drip.
3. If the kitchen is on a north wall and you're not sure of the protection to the pipes, open the cabinet under the sink to allow heat from the room in to help prevent freezing. You can also add a 100-watt bulb in a droplight to hang in the cabinet.
4. Remove all hoses from outside faucets, drain them, and store them inside.
5. Outside faucets should have a shut off valve. If not, or if it's not operable, wrap the faucet with several sections of newspaper, held in place by rubber bands. Cover this with a plastic grocery bag to keep the papers from getting wet.
6. Place a bucket or small garbage can upside down over the faucet. The dead air trapped inside is added protection.
7. If you have outside faucets that come out from the wall, buy special dome-shaped foam units that attach over the faucets.

What if it is too late? If you do have frozen pipes, you can help prevent a bursting pipe with these steps:

1. Open the nearest faucet to prevent a build up of pressure as the ice thaws.
2. Starting at the faucet and working away from it, apply heat to cause melting. Use a heat gun, heat lamp, hand-held hair dryer, heating pad, or electric heat tape.

Unfortunately, a burst pipe won't show up until the ice melts, so be prepared to quickly shut off the water supply at the main cut-off.

NOW LET'S TALK ABOUT OUTGOING-DRAINAGE PROBLEMS

CLOGS

The best time to combat clogs is before they happen. Here are some tips:

1. Minimize the solid garbage you send down the drain.
2. Even with a sink disposer, the tiny ground up food particles can start to build up on the pipe walls and cause problems. Don't grind up stringy foods like celery. Don't put non-food items such as cigarette butts into the disposer.
3. Never pour grease down the drain.

PREVENTIVE MAINTENANCE

1. Here is a kitchen sink drain formula you can mix at home:

   1 cup baking soda
   1 cup table salt
   1/4 cup cream of tartar

   Mix these dry ingredients in a glass jar by shaking well. Use ONLY 1/4 cup directly down the sink drain followed by 2 cups boiling water. After a minute, turn on the faucet to rinse out. Do this once a month and you may never have a kitchen sink clog! Or,

2. Pour 2 cups of white vinegar down the drain once a month. Or,

3. Pour a large pan of boiling water down the sink drain every month. This melts any grease in the lines. Or,

4. Use any of the commercial drain cleaners as suggested on the label for preventive maintenance.

THE PLUMBER'S FRIEND

This inexpensive suction cup is one of the oldest clog busters and still one of the best. It doesn't take a college degree to operate, but many people just give it a couple of quick strokes and if nothing happens, they give it up. Forget about needing a PHD, you just need PAD. That's Patience And Determination. Here's how to get results:

> **TEACHER'S TIP**
>
> Smear a little petroleum jelly around the rim on the bottom cup for a better seal.

1. The suction cup must be large enough to completely cover the drain opening.

2. There must be enough water in the sink to cover the bottom of the cup by about an inch.

3. Cover any other openings, like an overflow in a basin or the other drain in a double sink.

4. Now, with the plunger handle in both hands, start with an up and down motion. Give it 15 or 20 good strokes. Lift the plunger and hopefully the water will go swishing down the drain.

5. If it didn't work, go through the same routine several times. It's a great way to work off your frustrations, plus it's good exercise!

So, unless you know this is *not* where the problem is, let's remove the trap, a U-shaped part

> **REMEMBER**
>
> 57.3% of all kitchen sink clogs are in the trap.

in the drain line under the sink. The best and most effective way to clean the trap is to remove it and poke out the guck. Look at figure 4-23a and you'll see how the trap is attached. In removing it, have a bucket handy underneath because the trap will have water inside. If there is standing water in the sink, bail it out before removing the trap.

If the clog is not in the trap, having it out of the way gives you better, straighter access for taking the next best step, going into the pipe in the wall with an auger.

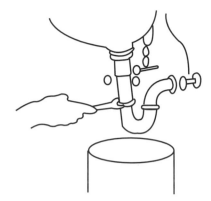

figure 4-23a

THE PLUMBER'S SNAKE
(a.k.a. the plumbing auger)

Many times, using this old stand-by will be the next best step. This flexible auger can wind around through the curves and turns of the drain line.

Using the snake is a sure-fire way to success IF you can get the head of the snake to the clog. As you feed the snake into the drain, keep twisting the handle (see figure 4-23b). This helps the snake to make all the twists and turns in the line.

When you actually reach the clog, it will feel different. Patiently work the snake back and forth to force it through the clog to break it up.

There are other places to introduce the snake into the drain. Usually, there will be a cleanout plug on an outside wall, usually near the kitchen (figure 4-24). A wrench will remove the plug.

After the clog breaks up, it may be a good idea to remove the snake and insert a garden hose into the drain. Then, with the water turned on, the debris will be flushed on down the line.

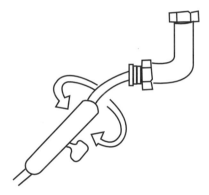

figure 4-23b

TEACHER'S TIP

After the water from the trap is in the bucket, don't get rid of it by pouring it into the sink. Don't laugh. It happens, even to smart people, like teachers!

SLOW RUNNING DRAINS

If water no longer swooshes out, the problem could be a partial clog or it could be a clogged vent stack. These vents are just open pipes that stick through the roof and are

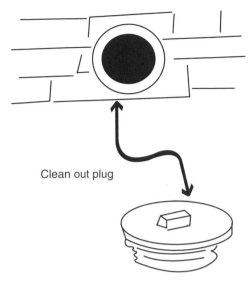

Clean out plug

figure 4-24

> ### A WORD OF CAUTION
>
> If this is a bad clog, water and garbage will be in the drain and when you remove the plug, this debris may spurt out all over you. (Don't you just hate it when that happens?) If you just barely loosen the plug, the water will ooze out until the pressure is relieved and then you can remove the plug.

connected to the various drain lines. If leaves or insect nests or small critters get into the pipe, the drain is slowed. It's just like when you put a soda straw into a coke. If you put your finger over the top of the straw, you can lift the straw out and the liquid will still stay inside until you lift your finger and let air help with the draining. You can poke a plumber's snake down the pipe or even a garden hose to clean out the clog.

A CLOGGED TOILET

Sometimes a toilet is just slow to drain and doesn't perform an adequate flush. This can be because the vent stack, as described above, is partially clogged. A plumber's snake or a garden hose down the stack can correct this problem.

However, if there is an actual clog, try either a closet auger or a plumber's friend. The closet auger is a small snake in a J-shaped housing that extends into the throat of the toilet and extracts or destroys the clogging material (figure 4-25). The best plumber's friend for toilets is one with an extension sleeve as in figure 4-26.

A less professional effort is to straighten a wire coat hanger, except for the hook, and use that to see if you can fish out any blockage. Be careful not to scratch the finish.

SEPTIC TANKS

Septic tanks, a.k.a. on-site sewage treatment systems, have been around for centuries. Simplified, they are an ingenious way of turning sewage into a more acceptable liquid that makes your grass turn green.

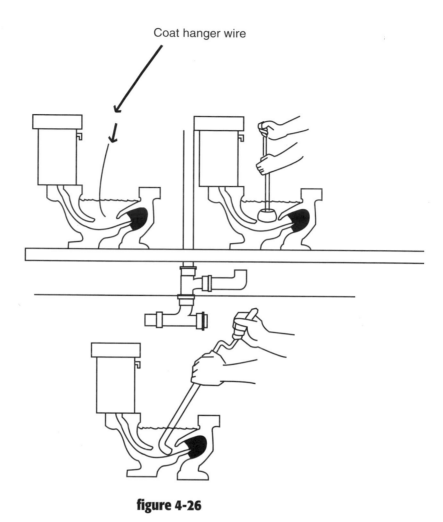

Coat hanger wire

figure 4-25

figure 4-26

Raw sewage flows downhill into the tank from the house sewer. The solids separate from the liquid and stay in the tank. Anaerobic bacteria that do not use oxygen from the air grow in the tank and work to decompose the solids to reduce their volume.

Periodically the solids need to be removed from the tank. That varies from system to system for a lot of different reasons.

Many systems will have a series of two or three tanks, each a little lower than the one before it. This helps the system work more efficiently.

From the last tank, there is an outlet pipe that caries the liquids out into a drainage field (figure 4-27). This is a series of pipes that run under the soil and have holes in them where the liquid seeps out into the soil (figure 4-28). These are installed in trenches that are lined with some sort of aggregate that will not cause the

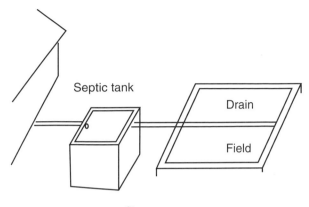

figure 4-27

drain lines to clog up. Some systems will have a junction box where these drain lines originate.

Special baffles allow scum to collect and remain in the tank rather than flow out into the drain field and clog the lines. This should be inspected when you have the tank drained to make sure it is still in place. Be careful if you snake your drains that you don't knock it off.

Within the tanks, there are three basic layers of material (figure 4-29).

1. The top layer is the floating scum layer. It collects wastes such as soap or detergent scum, cooking fats, and any other material that floats. Most of the material in the scum layer does not decompose readily through bacterial action.
2. The center zone is called the clear zone, which is liquid that contains suspended solids and bacteria. A deep clear zone is very important. As the other layers build up, more sludge is likely to drain out into the drainage field and can clog the lines.

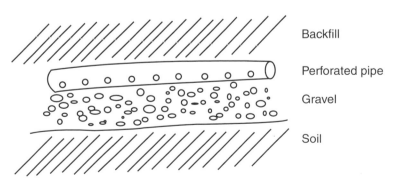

Backfill

Perforated pipe

Gravel

Soil

figure 4-28

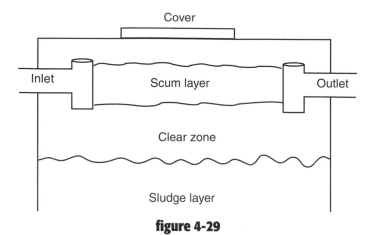

figure 4-29

3. The bottom of the tank is the sludge layer, which is the decomposing and partially decomposed solids which sink to the bottom of the tank.

Things you should not put in your household drains if you have a septic system:

1. Plastics
2. Antibacterial soaps
3. Household chemicals and cleaners
4. Bleach
5. Softened water—in certain situations, softened water can change the way your soil absorbs this drain water and your lines can become ineffective
6. Too much water—a leaking toilet or sink can fill your tanks up before you know it
7. Toilet paper that isn't as biodegradable as it should be

Toilet Tissue Test

Put some toilet tissue in a jar of water and shake it up—if it falls apart easily, use it, if not, switch to a brand that does. Colored toilet tissue doesn't seem to have an effect on septic systems, but some scented tissues don't work as well as the plain types.

---

8. Grease
9. Coffee grounds
10. Latex paint—wash your brushes elsewhere

11. Degreasers
12. Washing machine water—the soapy water is the problem
13. Ground-up food from a garbage disposer—better throw it away in the garbage can

Southern tanks usually work faster to break down waste than northern tanks because of the warmer climate. In some northern climates, insulation is placed over the tank tops to help keep them warmer.

Some miracle septic tank cleaners are designed to cause the sludge layer to become lighter and be washed out into the drain field—this will most likely clog your lines. Remember this—if it sounds too good to be true, it probably is.

Since the septic system depends on bacterial action, there are chemicals you can add to keep the system percolating. Here is an old family recipe for a homemade formula:

2 cups brown sugar
2 cups corn meal
2 packets of yeast powder
Dissolve in a quart of warm water

Pour this mix into the toilet and flush. There are also prepared mixes available in plumbing supply places.

THE PLUMBING CODE

There are ground rules for plumbing, and these are referred to as the plumbing code. Most repairs aren't covered by the code but nearly all additions are. There may be differences in the code in different communities. Be sure any plumbing work you do complies with the code. You may even have to apply for a permit and then have your project inspected by a plumbing inspector. These codes are there to protect you and your community, so make sure you abide by the rules.

CLASS DISMISSED! That's it for plumbing basics. We'll be covering the various appliances that are connected to the plumbing in chapter 14.

For now, these basics will let you experience what the **Super Sage said:**

"PERSON WHO IS HIS OWN PLUMBER WILL STOP LEAK IN HIS POCKETBOOK!"

Electricity 101

Most of us know of the many magical things electricity does in and around our homes. Many of us haven't a clue as to either how electricity happens or how it works.

Here's a thumbnail sketch of how it happens. Your local utility company delivers electricity to your house through a meter that measures the usage. It then goes into a box or service entry panel where it is distributed to the various circuits in and around the house. Today, standard service is of the three-wire variety . . . two wires carry 120 volts each and the third wire is neutral. This provides 120 volts for lights and wall outlets. When the two hot wires are combined, you get 240 volts for large appliances like ranges, dryers, and air conditioners (figure 5-1).

Well, now that we've mentioned "volts," we'll have to at least explain that and a few other terms used in the elec-

figure 5-1

tricity game. The current going through the wire is under pressure and this pressure is measured in "volts." The amount of current going through is measured in "amps." The amount of work that current can do, for example, lighting a bulb or ironing a shirt, is measured in "watts." "Kilo" in the metric system means one thousand, so a kilowatt is a thousand watts.

The power company bills you in a unit called the kilowatt-hour—the amount of work done by a kilowatt in an hour.

You'll be happy to learn that you don't have to know any of the technical stuff to accomplish many electrical fix-it chores. However, many people become totally fascinated by the field of electricity.

Those of you who labor under the misconception that only a licensed electrician can work on anything electrical will be pleasantly surprised that in most communities this is a myth. And, if you've always heard about the dreaded permit you have to get, in most cases, the repairs we'll learn about only require a permit from your spouse.

SAFETY

As the troops shouted during the Spanish-American War:

REMEMBER THE MAIN!

They were talking about the Battleship Maine. We're talking about the main shut off at the entry panel. It may be a pullout fuse block (figure 5-2) or an actual switch. This shuts off all electrical current to every circuit in the house. Knowing where this is and how to use it can save a life or prevent a fire. This entry box also has fuses or circuit breaker switches for each individual circuit.

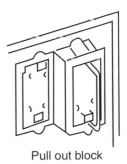

Pull out block

figure 5-2

If you have no current to the entire house, electrical repairs can be perfectly safe. If you can isolate the circuit you'll be working on and trip that breaker, the same is true. However, anytime you approach the entry panel, keep these safety rules in mind.

1. Since most service panels are in a garage or basement that has concrete floors, rather than standing on the concrete, which can hold moisture, stand on a 2x4 or wooden platform (figure 5-3).
2. Always wear rubber-soled shoes.
3. Do not touch any metal within the box.
4. Use only one hand. To be sure that you don't use the other hand, keep it in your pocket.
5. Put a warning sign across the front of the service panel alerting others to the fact that they should not mess with the box.

If you have a system with fuses, be sure you replace a blown fuse with one that has the same amperage (figure 5-4). You can just look at the fuse to know if it's blown. The glass top will either be black or, if not, you will be able to see the broken element.

FIXING A LAMP

Remember that with the lamp unplugged, you can't get shocked.

To find out why the lamp doesn't work, check these things:

1. Is the bulb burned out? Try a new one.
2. Is it getting current? Plug the lamp into another outlet on a different circuit. If it lights up, then you must determine if the outlet is bad or if the entire circuit is out.
3. While the lamp is plugged into a live circuit and the switch is turned on, wiggle the plug. If the light flickers, check the plug. If wires are loose, tighten them. If not, replace the plug. There are easy to replace plugs called quick-connects (figure 5-5). There is no splitting or stripping. Just snip off the old plug, push the wire through the outer body of the new plug, and sharp points stab the insulation to make contact. The white wire should be on the side with the wider prong.
4. Test the cord by flexing it. If you get intermittent light, either change the cord or cut out the bad section.

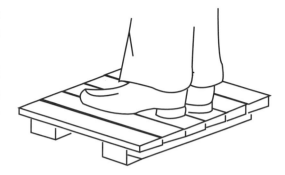

figure 5-3

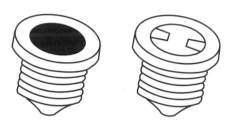

figure 5-4

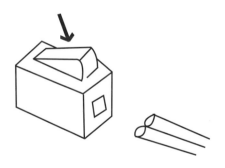

figure 5-5

TEACHER'S TIP

Before pulling the old cord out, remove the socket and plug and tape the bottom end of the old cord to the new. The new cord will be pulled up through the lamp and into place.

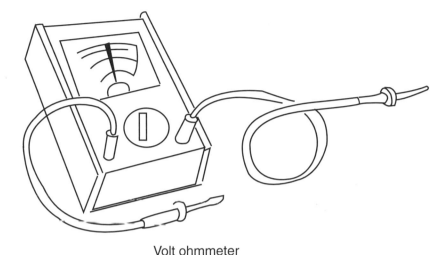

Volt ohmmeter

figure 5-6

You can also use a continuity tester to find out if the cord is the culprit (figure 5-6, 5-7).

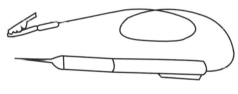

figure 5-7

5. After all that, if you haven't found the problem you can probably assume that the socket is bad.

If you have to replace the socket, it may be an opportunity for you to replace the old one with a three-way socket. Of course, you need to have a 3-way bulb. Or, maybe you'd like a dimmer switch. They are all wired in just like the old one. Here are the steps:

1. Unplug the lamp and remove the bulb.
2. Remove the old socket from its base by pressing the outer brass shell with your thumb and forefinger. If it's stubborn, pry with a screwdriver.
3. Remove the cardboard insulation sleeve (see figure 5-8).
4. Unscrew the two screws holding the wires (see figure 5-8).
5. Split and trim off the wires. Strip off about 3/4-inch of insulation. Tightly twist the strands on each wire to make it into one wire.
6. Before attaching the wires to the socket, tie an Underwriter's Knot, as shown in figure 5-9. This prevents stress from pulling the connections loose.
7. Curl each wire, as shown in figure 5-10, in a clockwise fashion so that when the screws are tightened, the wire is pulled into the screw.

8. Be sure to include the insulating sleeve as you put the pieces back together and snap it in place securely.

REPLACING A WALL SWITCH

If you enter a room and flip on the switch and you're still in the dark, you figure the bulb is burned out. Nine times out of ten that is the problem. If that's not the problem, you may be in need of a replacement switch.

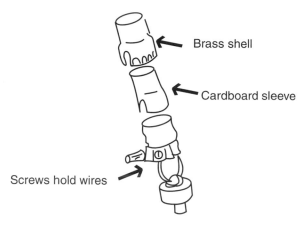

Brass shell

Cardboard sleeve

Screws hold wires

figure 5-8

First of all, if the switch is the only one that controls the fixture, it's what is called a single-pole switch (figure 5-11). Either replace it with another single-pole switch or, in most cases, you can replace it with a dimmer switch. Here are the easy replacement steps:

1. Shut off power at the service entry panel.
2. Remove the cover plate at the switch, pull the switch unit straight out of the box, and disconnect the two black wires. Most will be fastened with screws. Others will be poked into holes and released with a tiny screwdriver pushed into release holes indicated on the back of the switch. Since the switch is just an interruption of a hot wire, if one of the wires is white, it should be painted black

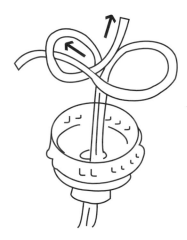

figure 5-9 step 1

figure 5-9 step 2

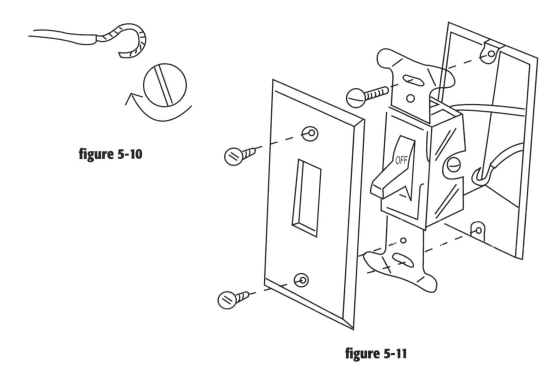

figure 5-10

figure 5-11

or marked with black tape. Generally, the black wire is the hot wire, the white wire will be neutral. If there is also a red wire, found in more exotic situations, it will also be hot. A green or bare wire will be a grounding wire.

3. Curl the wire as previously described and loop it over the screw in a clockwise direction.
4. As added protection against bare wires accidentally touching a metal box, run a strip of tape around the unit before pushing it back into place.
5. Install the cover plate and restore current to the circuit.

WALL OUTLET WOES

If you plug in your gadget and it doesn't work, most people blame the gadget. Yet the problem could be the wall outlet. You can use a tester or plug in a lamp that you know works to find out if it is the outlet. If the outlet is the problem, replacement is a snap. Here are the steps:

1. Select the proper type of replacement. If it is old, it may require a two-pronged outlet. Most, however, will be three-pronged, which should mean they are grounded.

2. Shut off power at the service entry panel, but then test to be sure there is no current to that outlet.

3. Remove the single screw holding the plate on. This will expose two screws that hold the outlet to the box. With these removed, the outlet may be pulled out.

4. Before disconnecting the wires, note exactly how the wires were hooked up. If there's any doubt, draw a rough diagram of where each wire goes. Generally, black wires will go on the brass screws and white wires on the silver screws. The green or bare wire will attach to the green screw.

5. Push the unit back in place, secure it with the old screws, and reinstall the plate before restoring power.

Q: What will happen if the old outlet just has two holes and you replace it with a three-holer? If you plugged in a gadget with a three-pronged plug, wouldn't that make it a grounded outlet?

A: Unless the outlet box is grounded all the way back to the service entry panel, it is not grounded.

FLUORESCENT LIGHTING

If you are interested in saving some energy dollars, you might wish to consider fluorescent lighting, particularly if you're going to put in new fixtures. Fluorescent tubes give light much more efficiently than incandescent bulbs. In fact, a 40-watt fluorescent gives out more light than a 100-watt incandescent while using less than half the current. While the incandescent bulb costs a lot less than the fluorescent tube, the fluorescent can last from ten to twenty times as long.

Why wouldn't everyone switch to fluorescent lighting? Buying the new fixtures would cost quite a bit, making the payback in savings a long time off.

However, there are now fluorescent bulbs that have a tiny built in ballast and screw into a lamp or fixture socket. This gives you an inexpensive way to try fluorescent lighting and see if you like the kind of light it produces. Some people don't.

FLUORESCENT REPAIR

If you turn on a fluorescent fixture and the tube doesn't light up, here are some things to check:

1. Is there current to the circuit? Check for a blown fuse or tripped circuit breaker switch.

2. If the tube isn't properly inserted in the lamp holder at each end, no electricity is reaching the tube (figures 5-12a-b).

3. If your fixture requires a starter (figure 5-13), replace it with the proper size starter.

4. If you have another fixture that uses the same size tube, switch them and you'll find out if the tube is burned out.

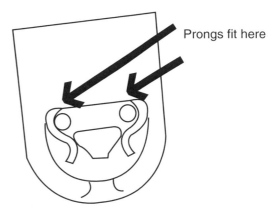

Prongs fit here

Twist tube so prongs make contact

figure 5-12a

Sometimes a fluorescent tube blinks or flickers. Before it drives you crazy, check these things:

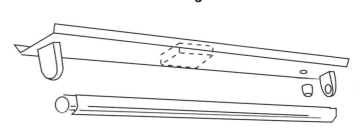

figure 5-12b

1. If it's a new tube, the problem should go away shortly. In fact, shut the fixture off and back on, and the problem may solve itself instantly.

2. Check the lamp holder and the pins on the end of the tube for corrosion. Light sanding will eliminate this. If the pins are bent, use pliers to gently straighten them.

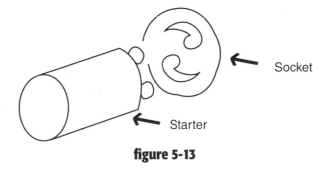

Socket

Starter

figure 5-13

3. The problem may be in the starter, or the tube may be going bad.

If the tube is just partially lighting—for example, the ends are dark, or there's no light in the middle, try these things:

1. Reverse the tube end for end.
2. Shut off power to the unit and check the wiring and all connections, starting at the ballast.
3. Try a new starter.

If the fixture starts to hum, it may mean the ballast is going out. Check the wiring, and if that doesn't help, be prepared to buy and replace the ballast. It should be wired in just as the old one was.

CEILING FIXTURES

When a ceiling fixture fails to light up, the vast majority of times the cause is a burned out light bulb. Most fixtures have a recommended wattage for the bulbs. Using a bulb with higher wattage will probably result in the bulb burning out before its time. This extra heat can also cause insulation to melt, and could result in fire or other problems.

If it's not the bulb, chances are it's either the switch or a loose wire. We've already talked about wall switches on page 38. To work on the wiring, you must trip the circuit breaker or remove the fuse for this circuit. While doing this, check to be sure the problem isn't at the entry panel.

To check the wiring, you'll probably have to remove a cover, followed by the removal of the canopy plate. This is called "dropping the fix-ture." These steps give you access to the wiring, which is in a recessed box. The wires from the box are usually attached to the wires from the fixture by solderless connectors called wire nuts.

> **WEATHER REPORT**
>
> Regular fluorescent tubes don't like cold weather. When the temperature gets below 50° F the light may blink. In extreme cold, it may not come on at all. There are special tubes that are made to be more cold tolerant.

Wire nut

figure 5-14

INSTALLING A NEW CEILING FIXTURE

A newer, more modern, or maybe more ornate fixture can change the look of a room and maybe give you better light. It's easy to do, and here are the steps:

1. Trip the breaker or remove the fuse to the circuit before dropping the fixture.
2. The wiring is just a repeat of the way the old fixture was wired. So, take notes if it looks confusing.
3. Strip the insulation back on the wires from the new fixture about 3/4 inch. Use the wire nuts to attach wire from the fixture to the wires from the box.

So much for wiring. But the fixture has to attach to the box and its canopy must cover the opening in the ceiling. You may need some additional gadgets, like a strap, a stud, a hickey, and/or a nipple. When you buy the new fixture, all the hardware will probably be included. If not, let the dealer tell you what you need and supply you with it.

CEILING FANS

While the ceiling fan is part of your home's heating, cooling, and comfort, installing one involves electricity. Actually, installing a ceiling fan that will replace a light fixture is a lot like replacing that light fixture. The same wires that come out of the box in the ceiling can be attached to the wires coming from the fan.

One difference, however, is that the fan is usually heavier than the light fixture. If the box will not support the weight of the fan, you must add bracing. If you can get into the attic, you can place a 2 x 4 between joists and position it so that the box can be firmly attached with screws into the 2 x 4. There are also metal brackets that can be put into the hole in the ceiling. The bracket has a box on it and can be installed from below the ceiling.

Many fans have a light kit included. If not, you can add lights to replace what you have lost.

You have several options as far as controls.

1. The switch that controlled the light will also turn on the fan. If there is a light kit, a pull chain will control the light.
2. Wire new switches from the fan and from the light so that each is controlled from the wall.
3. There are now remote control switches that will require no wiring . . . a little pricey, but a lot easier.

Ceiling Fan Maintenance

The ceiling fan is not normally a troublemaker, but sometimes it can start to wobble. This is usually a matter of balance. There are balancing kits that may solve the problem. Often the blade irons (figure 5-15) are loose. Tightening the screws may solve the problem. With the fan turned off, measure the distance from the tip of the blade to the ceiling.

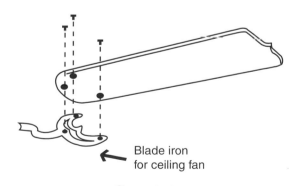

Blade iron
for ceiling fan

figure 5-15

Then, without moving the tape measure, rotate the blades by hand to check each blade. Add weights to the blades that are highest. Taping a dime or penny to the top of a light blade will weight the blade down.

DOORBELLS

It is amazing how many doorbells only work on Halloween or when the in-laws come to call. If you'd like for it to ding-dong all the time, it's an easy repair. There are only four components . . . the button, the chime or buzzer, the wiring, and the transformer.

Because there is a transformer, that means you are dealing with 12 to 24 volts. This can give you a tingle, but is not too bad. To play it safe, trip the circuit breaker or remove the fuse to that circuit.

The easiest component to get to is the button, and it is also the most frequent culprit. You can troubleshoot the button by removing the faceplate and disconnecting the two wires. If you touch the two wires together and the unit chimes or buzzes, you know the button needs to be replaced or that the connection was not good. If the wires have corrosion, lightly sand them. But what else could it be?

1. A faulty button is an inexpensive replacement.
2. Next, check the buzzer or chime unit. Inspect the wiring to be sure the connections are tight and the wires are not corroded.
3. The clapper or chime striker rods must be able to hit the bell or tone bars. Gently bend the clapper and clean the chime rod with rubbing alcohol.
4. Next, use a tester to be sure current is coming to the unit.
5. The next place to check is the transformer. Unfortunately, this is often in the attic or someplace else that is not easy to get to. Test the low voltage side and then the other side to see that power is coming from the power source. Keep in mind that the current coming into the transformer is 120 volts, and you must shut off the current before touching the transformer.

If you have a large home, and if the chime or bell unit can't be heard from remote spots, you can add a wireless system that plugs into wall outlets and chimes when the button is pushed.

OUTDOOR LIGHTING

Lightscaping is an important part of beautifying your landscaping at night. Having the extra light also makes it safer to walk around outside. Low voltage systems are easy to install and can be quite nice. Installation is a piece of cake. A transformer is plugged into an outdoor outlet. The lights are connected by cable and can be placed where they look best. Because they have low voltage, there is no worry about people or pets getting shocked, even if they chew on the wires.

Other outdoor lighting systems include HID, or high intensity discharge lighting. These include mercury lights, metal halide, and sodium vapor lights. These are usually security lights that really flood outdoor areas.

NONREQUIRED READING: THE METER

Most electric meters have four or five dials. Our example, figure 5-16, has five, and you'll note the dials alternate between clockwise and counterclockwise. To read this meter, start with the left-hand dial. This dial registers tens of thousands of kilowatt-hours. When a pointer is between two numbers, use the lesser number. In our case, that would be 5. On the next dial, the pointer is between 9 and 0. So jot down 9. The next dial is exactly 6. If the next dial had not yet reached 6, you would use 5. However, the pointer is past 6 so the reading is 6. The final correct reading is 59,627.

The dial on the far right measures single kilowatt-hours.

Why read the meter? If there is a sudden jump in the bill, there could have been a mistake on the part of the meter reader. If you read your meter regularly, you would spot the mistake and the utility company might come out for a second reading. Also, this makes some people more aware of the energy being consumed and they may make more of an effort to conserve.

As Ben Franklin once said: "When I asked about electricity, they told me to go fly a kite."

figure 5-16

Walls and Ceilings 101

6

The walls in your home are used to define spaces, give you privacy, and block out noise. And, let's face it, they are pretty much background for your decorative touches and a place to hang the life-sized portrait of your in-laws.

Most homes built since World War II employ hollow wall construction. This means the interior walls are hollow with only vertical studs inside. Hopefully, the walls that face outside have the proper insulation in the hollow spaces. The frame work is covered with drywall (also called plasterboard, gypsum board, Sheetrock, and a few other terms we can't use in a classy class like this).

Older homes often have plaster walls. These, too, involve studs, but wooden lath is attached to the studs and these are then coated with plaster.

Whatever type wall you have, it will cease to be background when it has holes or cracks. These flaws tend to stick out like a sore thumb.

Ceilings in most homes are just there. Unless somebody just happens to look up, they'd never know if it was crow's foot textured, swirled, or covered with ceiling tiles. But since stuff happens to ceilings, we'll talk about these things, too.

PATCHING

CRACKS

Whether the walls are plaster or drywall, the same patching compound will work for both. It's some stuff called "spackle." It comes already mixed in a small plastic tub. Spackle also comes dry so you can mix it yourself, but that's mostly used for really big jobs. Drywall joint compound is a very similar product that is made for covering joints between drywall panels. It is also called "mud" and is used to texture drywall.

Most cracks in walls and ceilings in either type of construction are from settling. New houses may settle just once and that's often the extent of it. However, if you have recurring cracks, read all about foundations in chapter 7.

Hairline cracks may seem insignificant, but if not patched they can grow. Here's what to do:

1. First remove any debris in or around the crack.
2. Dip a finger into the spackle and rub the compound into the crack.
3. Use a well-squeezed damp sponge to remove excess spackle. Wait until dry before touching up with wall paint. There is another form of spackle for hairline cracks and nail holes, called a solid spackle stick. To patch, just rub the stick along the crack or over the nail hole. Touch-up painting can be done immediately.

Larger cracks will do better if the edges are undercut. This means using a chisel to make the crack wider underneath (figure 6-1). Next, bring the patch almost up to the surface, but wait 24 hours before leveling it with the surface. At this point, you may have to texture the new compound to make it match the rest of the wall. We'll have some texture tips later in this course. Sand and touch up with paint to hide the repair.

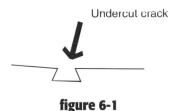

Undercut crack

figure 6-1

POPPED UP NAIL HEADS

You can try to drive the nail back in, but chances are it'll pop out again. The best way is either to use a ring-shanked nail or a drywall screw and install the new fastener about 2 inches below the popped nail, making sure the fastener pulls the drywall snugly against the stud. Then drive the popped nail back in, cover both heads with spackle, and when dry, use touch-up paint.

SPLIT OR LOOSE DRYWALL TAPE

The joints between sheets of drywall are covered with drywall tape and hidden with several layers of drywall compound that are feathered at the edges to hide the seam. If the tape is loose in a small area, try to work a little white glue under the tape and press gently to force out excess glue. If that doesn't hold, very carefully remove the loose or split tape down to where it's in good shape and well adhered. Try to avoid pulling or dislodging any bits of the drywall compound. Sand the base where the tape was removed and if there is a space between sheets of drywall, fill with compound. Cut the new tape to fit and carefully replace it with drywall compound, feathering the edges. You may have to add more compound when the first coat dries. When the patching is complete, apply your touch-up paint.

HOLES IN THE WALL

There are many ways to get holes in the wall. There's the doorknob hole from a too exuberant opening of the door. The doorknob makes a hole about the same size as a fist-sized hole. There are even bigger holes like the one caused by a runaway tricycle crashing through the wall. Patching any of these disasters may be easier than you think.

GOLF BALL-SIZED HOLES AND SMALLER

The problem with drywall holes is that there is no backing. The spackle can end up falling into the hollow space. With any hole, clean away any loose debris. For smaller holes you can usually use a putty knife to cover the hole with spackle. Smooth it, let it dry, and then touch-up with paint.

Another way to patch small holes is to crisscross small strips of self-adhesive fiberglass drywall mesh tape to cover the hole. Then apply a layer of drywall compound. After this coat dries, you'll probably have to texture it.

DOORKNOB-SIZED HOLES

For a hole of this size in drywall, you definitely need some backing. Fortunately, there are several choices. There are doorknob repair kits available that have everything you need for this job. These kits contain a small square of gypsum board, plastic clips that hold the patch in place, a small container of patching compound, and a putty knife. You use the patch as a template. Mark it off on the wall, covering the hole. Use a keyhole saw to cut the opening. Be on the lookout for wiring. Then with the patch clipped in place, you cover it all with compound and smooth it out, feathering the edges. When dry, sand the surface, texture it, and use touch-up paint.

Or, here's a way that costs nothing:

1. Cut a scrap of window screen a little bigger than the hole.
2. Run a piece of string through an opening in the center of the screen. Loop the string back through the screen.

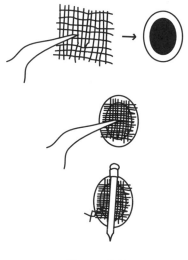

3. Now force the screen through the hole while holding onto the string.
4. Pull the screen up snug against the inside of the wall.
5. Tie the string around a pencil.
6. Twist the pencil tourniquet style to tighten the backing against the wall (figures 6-2).
7. Apply patching compound up to within 1/8-inch of the surface.
8. When this coat dries, snip off the string and fill with compound to the surface.
9. When dry, sand and texture to match the rest of the wall and then paint.

figure 6-2

For the doorknob sized hole in a plaster wall, here's the drill:

1. Clean away all loose material around the hole.
2. Cut a scrap of hardware cloth to fit inside the hole. (Hardware cloth is a wire mesh with about 1/2-inch openings.)
3. Staple the mesh to the wooden lath.
4. For bigger holes in plaster, use patching plaster instead of drywall compound. Fill in the hole with three applications, allowing drying time between each.
5. When dry and hard, sand, and either smooth or texture to match the rest of the wall. Then paint.

CRASH-HELMET SIZED HOLES

A large hole that takes up a good part of the width of the cavity between studs usually requires enlarging the hole. There are several other ways to tackle this chore but here's one we like. Just follow these easy steps:

1. Use a keyhole saw to cut out a rectangle that goes over the stud on each side. Don't forget that there could be wires within the cavity. Be careful!
2. Rather than cutting half the drywall off of the studs, cut two short 2x4 scraps to nail to the studs as shown in figure 6-3. These provide a surface for attaching the patch.

figure 6-3

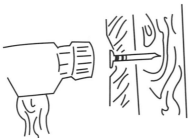

Dimple drywall nails and screws

figure 6-4

3. Cut the patch to fit, and nail or screw it in place. If nailing, be sure to dimple the nail heads (figure 6-4).
4. Cover the dimples and or screw heads.
5. Finish as described above.

CEILINGS

Most residential ceilings are either drywall or plaster. As we suggested, many of the same things that happen to walls also befall ceilings. The same general idea applies to ceiling repairs. However, dealing with the ceiling must often be done while you're on a ladder and in an awkward position. Also, there is the additional problem of fighting gravity. The patches must be well secured or they are liable to come tumbling down. Often this requires more drywall screws than for wall patches.

Plus, ceilings have some other problems, and there are many types of ceilings.

A SAGGING CEILING

This can be a minor thing or can be very serious. With either type, you'll do well to make a T-brace or maybe even a couple of them. To work, the T-brace must be about an inch longer than the ceiling height so it can be wedged in place to lift up and hold the ceiling at the sag.

With drywall, nails have probably come loose, and you may spot the areas where this has happened from the nail holes. The nail holes also help you see where the joists are. If so, install drywall screws into the joists. Use plenty of screws but remember that you'll have to patch over each screw head.

The sagging plaster ceiling can be more dangerous because of the weight involved. But with plaster, there are more places in which to fasten the ceiling back in place. In addition to joists, there are also lath boards. Use screws plus washers under the heads. All of these fasteners must be covered when the ceiling is secure.

CEILING TILES

Damage to a single tile usually calls for replacement. Hopefully, you saved some extras. Most ceilings use tongue and groove tiles that are either stapled or glued to furring strips. To replace:

1. Use a sharp utility knife to cut around the edges of the damaged tile.
2. If you need a better grip, cut out the center of the damaged tile.
3. Pull the tile loose from the staples and glue.
4. Scrape away the old adhesive and pull out all the staples.
5. Cut off the bottom lip of the groove edges of the replacement tile.
6. Apply new adhesive to the furring strips.
7. Ease the new tile in place. Be sure your hands are free of dirt or glue.

Speaking of dirt, that is about the only other ceiling tile problem. Since the tiles are usually white, a little laundry bleach will remove stains. If not, a neat cover up is to apply talcum powder with a powder puff to hide a stubborn stain. It won't last forever but it's easy to reapply.

We're often asked about painting ceiling tiles. Of course this can be done, but it does take away some of the acoustic qualities of the ceiling.

TEXTURING

Even though the sheets of gypsum board are very smooth, when installed there are uneven areas because of taping and bedding, nails, and uneven studs. Under certain lighting conditions, imperfections show up. Texturing tends to make these bad spots get lost. A good texturing tool is a paint roller. The length of the nap on a roller gives different textures. We prefer a short napped roller but that's a judgment call. It's a good idea to practice on a scrap of gypsum board. You can roll and then scrape it all off, trying different things until you get the right texture. Apply a thin smooth layer of mud with a wide drywall knife and then roll the surface.

Ceilings have a wider variety of popular texture patterns. Crow's foot is done with a special brush that you jab against the ceiling to make the pattern. Swirls can be made with a stiff broom.

There are no rules when it comes to texture patterns, so if you want to try something weird, use that scrap and practice. A notched trowel made for spreading floor adhesive can make an interesting pattern on walls or ceilings.

POPCORN CEILINGS

This is a very popular acoustical ceiling treatment that is sprayed on. There is also a roll-on version that is easier for the do-it-yourselfer to apply. From the name, you know exactly how it looks. It is generally not painted. In fact, efforts to paint this type of ceiling usually result in a lot of the aggregate being dislodged. This is a common problem with a popcorn ceiling. Fortunately, there is a patching compound made to replace the stuff that has fallen off. This compound comes in a small plastic tub and is applied with a putty knife. It comes in two types—"New" and "Old." New is very white and Old is off-white.

REMOVING A WALL

Sometimes the home you bought has a wall that is in your way. Maybe you want to open up an area and combine two small rooms into one bigger room. Demolition can be fun.

First it must be ascertained if the offending wall is load bearing. Load bearing means the wall is supporting and holding up other parts of the house. If it is, and if you remove it, the roof could fall down around your ears. There are ways to compensate for the structure being removed, but it may be a job for a pro. We'll talk about this later in the course. In most cases, all exterior walls are bearing walls. You can usually tell from the attic or basement which walls are the bearing walls.

In the attic, the joists will usually run perpendicular to the wall in question if it is bearing. You can be sure if the joists are spliced or lapped together over the wall.

In the basement, look for double joists perpendicular to the girders. A bearing wall will be directly above the double joist. Also, walls directly above a girder will usually be bearing.

If there's any doubt, seek the advice of an architect, builder, or other pro. Also see if a permit is needed.

Once you're sure everything is a GO, let the games begin—but not before you put on a hard hat and goggles!

Removing the actual wall is not that big a deal, but you must remember that there can be wiring, plumbing, and maybe even a gas line hidden in the wall. Here are the steps:

1. Trip the circuit breaker or remove the fuse for any electrical current to the wall. Water lines will have to be removed, so at some point the water supply must be shut off. A gas line should probably be removed professionally.
2. Remove all the trim, including door casings, shoe molding, and baseboards. If you are careful, you can salvage these materials.
3. There is little likelihood of salvaging the drywall or lath in a plaster wall, so use a hammer to break the surface material and a pry bar to rip it off.
4. Once the wall is stripped down to the skeleton of studs, remove the wiring and electrical boxes. Toss the wiring and save the boxes.

5. Use a sledgehammer to knock the bottom of each stud loose from the sole plate. Twist the stud to pry it loose from the top plate. Most of the studs can be salvaged after the nails are removed.

6. Take extra care in removing the end studs so as not to damage the wall any more than you have to. The same care should be used in the removal of the sole and top plates.

Now all you need do is patch up any damage and haul off a bunch of debris.

BUILDING A NEW PARTITION

If the kids have outgrown the playroom and you need a home office, you may want to install a partition. The basic wall is not all that difficult, but you do have to figure out how to best tie the new wall into the old house. There are several places where the tie-in can be made:

1. If the joists above run perpendicular to the new wall, the top plate can be attached to these joists. Nails or screws will do.

2. If the joists run parallel, place a nailing board between the joists on either side of where the wall will be. Then install 2 x 4 blocks between joists to back up the nailing board (figure 6-5).

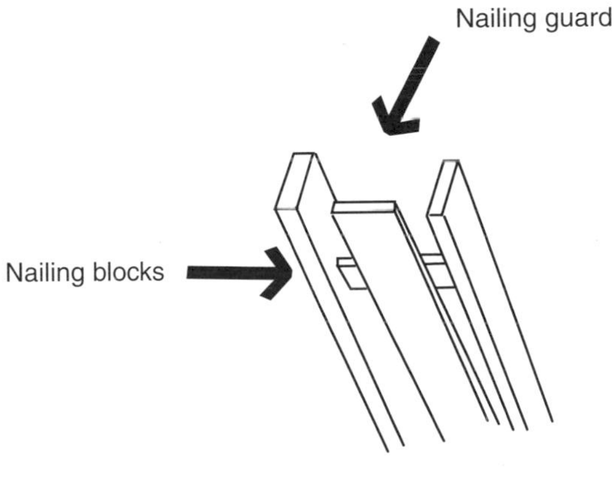

Nailing guard

Nailing blocks

figure 6-5

3. Remove enough wallboard to expose studs within the place where your new wall will be attached to this wall. If there is a stud in the right spot, attach the end stud of the new partition directly. If not, provide nailing blocks of 2 x 4s running horizontally between existing studs (figure 6-6).

4. If the new wall butts up to a masonry wall, as in a basement, use masonry nails or bolts into masonry anchors to attach the end stud to the wall.

5. Attach the sole plate to the floor using whatever the appropriate fasteners would be.

Often, you'll use more than one of these tie-in spots for the new wall. If space is adequate, you can construct the entire wall with all the pieces flat on the floor and then raise it up to be fastened into place.

Take advantage of the open frame-
work to easily install wiring, insulation,
or whatever else.

HANGING THINGS ON THE WALL

It's true: "What goes up must come down."
But that doesn't have to happen to things
you hang on the wall . . . even if it's a
moose head. The secret is in using the
proper hardware for the thing you want
to hang. If you have drywall, you know
that if you just drive a nail into the wall,
even the lightest hanging weight will soon
be on the floor.

If, however, you could drive the nail
through the drywall and directly into a
stud, you'd have no problem.

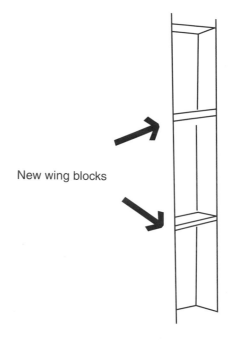

New wing blocks

figure 6-6

STUD FINDING

There are several ways that are almost as good as having X-ray vision when it comes
to locating studs behind the wall. Take your pick of these locator tips. It's best to try
in the center of the wall as opposed to the ends.

1. Electronic stud finders are probably best. They sense mass and can indicate
   where the stud's edges are.
2. Magnetic stud finders locate the nails driven into the studs to secure the gypsum
   board.
3. Rapping on the wall with a screwdriver handle can often detect the hollow
   spaces by the difference in the sound. Another sounding trick is to place the side
   of an electric razor against the wall. With the razor turned on, move it slowly
   across the wall, and you can tell the difference in sound when it crosses a stud.
4. Most electric wall outlets are attached to studs. Remove the cover plate and you
   can see the stud.
5. Another way is to drill an angled hole in the wall and probe with a length of
   straight coat hanger wire.

Once you locate one stud, you can usually measure 16 inches in either direction to find the next. If the 16-inch span doesn't work, try 24 inches.

Now that we've found all those studs, you should know they are never exactly where you wanted to hang things. That's where hardware comes in:

figure 6-7

1. Picture hangers (figure 6-7) hold more weight than you'd think. The angled nail plus the flat plate gives much better holding power than just a nail. But each package will specify the weight limit. Don't push it!

Molly bolt installed

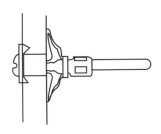

figure 6-8

2. Plastic anchors can be tapped into predrilled holes to accept screws. As the screw goes in, the plastic expands against the hole for a better grip.

3. As we go up on the weight scale with shelves or mirrors, consider a Molly Bolt (figure 6-8). They come in different sizes for differences in wallboard thickness and for different weights to be held.

4. For the moose head and other really big hang ups, there are various sizes of toggle bolts (figure 6-9). The flange is held closed until it's completely inside the wall. When released it springs out wide and when the bolt is turned, the flange is pulled tight against the inside of the wall. Keep in mind that once the toggle bolt is installed it can't be removed without the flange falling down into the hollow space. So, you must have whatever it will hold already attached to the bolt.

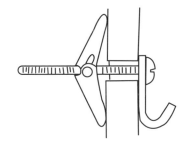

figure 6-9

5. An alternate to hardware is to attach a solid piece of wood as a bridge between studs. You can then nail or screw into this with good security.

6. If you need to hang something on a masonry wall, use a masonry anchor with an appropriate size bolt.

TEACHER'S TIP

After drilling the hole for the anchor, smear epoxy glue on the anchor for extra hold.

Structural 101

7

FOUNDATIONS AND BASEMENTS

Most homeowners don't pay a lot of attention to their home's foundation. However, when you stop to think about it, that foundation is holding up the entire house. That makes it a very important factor to the health of the home.

That having been said, let us now tell you that foundation repair is not a do-it-yourself project.

There are, however, things you can do to help prevent foundation failure. Here is your responsibility in the fight against foundation failure:

1. Since moisture has a huge effect on the well-being of your foundation, go outside during the next rain and walk completely around the house. Look for places where water is forming puddles close to the house. This means it isn't running off. This water will soak into the ground, and when it hits a layer of clay or rock or whatever, it will spread out, with some of it going under your house. Add dirt to change the grade at these low spots

2. Be sure that your gutters and downspouts are not dumping the water too close to the house. The use of extensions or splash blocks can help to solve this.

3. Fix all plumbing leaks ASAP, as water has a way of working under the house.

4. If you have a pier and beam foundation, go under the house to inspect for wet spots. The soil under a house should be 100% dry. If not, find out where the moisture is coming from.

5. With a pier and beam foundation, remove all vent covers, except during the cold times.

6. In dry periods, water around the entire perimeter of the house. Use a flat soaker hose, the kind with tiny holes on one side, and turn it upside down about 18 inches from the house. Turn the water on so it gently soaks into the earth. Move it every hour or so until you go completely around the house. This gives the soil consistent moisture content. Too-dry earth shrinks, which can cause foundation settling.

7. Inspect the foundation regularly and call in a pro if you detect failure.

Foundation repair is expensive, so it behooves you to get an honest, experienced, and knowledgeable contractor. See page 221 on selecting a contractor.

SIGNS OF FOUNDATION FAILURE

Several minor annoyances may indicate foundation problems. Look for cracks in both interior and exterior walls. Doors and/or windows that are hard to open or close may be bad news. Unleveled or sloping floors are another sign. Many foundation repair companies will inspect for free, but some will sell you expensive repairs that are not actually needed. That's why many people will pay a structural engineer to analyze the foundation. His small fee could save you on big bogus repairs.

BASEMENT REPAIRS

The most common basement problem is moisture, and that moisture doesn't have to be the result of a flooded basement to cause trouble. A damp basement can ruin items stored, can cause mildew and other fungal growth, and can make conversion of the basement into living space a little iffy.

A basement may be damp from condensation or from seepage. How can you tell? An easy test is to dry a spot on the wall or floor and cover it with a sheet of clear plastic. Even a trash bag will do. Use duct tape around all the edges. Leave it on overnight. If there is moisture on the outside of the plastic, you have a condensation problem. If there is moisture underneath, you have seepage.

CONDENSATION

Better ventilation can help. You can also use a dehumidifier. You may be amazed at how often you have to dump water the dehumidifier takes from the air.

If you have exposed pipes in the basement, it's good to insulate them completely with pipe wrap to stop dripping. Wrapping would also be a good idea for air-conditioning ducts.

SEEPAGE

There are waterproofing compounds available that can be painted on the inside of the basement walls. Some can be sprayed but most require rolling or brushing. Be sure to follow all label directions as to drying, curing, and number of coats.

LEAKS

If the basement is flooding you will probably see cracks, gaps, or holes. These can and should be patched. Water can also come through the concrete or concrete block walls. After all, concrete is very porous. The inside coating mentioned above is certainly worth trying. However, the real place for waterproofing is the exterior wall, and that means digging down to gain access to the actual wall. Since this is usually done with excavating equipment, it's probably a job for a pro. In addition to waterproofing the exterior walls, it might be good to add a drain system below ground.

HIGH WATER TABLE

You can try all of the above, but this situation probably calls for the installation of a sump pump. Since this involves digging a sump pit, a hole has to be cut in the concrete floor, and this is generally a job for a pro. The sump pump is activated when water rises in the pit (figure 7-1). This causes a float to rise, turning on the

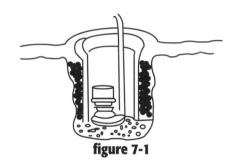

figure 7-1

pump. The unwanted water is pumped out to a drain line. It's a good idea to have battery back-up power to the pump.

In picking out a professional for waterproofing, be sure you select a company that has been around, has a good reputation in the waterproofing business, and stands behind their work. See page 221 on selecting a contractor.

OTHER STRUCTURAL PROBLEMS

Sometimes a rafter in the attic will crack. It could be from shifting or maybe even from faulty lumber. Usually you can prevent a worsening situation with a little reinforcement in the form of "sister rafters." These are two boards of the same width and thickness as the rafter. Cut them to a length that will cover the crack and extend a couple of feet beyond the crack. Nail one piece to the rafter using nails long enough to go through both the sister and the rafter and stick out an inch or so. Clinch the protruding points, then attach the second sister on the other side.

It's not a thing of beauty, but who is going see it?

Furniture 101

8

We probably should add this course in our "FunEd" catalog. Furniture finishing and refinishing is usually a lot of fun. At the same time, it's excellent therapy. So, instead of spending all that money on a shrink, use the same amount on a field trip to a few garage sales and pick up some treasured old furniture pieces.

What do you think most people do when they get home with that old piece of furniture? If you guessed "paint" or "refinish" you'd be right! However, many times that would be the wrong thing to do. There may be an easier way . . .

FIRST AID

TERMINAL DIRT

Often an old piece of furniture looks grungy because its got several layers of dirt on it. Many times the reason for the coat of filth is old wax, combined with airborne grease from cooking. Dissolve the gook and the dirt comes off. One great cleaner for this is plain old mineral spirits paint thinner on a rag. Wipe it on and wipe off the residue. Paint thinner won't do any damage to the finish. It is flammable but not highly volatile. Have plenty of ventilation, and don't smoke!

In many cases your drab old piece will suddenly look great. Then all you have to do is either apply another coat of paste wax or cover the piece with a good furniture polish.

WATER SPOTS

Those ugly white rings from a wet glass look like permanent damage on a table. In fact, they are amazingly easy to remove. The process requires a little rubbing with a mild abrasive and a lubricant so that the abrasive is not too dry.

This may sound a little coo-coo, but toothpaste is a mild abrasive and is not dry. Wrap a damp rag around a finger, dip into a squeeze of toothpaste—not the gel kind—and start rubbing. You can speed up the process just a bit by sprinkling some baking soda or salt on the mess. Use a clean rag to remove the stuff, and when the ring is gone, treat the table top to a dose of furniture polish.

Other weird abrasives include cigar ashes, silver polish, and 0000 steel wool. The lubricant can be olive oil, cooking oil, mayonnaise, or a pat of butter.

HEAT MARKS

A hot dish on the dining table leaves a white blush mark similar to a water spot. These goofs respond to the same treatment as water spot. However, there is an even easier way to fix a heat mark. Cover the spot with a coat of petroleum jelly and leave it on overnight. The next day, when you wipe away the goo, the blush mark will also have disappeared.

SCRATCHES

Many times this type injury can be hidden. If the scratch doesn't go down to the wood, a coat of wax or furniture polish will probably do the job.

A deep scratch needs to have some color added. Here are some things to try:

1. A kid's crayon may do the job.
2. Liquid shoe polish may be the right shade.
3. Often a nutmeat, like a pecan or walnut, rubbed over the scratch will hide it.
4. There are also wax melt sticks that offer a wide variety of colors.
5. The right felt marker might work.

BURNS

Use super fine (0000) steel wool to remove the black charred stuff. If the spot is too deep from the char removal, use stick shellac to fill. Otherwise, put stain on to match the rest of the finish.

PAINTED FURNITURE

Lots of folks are anti-painted furniture. Their credo is: "If you can't see the grain, it might as well be plastic." One thing about painted furniture is that it's less likely to have the injuries we find in other finished pieces. If you do have problems, chances are you can paint right over the problem. If you get tired of the color, you just give it a new coat.

The same general steps in painting furniture are those we talk about in our course on painting in chapter 15.

REPAIRS

LOOSE JOINTS

The most common repair problem with old furniture is a loose joint. Most of these problems just require re-gluing. A loose rung on a chair is a good example. Amber wood glue is fine for this repair. If there is no moisture involved on indoor furniture, even white glue will work. It's best to remove the old glue from both the end of the rung and the hole into which it fits. Sanding and/or scraping will do this.

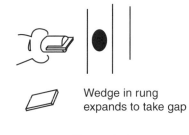

Wedge in rung expands to take gap

figure 8-1

If there is a reasonably good fit, apply the glue, clamp the work, and then wipe off any excess glue. If the wood has worn away and you don't think the glue will fill up the gap, try sawing a slot into the end of the rung and inserting a wedge, as in figure 8-1. The wedge will spread the end, but be careful not to split the rung. Wrapping the end of the rung with unwaxed dental floss (figure 8-2) will also fill up the gap.

Unwaxed floss takes up gap

figure 8-2

When clamping a glued joint in a chair, use a web, belt, or band clamp. Or, make your own tourniquet-type clamp from rope and a stick, as shown in figure 8-3. If several joints are being glued, wrap the rope around all four legs.

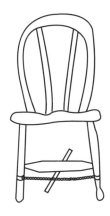

figure 8-3

VENEERS

A veneer is a paper-thin sheet of attractive wood often used on large surfaces such as a tabletop. Because it is thin, it can have problems, but because it is beautiful, it is worth fixing.

A vulnerable part of veneer is around the edges. The first thing to try is called the "heat-and-weight-and wait" method of fixing cracked edges. Put a cloth over the affected area, press it with a moderately warm iron, and then put a stack of encyclopedias on top and leave it alone for a while. The idea is that the heat will reactivate the adhesive and the weights will hold the veneer down until the glue takes hold again.

If that doesn't work, try using something like an artist's pallet knife to work some glue into the cavity. Use the weights, and it should solve the problem.

Another veneer problem is the blister or bubble that happens in the middle of a table. The glue has let go at that point. Here again, try the heat-and-weight-and-wait trick we just discussed. If that doesn't work, use a very sharp X-acto knife or razor blade to cut an "X" in the center of the bubble. Dampen the flaps to make them more flexible and gently pull them back to allow you to scrape away old glue. Vacuum away the debris. Insert new glue and press the flaps down before adding the weights.

REFINISHING

Sometimes the old piece is too far gone for first aid and the verdict is to refinish. This is not the end of the world—it can be a fun project. The first step is:

STRIPPING

No, this is not an anatomy class. We're not talking about removing clothing . . . just removing the old finish on the old furniture!

If the finish is dull but sound, restore rather than strip. Try one of the so-called "refinishers" that claim they allow you to refinish without stripping. There are several such products on the market, such as Formby's Refinisher. These products dissolve the finish enough so all the guck is loosened and removed but still leave a layer of whatever finish was there. The piece can then be protected with a coat of tung oil or lemon oil polish.

There is an elective here . . . your choice of two different ways to strip furniture. There's the hard way, which is sanding, scraping, and cursing. Or, the easy way, "better living through chemistry!" A chemical paint and varnish remover does the work. Here are some important points to keep in mind:

1. There are two basic types of paint and varnish removers—liquid and paste types. If your furniture piece has a lot of vertical surfaces, the liquid will be too runny so use the paste. The thicker stripper also doesn't evaporate as rapidly so it does a better job.
2. Strippers can be dangerous! Read all the caution notices. Have plenty of ventilation.

TEACHER'S TIP

Add cornstarch to the liquid stripper. Mix until it's about the consistency of pancake batter. This makes it less runny and longer lasting.

Wear protective clothing including rubber gloves and safety goggles.

3. Protect the floor underneath. Also put legs in empty tuna cans (figure 8-4). Even some of the paste types can run down a leg. This run-off can be reused by just dipping you brush into the can. This trick also saves what is underneath.

4. Use old brushes to apply stripper, and brush only in one direction. Going back and forth disturbs the film that retards evaporation.

5. Read the label for any special instructions for your particular stripper. It will also tell you when to start checking to see if the sludge is ready for removal.

6. When the finish has softened, scrape the mess away. Grind off the sharp corners of your knife as shown in figure 8-5. Otherwise, you might gouge the wood. In round, curved, or carved places, use steel wool to remove the sludge.

7. The last step for many strip jobs is to clean with a solvent to remove all traces of the wax that is mixed into many removers to retard evaporation.

Drip run-off into tuna cans

figure 8-4

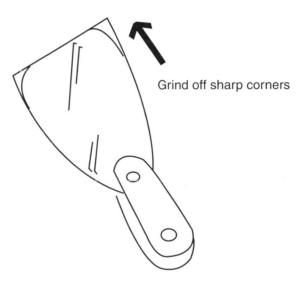

Grind off sharp corners

figure 8-5

If there are any stubborn places where the old finish remains, spot treat.

TO STAIN OR NOT TO STAIN?

A very common reason for staining is if you want darker furniture. Another reason is because some woods are so lacking in color and character that they need to be enhanced by staining. It's kind of hard to tell what the furniture will look like by just looking at the newly stripped wood.

But there is a way to see into the future! Dampen a clean rag with paint thinner and apply enough to make a spot about the size of a dinner plate on the wood. While it's still wet and shiny, it will bring out the grain and color and show the contrasts. It will look very much as the piece will with a clear finish. If you like what you see, forget about staining. Go directly to Finishes.

There are a number of different types of stains and a wide variety of shades.

Keep in mind that a stain will look different on different types of wood.

Pigmented wiping stains are easy to use and even a novice will get good results. Here are some things that will help ensure a good job:

1. If the grain was raised during stripping, lightly sand to remove the whiskers.
2. Make sure the surface is clean, dry, and free of wax.
3. Application is not critical, just be sure you have complete coverage. Use an old brush or rag.
4. Start on an obscure spot to be sure the stain is what you had in mind.
5. Stir well before you start and often during application.
6. When the surface starts to lose the wet look, it's time to do the wiping. Use an absorbent cloth and rub hard to remove as much surface stain as possible. Refold the cloth or change often.

The beauty of this type of stain is that if you don't get the right results to begin with, you can start over. If it's too dark, take a rag and paint thinner and you'll be able to remove nearly all traces of the stain. Then buy and apply a shade lighter or thin what's left of the old can. If it needs to be darker, apply another coat of the original or one a bit darker.

When the stain is right, let it sit for at least 24 hours, and you're ready to put a finish on.

FINISHING

The two main reasons for applying a finish are to protect the surface and also to enhance the beauty of the piece. The most popular finishes today are varnish, lacquer, and polyurethane. Shellac used to be popular, as were oil finishes. However, shellac was not as protective as would be preferred, and oil finishes took a lot more time and work than most people wanted to expend. So, let's talk about the current big three.

VARNISH

This finish is popular because it's tough, and is both water and heat resistant. One big disadvantage is that it's slow to dry, which means the tacky surface can, and probably will, pick up airborne lint. Also, if not done right, varnish application may show bubbles and brush marks. Here are some thoughts on how to get a better varnish finish:

1. Use a dust free room. Wear lint free gloves and clothing. (Nude varnishing is popular in some circles.) If you have heat or air in the area used, turn off the blower fan for at least an hour to let the dust settle before varnishing.
2. Wipe the entire surface with a tack rag before starting.
3. Have a light source on the opposite side of the piece so you'll avoid any skips.
4. Unlike James Bond's martini, varnish should be neither shaken nor stirred. Either action would create bubbles.
5. Don't overload the brush and use slow strokes, as few as possible. Always work against the wet edge of the previous stroke and brush with the grain.
6. Pick up the brush just as you reach an edge to avoid creating a ridge of excess varnish.
7. Be sure each coat is dry before applying the next.
8. Lightly sand with 0000 steel wool before the next coat.

Two or three coats of varnish are desirable to ensure good protection.

LACQUER

This is a wonderful finish because it is fast drying. It is a terrible finish for the novice for the exact same reason. Lacquer is best applied by spraying, which requires an expensive rig and more experience than most of us have. Aerosol cans of lacquer are great for the do-it-yourselfer, but for a medium-to-large piece of furniture, that gets expensive. So, unless we're talking about a small footstool or a picture frame, we're going to suggest you skip lacquer until you go for a masters degree in furniturology.

POLYURETHANE

This is a synthetic varnish, but to the purist it's just plastic. However, in the real world, the urethanes dry much faster than varnish. They are highly resistant to almost any kind of damage, and are easier to use than varnish. So, the urethanes are faculty approved.

CLASS MOTTO

"Make sure your furniture is finished . . . Not done for!"
—Billy Bob Hepplewhite

EXTRA CREDIT

Raise your grade with one of these fun out-of-class endeavors!

TACK RAG

We mentioned the tack rag and nobody in class even asked what we were talking about. Not only are we going to tell you what a tack rag does, we'll tell you how to make your own.

The tack rag has a tacky feel that, when rubbed over a wood surface, will pick up any dust and lint. This is a much-needed cleaning task that should be done just before applying a finish. You can buy a tack rag at the paint store, but here are the easy steps for making a tack rag:

1. Use a well-washed old handkerchief, diaper, or similar lint-free cloth.
2. Dip the cloth in hot water and wring it out as completely as you can.
3. Soak it in turpentine and wring it out once again.
4. Lay the cloth out on a clean, flat surface and drip varnish in small dots about two inches apart and covering the entire surface. A large eyedropper works well.
5. Fold the cloth over varnish to varnish. Then roll it and wring it. Keep doing this until when you unroll it there is a uniform coat of varnish all over. The goal is to have a rag that feels tacky but does not leave varnish on your hands.

Store your tack rag in a tightly sealed jar between uses. When the rag begins to lose it tackiness, drip on more water and turpentine, wring and roll to restore it.

ANTIQUING

Making furniture look old is fun and rewarding. The two basic steps in faking antiques are distressing and finishing.

DISTRESSING

Old furniture will show a certain amount of wear. Sharp edges and square corners will have been worn away over the years. You can wear them away in minutes with a rasp and sandpaper.

You can simulate wormholes without having a trained worm by using an ice pick. Don't get carried away. Too many holes can weaken the piece.

Dents and dings give the furniture character. Beat it with chains and tap it with a ballpeen hammer. Again, use moderation.

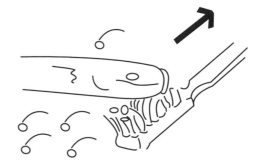

Make fly specks with a toothbrush, some black paint and a Popsicle stick. Dip the brush in the paint and rake the stick across the bristles, which are facing up pulling it toward you (figure 8-6). This action will fling tiny droplets toward the

figure 8-6

furniture. Practice first to get the technique. If you're going to glaze, as we discuss below, be sure the glaze won't dissolve the black specks.

FINISHING

You have a choice here. You can stain, but to have an older look, we suggest you try glazing over a painted surface. Semi-gloss enamel is good. The color is up to you. Paint several scraps of wood to practice with the glazing.

Your paint dealer will have glazing products in various shades of mostly earth tones. Or, you can make your own. Use a clear varnish and tint this with a squeeze from a tube of artist's oil paints. Brush the glaze on a painted scrap. When it starts to haze over, wipe it off. How much you remove determines the overall look. This test also lets you know if the tint looks right.

If your project looks really old, make up a story about the piece . . . like maybe George Washington slept on the table?

THE SUPER SAGE SAYS

Not all antique furniture is as old as it is cracked up to be!

Home Security 101

9

With a break-in of some sort happening every few seconds in this country, it is no wonder that people have become more security conscious. However, we must tell you that there is no way to make your home totally burglarproof. About the best thing you can do is make it more difficult for the crook to get in. After all, the perp went into this line of business because he didn't want to work. By "hardening the target" he or she may go on down the block where the pickings are easier.

If someone will dim the lights, we'll play a videotape of an interview with an actual burglar. Since he is still around, he is wearing a ski mask.

"First of all, I want you to know that I'm not a dangerous criminal. I never carry a weapon. I try to break into unoccupied houses. Most of my jobs are done during the day when everyone is away at work or school or shopping.

"Also, I'm not some clever person who can pick locks. I couldn't pick my way out of a pay toilet. I don't have to, because there are so many cheap locks that I can open in 30 seconds.

"In fact, lots of times I find doors that are not locked at all. More often than that, I find a hidden key in the mailbox, under the doormat, or up on the ledge above the door.

"However, if the door looks like it might make my entry a little difficult, I can get in through lots of different types of windows even quicker. Here again, I find many easily accessible windows are left unlocked and often even partially open. Even when locked, many double hung window locks can be easily jimmied.

"I try to avoid breaking glass to get past a window because the sound might alert a neighbor. But I've done it many times and have yet to get caught because of that.

"If there is a dog, even a wussie little dog, I'm on down the block. Not that I'm afraid of dogs—it's mostly the noise factor. But I still wouldn't want to get bitten.

"I don't spend much time inside after entering a house. In fact, I grab all I can carry and exit within four minutes. I actually time myself. Even if I've set off an alarm, by making it a quickie job, I'm long gone by the time the cops arrive. That said, if I can tell that there is a security system in the house, I'll pass.

"I look for TVs, stereos, cameras, computers, hand guns, and office equipment. Things that are easy to fence and easy to carry. And of course, any cash that's lying around. But I wouldn't even think of trying to crack open a safe. Once I did carry off a small safe on rollers. When I finally got a safe cracker buddy to open it, we found nothing but insurance policies and other papers that were worthless to us.

"People have asked me why I do this. Well, I make a good living. I set my own hours. I'm my own boss, and the risk is minimal. If I do get caught, I'll probably beat the rap and if I do time, the jails are so crowded that they'll probably let me go in a few months."

There you have it! Our goal is to make it more difficult for this bozo to make a living and also give you greater peace of mind.

MAKING YOUR HOME LOOK OCCUPIED

Our burglar friend is looking for homes where the family is gone. Here are some techniques to fool the bad guys when you're on vacation:

1. Stop the newspaper delivery and the mail. Or, have a friend or neighbor pick up these tell-tale signs that you're gone. The same goes for deliveries.
2. Use timers to turn lights on and off at appropriate times. You might also put radio and TV sets on timers. Timers or an electronic eye should control outside lights.
3. Arrange to have the lawn mowed and shrubs trimmed.
4. Keep the thermostat set at about 55° F in winter and about 82° F in summer.
5. Don't have all the shades down or blinds completely closed. That makes the house look empty.
6. If your garage doors have windows, cover them with opaque peel & stick shelf paper.
7. If possible, have a friend or neighbor leave a car parked in the drive at night.

COMMONSENSE CRIME FIGHTERS

1. When you leave, even for a few minutes, lock the house and set your alarm if you have one.

2. When you're outside doing yard work, lock all entry doors.

3. Do not leave a ladder or any tools outside that might help a burglar do his thing. If there is no storage space for a ladder inside, chain and lock it to the fence.

4. Examine shrubbery and other landscaping to see if it shields doors and windows from view, allowing a crook to break in without being seen.

5. Put a wide-angle viewer on every exterior door so that you can see who is calling without opening the door. If there is an attached garage, include the door from the house to the garage. If there are children old enough to be responsible, add a second viewer at their eye level.

6. Use an electric engraving tool to mark IDs on tools, appliances, and other things likely to be stolen. This aids in retrieval and deters many burglars from even taking the items.

7. Talk to your neighbors and form a neighborhood watch group. The local police Department may have suggestions and guidelines.

8. Consider getting a dog. Not only is this a good alarm factor, but you'll also have a good companion.

9. If you can afford one, put in an alarm system. Do-it-yourself systems can be less expensive and many are easily installed. Having your system monitored is an additional expense but we consider it well worth it.

DOORS & LOCKS

1. Hollow core doors are a no-no as exterior doors. One good kick from even a small person can shatter the door. Metal doors are best, but solid core heavy-duty exterior doors are also good. (See chapter 11 for more information on doors.)

2. All exterior doors should have a deadbolt lock. Learn how to install a lockset below.

3. Many of the screws used on door hardware are small. Add longer screws to the strike plate to make it a little tougher to kick in.

4. Sliding glass doors can often be lifted up and, even though locked, may be taken out of the track (figure 9-1). This makes illegal entry a snap. Make this trick impossible by installing several sheet metal screws in the upper track. They should stick down far enough so that the door can not be lifted but not so far as to impede the movement of the door to open and close. To do this, open the door and space the screws out over the exposed track. Another sliding door problem lies in the fact that many can be jiggled to unlock. Put a pipe or dowel in the track to make it impossible to slide the door open even when unlocked.

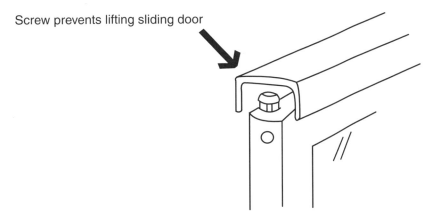

Screw prevents lifting sliding door

figure 9-1

INSTALLING A DEADBOLT

Rather than replace the old locksets, we suggest you install a deadbolt cylinder lock above the old unit. The two locks may cause you to spend a little extra time getting in, but that gives you extra protection. Here are the installation steps:

1. Be sure the new lock has a paper template to let you drill the necessary holes. Tape the template on the door as shown (figure 9-2). One hole goes in the side of the door and is for the cylinder. The other goes into the edge and is for the bolt. They must be lined up properly for the new lock to work.

2. The best tool for the cylinder hole is a power drill and hole saw (figure 9-3). Then use a spade bit (figure 9-4) for the hole that will house the bolt. The template will tell you what bit size is needed for each hole.

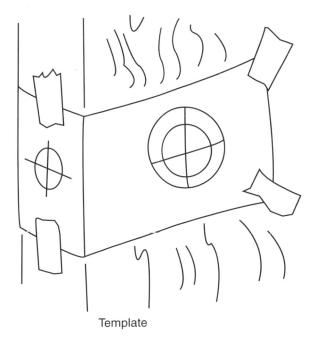

Template

figure 9-2

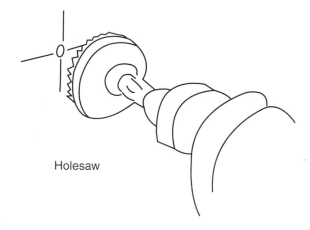

Holesaw

figure 9-3

3. Drill the cylinder hole first. When the point of the hole saw comes through on the other side of the door, stop and move to the other side to finish the hole.

4. When you drill the hole for the bolt, continue until you have reached the cavity of the cylinder hole.

5. Insert the bolt in the hole and mark the spot for the plate.

6. Use a chisel to mortise out for the plate. Use the plate to mark spots for drilling pilot holes for the screws that hold the plate.

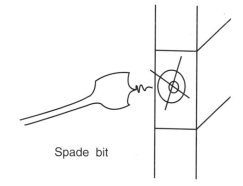

Spade bit

figure 9-4

7. With bolt secured in place by the plate, insert the exterior part of the cylinder so that the connecting arm fits into the bolt unit.

8. Attach the inside part and secure it with the bolts.

9. All that's left to do is to mark the site for the strike plate on the doorjamb, drill the required size hole, and mortise.

The other way to handle this is to replace the entire old unit with a new deadbolt type. Try to find one that will fit into the old holes. If this isn't possible, you can enlarge the old holes and maybe get a decorative plate to help cover exposed areas.

WINDOWS

Without windows, we might just as well still be living in caves. However, the trade-off for having more light, a good view, and maybe some fresh air is that windows are not very secure.

The first reason is—and this isn't exactly a news flash—glass is breakable. A quick tap and the crook can reach in and unlock the window, raise or slide it open, and then crawl in.

One solution is to install burglar bars. This iron grillwork is only as good as the fasteners that hold it in place. Use large lag screws and then fill the slots with solder or epoxy glue to render them tamper-proof. A big downside to burglar bars . . . in case of fire, you could be trapped in the house.

The addition of storm windows adds another layer to be reckoned with, and often the thief will just go elsewhere, looking for an easier target.

The replacement of the glass with a plastic such as Lexan or Plexiglass is a good option. These acrylics are many times more impact resistant than glass. The thicker the plastic, the greater the resistance.

A conventional double hung window, either wood or aluminum, can be made more difficult for an intruder by merely drilling a hole into both the lower and upper sash. Do this with the window closed so the holes match up. Drill from inside but don't go all the way through the second sash. By putting a large nail into the holes, the sashes can't be moved (figure 9-5). As you can visualize, this little trick can also work on a sliding glass door.

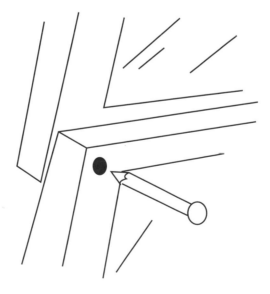

figure 9-5

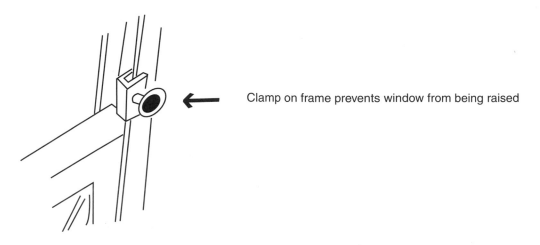

Clamp on frame prevents window from being raised

figure 9-6

A trip to your local hardware dealer will allow you to see all sorts of very inexpensive locks to add to windows. The one in figure 9-6 requires no tools. It fits on the track of an aluminum window and the thumbscrew locks it in place so that the movable sash can't be moved. Of course, that doesn't keep the perp from breaking the glass.

JUST IN CASE

All of the things we've learned in this class may not prevent a break-in. Sometimes the stolen goods are recovered. You can help the authorities by making a detailed list of all your goodies. Include the make, model, serial numbers, appraised value, and a detailed description. Take pictures of tools, appliances, paintings, furs, and jewelry.

Keep your list updated. Not only can this help in recovery, but it may also come in handy with your insurance claim.

We hope you never have to use it.

We also hope what you've learned in the class will help you and your dog take a bite out of crime . . . or at least out of a criminal!

Floors 101

10

Why is it that floors always seem to be underfoot? Many floors squeak. Carpets gather spots that not even dynamite will remove. Vinyl floors curl up at the seams. In this course, we'll learn floor care. The ease with which you can remedy these problems will floor you.

CARPET CARE

Carpeting is usually a fairly expensive item in most homes. We abuse it by walking all over it, and we also subject it to spills and dirt. Both dirt and stains not only take away from the beauty of the carpet, they can also shorten its life. Dirt particles act as an abrasive and wear away at the carpet fibers. Here are the simple steps of carpet care:

1. There is no such thing as too much vacuuming. Vacuum at least once or twice a week, depending on the amount of foot traffic. Make a half dozen passes over each area to remove both embedded and surface dirt. Between vacuuming use an unpowered carpet sweeper.
2. Get on spills and spots as soon as they happen. However, test any spot remover on a scrap or an inconspicuous section. After the cleaner has been there for a minute or so, dab at it with a tissue. If there is even a tinge of color on the tissue, find another solution. (Check with our spot remover guide below.)
3. From time to time, rearrange the furniture to change traffic patterns.
4. Use area rugs over high traffic areas.

5. If you see a loose carpet fiber sticking up, snip it off with scissors. If you pull it, you could unravel the entire carpet.

6. Have the carpets shampooed at least once a year before they get too dirty. Vacuum just before shampooing, and move all furniture out. If you replace the furniture before the carpet is completely dry put squares of aluminum foil under each leg.

SPOT REMOVAL

There are three key words to spot removal: *test* (which we've already covered); *speed*, because you should get on spills as quickly as possible to prevent them from becoming stains; and *blot*, to prevent over-wetting the carpet. Here are some tips on handling common spots:

GENERAL RULES

When using liquid cleaners, do not over-wet. Don't apply the liquid directly to the carpet: apply it to a sponge or clean white rag and then blot it on the spot.

Work from the outside edge of the spill toward the middle.

Stain removal guide:

1. **Acids**—Neutralize quickly with club soda. Blot as you pour.
2. **Blood**—Dampen with cold water. Then use carpet shampoo, blotting with white paper towels as you go.
3. **Butter**—Use a chemical carpet spot remover product or a dry cleaning solution made for fabrics.
4. **Chewing gum**—Put a couple of ice cubes in a plastic bag and hold the bag against the gum. The cold makes the gum brittle, and it can then be scraped away with a spoon.
5. **Chocolate**—Start with carpet shampoo followed by a mild ammonia and water solution. Blot well.
6. **Cigarette burn**—If it's not burned down to the backing, sometimes you can use fingernail scissors to trim off the charred ends. If the carpet spot looks too bare, snip fibers from a scrap, pour some white glue into the spot and stick the fibers into the adhesive. Done carefully, the problem may be well hidden. If this hasn't worked, see page 77, on patching.
7. **Coffee**—Carpet shampoo mixed with a little vinegar and blotted well.
8. **Crayon**—A carpet spot remover will usually remove both the wax and the color.

9. **Eggs**—Try a solution of half water and half white vinegar followed by carpet shampoo.

10. **Grease**—See Butter.

11. **Ice cream**—Scrape up as much as possible and blot any liquid that results from melting. Then use carpet shampoo.

12. **Lipstick**—Chemical spot removers should work. If not, equal parts of white vinegar and water with lots of blotting

13. **Mayonnaise**—See Butter.

14. **Paint**—If the paint is latex there are two products that remove only latex. They are called OOPS! and Goof-Off. For oil based, use a carpet spot remover.

15. **Pet accidents**—Get right on it! Scrape up solids and blot up liquids. The pet store or your vet will have some enzyme-based products that remove the spot and the odor.

16. **Wine**—Blot up and then use a carpet shampoo, avoiding over-wetting.

17. **Wax**—There are two ways to remove wax from a carpet. Use a blotter and a warm iron. The blotter will absorb the melted wax. However, if the wax is colored, don't try this. Use ice cubes in a plastic bag. Hold the bag against the wax and it will become brittle; you can then use a spoon to chip the wax away.

> **SPOTLIGHT ON THE FUTURE**
>
> There is a new two-step spot removal system that has a slightly acidic rinse. After the spot remover does its thing the rinse removes all residue. Otherwise, the residue, being sticky, will attract airborne particles to make it appear that the stain has come back. Look for it.

THE PATCH

When the magic formula doesn't get rid of the spot or if the carpet is damaged (for example, a cigarette burn) try the patch. You need to cover the bad spot with a geometric shape. We like using a round lid from a plastic butter dish. Drive a pair of two-headed nails through the lid and carpet into the subfloor (figure 10-1). Use a utility knife with a new blade to cut around the lid through the carpet, but not through the padding.

Remove the lid and use it again to cut out your patch. If you didn't save any scraps, find an obscure place like in a closet or under the sofa.

Cut a strip of double-sided tape and work the edges under the carpet. Press the patch in place, making sure the nap runs the same way as the rest of the carpet. Weight it down overnight with several encyclopedias.

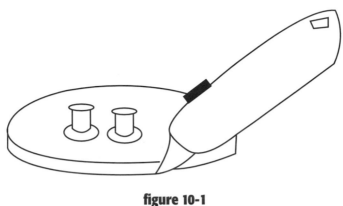

figure 10-1

CARPET INDENTATIONS

When we move the big couch to the other side of the room, we can see the footprints. Use the end of a spoon to fluff up the nap. Get it the rest of the way up by holding a steam iron an inch or so above the surface while using the spoon again.

SQUEAKING FLOORS

The reason a floor squeaks is because of movement that lets boards rub together or against something. Stop the movement and you stop the squeak. But first:

QUICK FIX TRICKS

If the flooring is hardwood, sprinkle talcum powder over the squeak area and sweep it back and forth. The talc goes into the cracks and acts as a lubricant. Not a permanent cure but it works. Or, flow liquid wax or all-purpose glue into the cracks.

If you can see that the floorboards are moving, drive a few flat glaziers points into the crack and this should stop the movement. Glaziers points are little metal points used to hold window panes in place.

When you see movement, another way to fix it is to drive finishing nails into the board at about a 45-degree angle. It's best to drill pilot holes and use a nail set to drive the heads below the surface. Cover the nail heads with wood putty.

If you have access to the underside of the floor, like in a basement or crawl space, this is the best place to attack the problem.

Have someone up in the house walk back and forth over the squeaking spot. Once you spot the movement you should be able to stop it. If you don't see it, use a magnet above and a magnetic compass below to point out the spot.

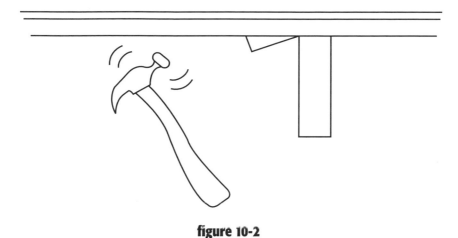

figure 10-2

Often, driving wedges between the subfloor and the joist (figure 10-2) can stop the movement.

Or, you can try a wood screw up through the subfloor and into the hardwood floor. The screw should pull the two layers tightly together (figure 10-3).

Bridging between joists is another way to silence a squeak (figure 10-4).

If the floor above is carpeted and there's no way to get at it from underneath, you can try to find an ingenious kit called Squeeeek No More. It comes with a device that locates the joists under the floor and includes nails that have breakaway heads that are removed after they are driven through the carpet.

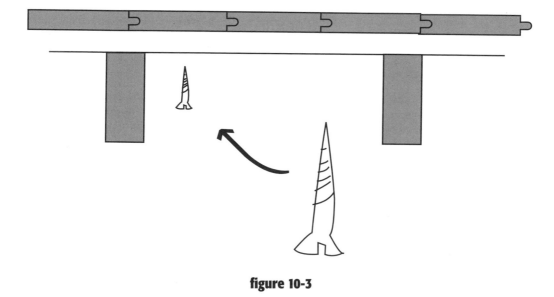

figure 10-3

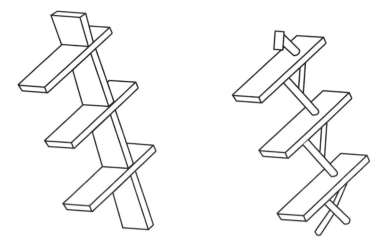

figure 10-4

HARDWOOD FLOORS

Adventurous families are buying older homes and want to bring these abodes into the twenty-first century. One of the most pleasant surprises is when the new owners remove the old orange shag carpet and find a hardwood floor underneath. Often the floor needs a little refurbishing to take care of tack strips from the carpet and may also need a refinishing job. Newer homes are featuring hardwood floors that need only minimal maintenance. Hardwood is beautiful, and here are some steps to keep it that way:

1. Wood and water do not mix. Any water spills and/or plumbing problems should be dried as soon as possible. A wet/dry vacuum can remove large amounts of water in a hurry. Use fans and maybe a dehumidifier to complete the drying.
2. Never damp mop the hardwood floor.
3. Spills should be wiped up as soon as possible so that they don't become stains.
4. Don't use over-the-counter general floor cleaners. Get cleaners that are specifically formulated for hardwood floors.
5. Sweep or vacuum the floors regularly. Tracked-in dirt can act as an abrasive and scratch the finish.
6. Keep indoor pets' toenails clipped.
7. Avoid moving heavy furniture and appliances across the bare floor. Put down a throw rug or use glides that protect the wood.
8. Be sure your home has proper ventilation so that the humidity remains in the acceptable range.

9. If you have a new pre-finished floor, get the manufacturer's guidance on whether to use wax or not. If wax is OK, use only a paste wax that is applied by hand and then buffed to a shine. Since the hardwood floor lasts for a long, long time, go ahead and buy an electric buffer.

REPLACING A DAMAGED BOARD

Since most hardwood flooring is of the tongue-and-groove variety, each board is locked together with the board on each side. Removing the single bad board would seem to be a challenge. It's actually not that difficult. Here are the steps:

1. Drill a hole near each end of the board to be removed (figure 10-5).
2. With a circular saw, plunge cut in the center of the board and all the way between holes. Set the blade depth so it cuts just through the board and not into the subfloor.
3. Use a chisel to split the board at each end.
4. A pry bar can be used to carefully lift the two pieces up and out.
5. Remove all nails left in the cavity.
6. Carefully measure and cut the new board.
7. With the board upside down, use a chisel to remove the bottom lip of the groove (figure 10-6).

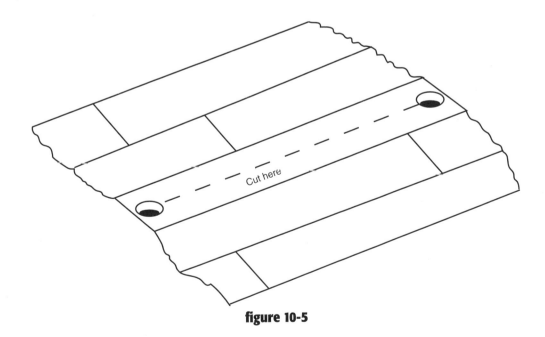

Cut here

figure 10-5

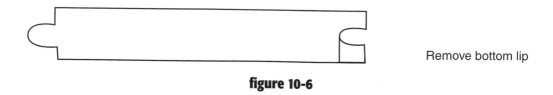

Remove bottom lip

figure 10-6

8. Coat both the tongue and half groove with wood glue.
9. Angle the tongue into the adjacent board and the other side can easily be pushed in place.

REFINISHING HARDWOOD FLOORS

Done properly, refinishing can make an old floor look brand new. You'll need to rent a drum sander and an edge sander. You'll also need to spend a little time with the rental guy to be sure you know how the thing works and how to use it. Describe your floor in detail so that he can tell you what grits of sandpaper to use and how many passes you'll probably have to make. Then when you get home, you should practice on an old sheet of plywood. When you've conquered the equipment, here's the routine:

1. Remove all the furniture.
2. Weather permitting, open doors and windows.
3. Seal off adjoining rooms with plastic drop cloths.
4. Wear safety goggles and a respirator.
5. Pry off the shoe mold and baseboards.
6. Closely examine the entire floor for popped nails and reset them.
7. All passes should be made with the grain. Start with coarse grit. Begin about 6 inches away from the wall and with the sander tilted back so that the drum is not touching the floor. As you turn on the sander, start to move forward, lowering the drum down to the floor.
8. Rock the sander back at the end of the pass.
9. Overlap half of the previous strip with each successive pass.
10. When the entire floor has been sanded, vacuum and use a tack rag to remove fine dust.
11. After completing the floor with the coarse abrasive, switch to medium grit and do it again.
12. The third cut should be with fine grit.

13. Use the edge sander to remove the finish along the borders.

14. A hand scraper will remove the finish from tight spots. Hand sanding can blend the area between the different sanders.

15. You are now ready to apply a stain, if needed, followed by a new finish.

Polyurethane is a good choice for a clear and durable finish. We suggest at least two coats. Pros may use as many as four. You do not apply floor wax to polyurethane.

VINYL FLOORS

What some folks still refer to as linoleum is mostly vinyl. It's beautiful, sturdy, is mostly water- and stainproof, and is practically maintenance-free.

This flooring is available as tiles or as sheet goods. Sheet good often means an entire room can be covered with no seams. With a vinyl tile floor, the room is a checkerboard of seams.

LOOSE AND CURLING SEAMS

We start with seams because this is a common vinyl floor problem. With sheet goods, you need to warm the flooring, as the heat often reactivates the adhesive underneath. Use a heat gun, hair dryer, or even an iron. Hold the iron close to the material without touching and keep the iron moving. When the edges are flexible, they should once again lie down flat. Then, by placing weights over the floor along the seam, the newly activated adhesive should hold it in place.

If that didn't work, heat the edges again but this time peel them back so you can scrape out the old adhesive and apply new glue. Press the edges in place and wipe away any excess adhesive. Place wax paper over the seam in case more glue gets squeezed out.

The permanent way to cure the seam problem is with a product called seam sealer. It is applied to the edges and chemically welds the flooring edges together.

SCRATCHES

Often a scratch will heal itself. To help this happen, take a penny or nickel and press hard as you rub it along the scratch. Seam sealer can also close cracks. Or, hide the scratch with wax.

GOUGES

Small holes can be filled with a patching compound you can make. Take a scrap piece of the flooring and use a food grater to create a fine powder. Mix this in lacquer to form a putty-like paste that will match the color of the floor to form a perfect patch.

Larger gouges may require patching. If the floor is tiled, just remove the ruined tile and replace. Use a heat gun or even a propane torch in the center of the tile. Heat will soften the adhesive and allow you to go to work at the gouge with a chisel or putty knife to rip up the old tile. Be careful not to damage the edges of surrounding tiles. With the old tile out of the way, scrape up the old adhesive, apply new glue, and press the replacement down. Put weights on it overnight. If the floor is sheet goods, cut out a square or rectangle and use the same heat treatment to get the old vinyl up. Lay this piece on a scrap of the flooring and line up the pattern. Carefully cut out the patch and set it in place over new adhesive.

STAINS

Spills on vinyl flooring usually don't become stains if you wipe them up immediately. Your best guide for removing stains is the manufacturer's material that came with the flooring. If you've lost it, here are some common stains and some uncommon solutions:

1. **Heel marks** can usually be removed by dipping 0000 steel wool into liquid wax and lightly rubbing. Don't press too hard.
2. A spritz of hair spray will get rid of some ballpoint **ink spots.** Or, make a compress from a folded paper towel saturated with rubbing alcohol.
3. For **tar** or **chewing gum** hold a bag with ice cubes against the spot. The substance gets very brittle and can be chipped away with a plastic putty knife.
4. **Candle wax** will dissolve when wiped with a rag dipped in paint thinner. If any color is left, apply a compress with hydrogen peroxide for a few minutes.
5. If **paint spots** are latex, use either Goof Off or OOPS. If oil based, use the 0000 steel wool and liquid wax treatment. See **heel marks** above.
6. **Fruit stains, mustard,** and **coffee stains** respond to a compress of hydrogen peroxide left on for a few minutes.

CERAMIC TILE

Ceramic tile used to be found mainly in kitchens and baths, and even then it might only have been used on walls and countertops. Now it is found in rooms throughout the house and is said to be the fastest growing flooring material today.

Glazed ceramic tile is very nearly maintenance-free. The glaze seals the tile against stains, and cleaning is usually done simply by damp mopping. The grout between the tiles is a possible dirt problem, but a grout sealer will prevent this problem. Sealing also precludes moisture entering the grout and causing mildew.

REPLACING A CERAMIC TILE

If you drop your bowling ball on a ceramic tile floor, you'll probably have to replace a tile. Probably the most difficult part will be finding a replacement to match. Try the tile companies. Then try the salvage yards. Then try to figure out what will closely match or something different that would make a nice contrast. Here's the easy part:

1. Remove the grout around the tile to be removed. You can use an inexpensive tool called a grout saw. Or, there's a new attachment for a rotary tool that lets you use power to remove the grout.
2. You must break the tile to remove it. Using a glass-cutter, score two diagonal lines to form an "X" (figure 10-7a).
3. Using a masonry drill bit, drill a hole in the center of the "X" (figure 10-7b).
4. Now take a hammer and chisel and go to work at the center. The tile will usually crack along the scored lines. Take care not to damage the surrounding tiles.

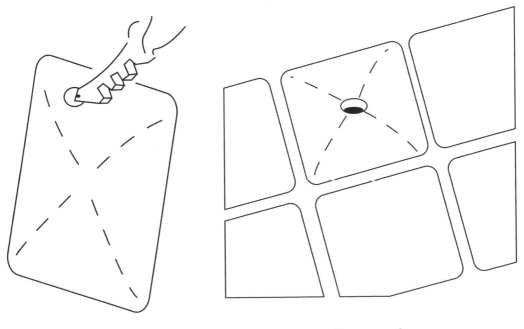

figure 10-7a   **figure 10-7b**

5. With all the pieces gone, vacuum the cavity.
6. Scrape away the old adhesive and vacuum up all the particles.
7. Butter the back side of the replacement tile with thin-set mortar. When the piece is in place, make sure it is level with the surrounding tiles and that the spacing for grout is equal all the way around.
8. After the mortar has set up, spread new grout using a grout float held at about a 45-degree angle and working in all directions.

YUCKY COLORED TILES

Fifty years ago, green, pink, and gold tiles were the rage. Now you'd like a different color. Tiles can be painted. The best category of professional to do this would be a bathtub refinisher. Get one that's been in business for some time and check references.

If you want to do it yourself, use a two-component epoxy paint and follow all the directions as to preparation and application. If it calls for acid washing to etch the glaze, be sure you are properly protected and that you have lots of ventilation and wear a respirator.

THE SUPER SAGE SAYS

"You can't just sweep floor problems under the rug!"

Doors 101

11

Doors provide privacy, security, and sometimes frustration. Some doors swing. Other doors slide. As long as they do these things, we pretty much take them for granted. But when the time comes that they start squealing, get stuck in the closed position, or the handle comes off in your hand, you're in for some hand-to-hand combat with your doors.

DOOR MAINTENANCE

Doors don't need much coddling. However, we suggest you keep the locksets and hinges properly lubricated. Lubricating them once a year is usually enough.

Keyed locks are easy to lubricate. Just rub the key across the point of a soft lead pencil. (It is not really lead but graphite.) Then insert the key in and out of the lock and turn it several times. This will distribute the graphite inside the lock. You can use graphite in a squeeze tube that sprays the powder inside. By turning the handle, the striker retracts and you can spray graphite in around the strike.

Lubricating hinges can silence a squeal. It's best not to squirt oil on the hinges because it can drip off onto your carpet. Remove the hinge pin by tapping a large nail into the opening at the bottom of the hinge barrel. Coat the pin with either petroleum jelly or graphite before putting it back in place.

Loose hinges are caused by screws that have come loose. From time to time check the screws for tightness. Sometimes the screw cannot tighten because the screw hole has become enlarged. Despite this, you can make the reamed out hole work by poking wooden toothpicks, dipped in glue, into the hole (figure 11-1). Pack them in, and when the glue sets, use a utility knife to cut the toothpicks off flush. The screw will go back in just like it was new piece of wood.

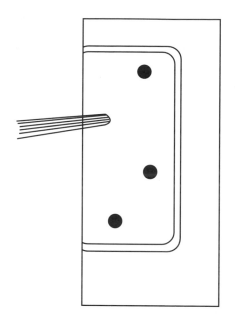

COMMON DOOR PROBLEMS

Door sticks—We'll attack this problem in detail in the next section.

Door won't latch—You may have to use a file to enlarge the opening in the strike plate or else file off the edge of the strike so it fits. Sometimes you have to move the strike plate, which will then include mortising out the jam so the plate is flush. You can fill in the low place from the previous mortise with wood putty and some paint.

figure 11-1

Door rattles—If it's just a loose fit, try weather stripping around the door. If the striker doesn't engage in the strike plate, adjust the plate or file off either the plate or the striker.

Door doesn't stay closed—It is probably the same problem with the striker as above.

Door drags on new flooring—Saw off a portion of the bottom of the door. Remove the door. Clamp a board to the door to use as a fence for a circular saw. Also, score the cut line on doors with a veneer cover to deter chipping. Paint over the bare bottom so that moisture doesn't enter the unprotected wood.

ENTRY DOORS

The front door is often the first impression most people have when coming to your home. It and other entry doors are out there and exposed to the elements. As a result, they require different maintenance than the doors inside. In fact, the inside portion of an entry door is treated differently than the outside.

The painting of an exterior door usually needs to be redone more often. If the door faces west or south and gets large doses of sunshine, it needs to have protection against ultraviolet rays. See if the type of finish you want for these doors is available with UV protection. If the entry door has a natural wood finish, consider using a marine varnish.

Since entry doors have locks, this element can present problems. Here are some of these lock losers:

Key broken off in lock—Straighten out a tiny fishhook to use in getting the piece of key out. A coping saw blade may also snag the key. If part of the key is sticking out, grab it with needle-nose pliers.

Key won't turn—If the key is a duplicate, it may be a bad copy. There may also be dirt in the slot. Another possible problem is that the cylinder has gotten out of place.

Key turns but bolt doesn't move—If it's a good lock, a locksmith will be able to fix it. Otherwise replace the lock, which is something you can do.

Lock is frozen and ice won't allow key to enter—Grab the key with pliers and hold it over the flame from a cigarette lighter. Stick the hot key in the slot. As the key cools, remove and repeat until the key goes all the way in. A shot of anti-freeze in the lock will prevent future freeze-ups.

HARD TO OPEN AND CLOSE

Often the first thing many people do is get out the plane and start shaving. That may be the solution, but here are some other things to check.

1. If possible, close the door and spot the sticking point. Look for a gap by examining the opposite edge. If you spot one, the problem is probably in the hinges. Here's what you do:

   a. Check to be sure the screws are tight. If one screw turns without ever getting tight, the hole is reamed out. You can try a larger screw or perform the toothpick trick as described above under "Loose hinges" (figure 11-1).

   b. Next, look at the door in the closed position again and if there is space all the way around except at a single binding spot on the latch side, shims may be needed. If the sticking point is toward the top, shim out at the bottom.

   c. Poster board can be cut to the hinge size. Cut slots where the screws are (figure 11-2).

   d. Loosen the screws and slide the shim in place. If one thickness isn't enough, add another.

   e. If the sticking place is at the door bottom, shim the top hinge (figure 11-3).

2. Next, with the door open, use a square against the frame at the top. If the frame is not squared, the house has probably settled. Here's what to do:

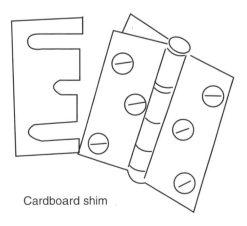

Cardboard shim

figure 11-2

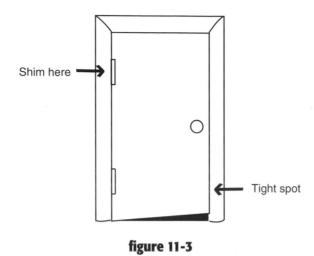

Shim here

Tight spot

figure 11-3

   a. Sometimes, as soil conditions change, the problem will cure its self. Look at chapter 7 to see how to better help your foundation.

   b. Use a padded 2 x 4 scrap, and hit the block all around the doorframe with a hammer to see if you can knock it back into alignment.

3. If there are no gaps anywhere, the door is probably swollen from moisture that has penetrated the paint and entered the wood. Now you can drag out the plane and take these steps:

   a. Mark all the binding spots with chalk.

   b. If the sticking is only on the top of the door, you can plane without removing the door. Otherwise, remove the door.

OPENING THE DOOR TO PLANE TALK

When planing a door top or bottom, plane from the edge toward the center. Otherwise the plane might catch the edge of the side rail and rip off a splinter. When planing the sides from the center toward the edges, keep in mind that the latch side of a door has a slight bevel to prevent the edge from striking the frame when closing. Maintain that bevel, or better still, plane as much as possible from the hinge side.

---

   c. Steady the door for working by clamping it to a big wooden crate (figure 11-4). Or, with the door on its side, push it into an inside corner.

   d. When you've planed away all the chalk marks, reinstall the door for a test. If it's still not right, take it down and plane some more.

e. When the job is done, be sure to paint over all the bare spot so no new moisture gets in.

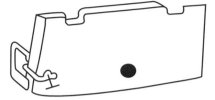

Door clamped to crate for planing

figure 11-4

REPAIRS

Most interior doors have hollow cores. Almost any sharp blow can knock a hole in the veneer. If the door is painted, a quick fix for a hole is to remove all the loose material and fill the cavity with automobile body compound. When this sets up, it can be sanded smooth with the rest of the surface and then painted. With a good paint job, you cannot see where the patch was made.

A WARPED DOOR

There are several steps you can take to straighten a warped door. If one method doesn't work, you may have to try them all.

1. With door closed, see if there is any play between the door and the doorstop. If there is, very carefully pry off the doorstop on the latch side of the door. Push the stop up tight against the door and reattach it.

2. If the door currently has only two hinges, install a third hinge in the middle of the door. This can force the door to straighten up its act.

3. Remove the door and lay it on a flat solid surface with the bowed side sticking up. Protect the surface with a tarp. Put heavy weights such as concrete blocks or bricks on the door for several days. Unfortunately, even if this does take away the warp, sometimes it comes back.

4. Use a turnbuckle, a block, and wires as shown in figure 11-5 to force the door back in shape.

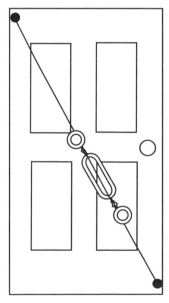

figure 11-5

SLIDING GLASS DOORS

The biggest problem with these door systems is that they balk, making it impossible for anyone but an NFL middle linebacker to move. Here are some causes for the problem and their solutions:

1. There is an upper and a lower track in which the sliding panel moves. If either track is bent, the door can bind and be difficult to slide. Inspect for these places and use a hammer and wood block to straighten out the kink (figure 11-6).

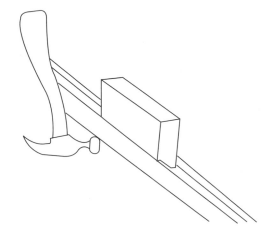

figure 11-6

2. Dirt or debris in the lower track could be the problem. Use a whisk-broom or a vacuum cleaner to remove the stuff.

3. Most of these systems have large rollers that stick out of the bottom of the door. On each edge of the door, near the bottom, there will be a couple of screws (figure 11-7). The top one usually holds the frame together. The bottom one lowers or retracts the rollers at each end. If the rollers don't stick out far enough, the door won't roll. Trying a couple of turns with a screw-driver may solve the prob-lem.

4. If it doesn't, retract the rollers all the way, and remove the door by lifting up and out. Since these doors are heavy, it's a good idea to have a helper. With the door out, you can actually inspect the rollers. Make sure they

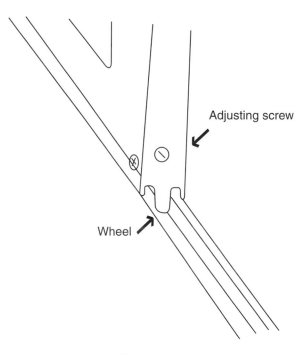

Adjusting screw

Wheel

figure 11-7

will roll. They may need cleaning or lubrication. If the rollers are worn, you can get
replacement rollers.

REPLACEMENT

If the old door is on its last legs, replace it! If it's
a standard sized door, you should be able to find
a match to fit with only a few alterations. Here
are the steps:

> **TEACHER'S TIP**
>
> Never cut more than
> 3/4-inch from either end.
> Too much can weaken the
> structure of the door.

1. First, check the frame for squareness.
2. If the new door is too high, you can saw it off. Allow 1/8-inch clearance at the
   top and 3/8-inch at the bottom.
3. Put the new door in place in the opening, using shims to lift the door off the
   floor. If the frame doesn't have doorstops, use shims on the sides, too.
4. If you can use the old hinges, mark the door where the old hinge plates are.
5. Mortise out on the door edge for the hinge plates. Then install the hinge plates
   and connect them with the hinge pins, and the door is hung.

THRESHOLD

All entry doors have a threshold that
runs horizontally along the floor
directly under the door. The door
closes against this piece to stop
air infiltration, and to keep out dust
and insects. After being walked on
for years, the threshold may have lost
its shape and should be replaced. If
it's a hardwood piece and is under
the frame and stops, rather than dismantling what is in the way, use a
back saw and cut the threshold at
each end (figure 11-8). Now you can
pry out the center part. We suggest

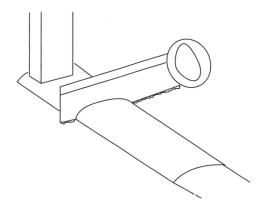

figure 11-8

you replace it with a new aluminum threshold that has a vinyl weather-strip piece
that fits into a channel and sticks up to seal against the door (figure 11-9). The

aluminum can easily be sawed to size with a hacksaw.

HARDWARE AND LOCKSETS

We've already covered the installation of locksets in chapter 9.

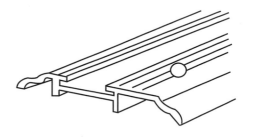

figure 11-9

THE SUPER SAGE SAYS

"With your new knowledge on doors, those doors that aren't adorable can soon be whipped into shape."

Windows 101

If we didn't have windows in our homes, we might just as well still be living in a cave. Windows let in light to brighten up our lives and our homes. Windows let us see what's going on outside in our neighborhood. Windows also allow others to look in. They can cut down on our energy efficiency, too.

First, let's talk about maintenance for windows, and then we'll get into replacing old windows.

CLEANING WINDOWS

The battle cry of lots of domestic help is, "I don't do windows." You may find that members of your family have the same motto. In that case, you know who is going to do the windows . . . YOU! People frequently ask how often we should clean our windows. The answer is "Whenever they are dirty!" Also, you'll be glad to know you don't have to clean both inside and out each time.

Maybe these window-cleaning tips will take the pain out of this chore:

1. Make your own window cleaner solution to save money. Add a tablespoon of household ammonia to a quart of hot water.
2. Sponge it on.
3. Squeegee it dry, wiping the squeegee blade often.
4. Use crumpled up wads of newspaper to polish the glass to a shine.
5. For cleaning outside windows that are hard to reach, such as on a two-story house, use a hose-end sprayer. Pour in liquid dishwasher detergent and turn the water on full blast.

6. Rinse well. This won't do a perfect job but it is a lot better than climbing or not cleaning.
7. If you're buying replacement windows, consider the type that allow you to do all of the cleaning from inside.

Although our magic formula is very diluted, it won't hurt to protect your skin with rubber gloves. Try to avoid cleaning outside in direct sunlight as the solution may dry before you squeegee it and leave streaks.

TEACHER'S TIP:

If both inside and out need cleaning, get a helper to work on the opposite side of the glass. On one side, use up and down strokes. On the other side, go back and forth. Any streaks will be highly visible and you'll know which side to touch up—as well as who to blame!

REPLACING A PANE

No matter what time of year, kids across the country are trying to set a new home-run record or complete a screen pass. Usually the thing that breaks is not a record, but a windowpane when the ball hits it. Putting in a new pane is painless—we'll lead you through it:

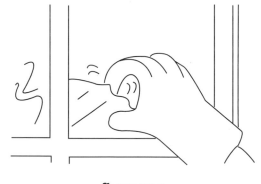

figure 12-1

1. Wearing gloves and safety goggles, carefully remove the shards of glass by wiggling them (figure 12-1).
2. When the glass is out, scrape away the old putty. Brush linseed oil over hardened putty to soften it up. Or, use heat from a heat gun or propane torch. Keep the torch moving so that you don't burn the wood. Try to retrieve the little metal points that held the glass in place. Metal-framed windows won't have the tiny glazier's points. Instead, the pane will be held in place by a spring that fits in a slot in the frame. Don't lose these.
3. Use a wire brush to get the last crumbs of putty.
4. Coat the bare wood with linseed oil.
5. Measure up, down, and across and subtract 1/8-inch from both the vertical and horizontal measurements.
6. Then measure again to be sure!

7. The retailer will cut the pane to size. While there, also buy a can of glazier's compound.

8. Roll the compound in your hands to form a long string about as big around as a pencil (figure 12-2).

9. From outside, push the string of compound against the frame where the pane is to go.

figure 12-2

10. Push the pane of glass against the compound. Don't worry if some squeezes out.

11. Using a putty knife, firmly embed the glazier's points every 6 to 8 inches around the wooden frame (figure 12-3).

12. Next, put blobs of the compound against the glass and use the putty knife to spread, smooth, and bevel it so that it rescmbles the putty around the rest of the panes.

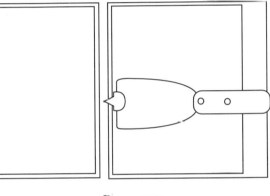

figure 12-3

13. Let the putty cure for three days and paint it. Let just a little of the paint get over onto the glass so the putty is sealed.

If you wish to make sure that pane isn't a target again, consider replacing with an acrylic instead of glass. It won't break!

REPLACING A SASH CORD

Older wood windows have a system involving ropes, pulleys, and weights that makes the windows easier to raise and lower, and also lets the window stay in any position along the track. The ropes are attached on either side of the moving sash. Each rope extends up and over a pulley in the upper part of the track. The rope is attached to the weight that is inside a hollow place on each side of the window (figure 12-4). These old windows are usually "double-hung," which means that both sashes are movable. This also means there are two sets of weights, ropes, and pulleys on each side. Everything is fine until the rope breaks or the pulley gets balky. The pulley might just need a shot of oil. Here's how you replace the rope:

1. Carefully pry off the stop molding on the side where the rope is shot.
2. You may have to use a razor blade to cut the paint seal along the stop.
3. Move the sash out a tad to expose the pocket where the knotted rope has been held.
4. Untie and remove the rope.
5. Work the sash out from the track on the other side and untie it, being careful to put the entire sash in a safe place.
6. Now comes a possible hard part. As you can see from figure 12-5, there is an access plate in the track down near the bottom. It is held in place with a couple of screws, and probably a dozen coats of paint as well. You may have to remove paint to find this. Once you do, remove the plate and you should see and retrieve the weight.
7. Untie and measure the two pieces of rope to cut the replacement rope to length.
8. Feed the replacement rope in over the pulley and keep feeding until you can spot the rope in the access opening.
9. Tie the weight on.
10. Put the sash back in place on the side opposite to the side you've been working on and reattach the rope on that side first.
11. Install the rope into the slot and knot it.
12. Hold the sash against the strip separating the tracks for the upper and lower sash as you raise it to the top.
13. Look at the weight in the access hole. It should be suspended about 3 inches from the sill. If not, adjust the rope in the sash.

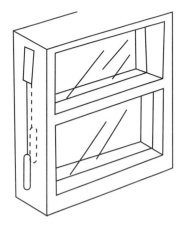

figure 12-4

figure 12-5

A BETTER IDEA

The rope could break again. Oh no! Why not replace it with a sash chain that will not wear out, break, or stretch? Your hardware dealer will have this replacement.

Once it's adjusted, replace the stop and the access cover.

Not all windows are old or wooden. Many windows are aluminum frames and don't have the rope, pulley, and weight balance system. If one of these windows suddenly stops keeping the position you set it at, look for a spiral rod coming from a metal tube in the track on one side of the moveable sash. Most of these rods have a small metal rod that sticks out on each side down near the bottom. This should fit into a slot inside the tube. It needs to be twisted and pushed up into the tube at the same time. Use needle-nosed pliers to do this, and as you get the rod up into the tube, move it around until it slips into the slot. If it doesn't operate properly, disengage the rod and twist some more.

In another variation, the tube is held in place by a screw at the top. The tube must be removed, and it is twisted to adjust the spring.

> **AN EVEN BETTER IDEA**
>
> You can replace all the ropes, pulleys, and weights with little devices called "sash balances." All you do is let the rope fall down into the cavity along with the weight. The balance unit replaces the pulley, and a metal tape attaches to the sash.

WINDOW PAINTED SHUT

Windows are not all that smart. Sometimes the window will mistake a paint job for a glue job and the window will not budge. Here are the simple steps in out-smarting the stubborn window:

1. First, check to be sure that the window is not locked. Duh!
2. Take a close look all around the frame to spot places where the paint is sealing.
3. Use a sharp knife to cut the seal. There is a special little tool called a "window zipper" that works well, but even a sharpened putty knife will do. If the window was painted inside and out, the seal must be cut on both sides.
4. If cutting the seal doesn't work, look for too thick a coat in the track above the used-to-be-moveable sash. Scrape, sand, or use a paint stripper to remove a few coats.
5. Spray a lubricant or silicon down the track from the top of the sash.
6. Next, try a small, flat pry bar with a small wood scrap for extra leverage. Outside is the best place for this.

> **SUPER SAGE SAYS**
>
> "If at first you don't succeed, pry, pry again!"

7. Another effort is to use a 2 x 4 block and a hammer to tap the window frame. If it moves even slightly that may solve the problem.

REPLACING A WINDOW

Old single-pane windows of poor quality probably need to be replaced. You can get your money back in energy savings. In many cases you can opt for windows that will never have to be painted . . . a saving in time and money. Your home may look a lot more beautiful, and the new windows may block out a lot of noise.

After you've figured what you want in the new window, here's how to get rid of the old one:

REMOVING A WOOD WINDOW

1. Start on the inside removing the casing and stop.
2. With this trim out of the way, you can measure the opening so that you can order the right size window.
3. It's best not to proceed until you have the replacement actually on site.
4. When you're ready to continue, cut the rope and remove the weights separately. This lessens the load so it is easier to handle.
5. Remove the apron.
6. If it's a large, heavy window, remove the sashes.
7. Move to the outside and remove the outside casing.
8. Using a hacksaw or a reciprocating saw, cut through the nails holding the jambs to the studs and any other nails involved.
9. The entire unit should come out when you pull on it. If you are on a ladder, be very careful that when the unit lets go it doesn't make you lose your balance.

REMOVING A METAL WINDOW

Many metal windows have flanges or fins all around, and the window is attached by nailing through these fins. Remove any outside trim; you can usually do this by just prying it off.

TEACHER'S TIP

Out-smart the window on your next paint job. Raise the sash a few inches. After painting, but before the paint sets, move the sash a few inches. The dreaded seal won't form, the window won't stick, and your blood pressure won't rise.

HISTORY LESSON

If you're doing a lot of windows, it may pay to rent scaffolding as a safer way to get up for the job.

At this point, you should be able to see how the window is attached. If you see that nails or other fasteners are driven into the sides of the windows and into the framing, use a reciprocating saw with a metal cutting blade to cut the window loose.

If you see that the fins are involved, you'll probably also see that the exterior siding is covering the nails. In order to remove the nails, you'll need to remove some of the siding. Since most window fins are 1-inch wide, you should remove 1½ inches all around. Measure and strike chalk lines all the way around. Then, set the height of the blade on a circular saw to 1/8 inch deeper than the thickness of the siding and cut this out. Now remove the nails and lift out the old window.

INSTALLING THE NEW WINDOW

Finally we're ready for the new window! The most popular windows are wood, aluminum, and vinyl. Each manufacturer will have specific instructions, but all have generally the same steps.

Prehung windows come with the entire unit put together. This makes your job easier because the unit goes into the opening left by the old window. Here are the steps:

1. With the unit in place, insert shims under the bottom jamb.
2. Check it for plumb and level, using more shims if necessary.
3. Draw an outline of the brick mold (brick mold may have nothing to do with brick. It is just the boundary of the window for brick or any other type of siding) on the siding. If the siding is metal or vinyl, you will have to allow extra for the J-channel.
4. Remove the unit and use a reciprocating saw to cut around the outline.
5. Put the window back in place and recheck plumb and level.
6. From inside, place pairs of shims into the gaps along the sides of the windows, about a foot apart. The shims should be snug, but not tight enough to cause bulges in the jamb.
7. Drive nails through the jamb and into the framing at each shim location.
8. Put on gloves and fill all the gaps with scraps of fiberglass insulation. Wear gloves and safety goggles.
9. Using a back saw, trim the shims flush with the framing.
10. Predrill pilot holes in the brick mold and into the framing. These should be about a foot apart all the way around.
11. Use a nail set to drive all nails below the surface.
12. Replace trim inside and seal with caulk all around the window outside.

WINDOW SCREENS

At certain times of the year, you want to open up the windows and let the fresh air and light come in but keep the bugs out. That's when you find out that a small rip can let every species of insect known to man into your house. Let's start patching:

1. For a tiny hole, you may be able to use an ice pick to move a few strands of wire over to close the hole.
2. If a strand or two of wire is broken, a dab of clear fingernail polish closes the hole.
3. A hole too big for either of the above needs a patch. Cut a square two inches bigger than the hole. Remove strands on all four sides. Fold the unwoven edges forward as in figure 12-6. Poke these ends through the openings in the screen around the hole and bend them in toward the center.
4. A long rip can be sewn up with a strand of wire. It won't look perfect, but the bugs are left out (figures 12-7 and 12-8).

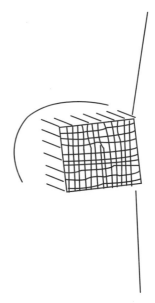

figure 12-6

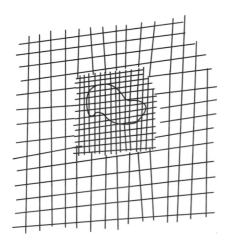

figure 12-7

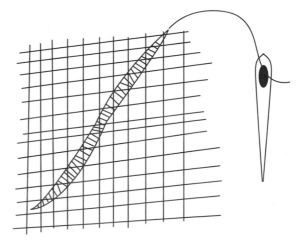

figure 12-8

If you need to replace a screen, here's the routine for a wood-framed window screen:

1. Buy a roll of screen the width of the old screen.
2. Carefully remove the molding from around the edges.
3. The old screen will be held in place by either tacks or staples. Pull the screen off and make sure you get rid of all the small fasteners.
4. To get a tight screen, you can bow the frame by putting it on a table. Put a 1 x 4 wood strip under each end.
5. Clamp the center of the frame to the table (figure 12-9).
6. Use a staple gun to attach the screen at each end.
7. Release the clamps and the screen will be very tight as the frame straightens out.
8. Staple the sides, trim off any excess, and then reinstall the molding.

For a metal frame window screen, the wire mesh is held in place in a groove in the frame by a spline that is sort of like a thin, flexible rope. There is a small, inexpensive splining tool you should buy (figure 12-10). Here are the steps:

1. If the spline is still in good condition, carefully peel it out of the slot in the frame and remove the old screen.
2. Buy or cut replacement screen that is about the same size as the entire frame.
3. Use the convex roller at one end of the tool to push the screen down into the groove. Once in all the way around, the screen should be fairly tight.
4. Now use the other roller that is concave to force the spline down firmly into the groove. Trim off any excess screening . . . and you've passed your screen test.

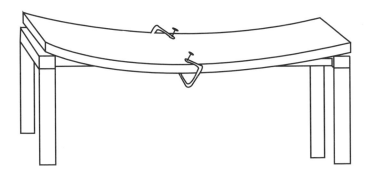

figure 12-9

103

figure 12-10

WINDOW TREATMENTS

Window treatments may be considered a decorative endeavor, but if the shades won't raise or the drapery hardware keeps falling to the floor, it's a fix-it problem. If the blinds won't close and the neighborhood peeping Tom is getting his jollies, it's a privacy problem. If the sun is fading your Persian rug, it's another pesky problem. We'll talk about the nuts and bolts and let you decide on the décor.

Shades—The shade mechanism is inside the wooden rod. There is one end that is hollow and contains a spring. It is held in place by a couple of brackets (figure 12-11). As you can see, one bracket has a round hole. The other has a slot. On one end of the wooden rod there is a

figure 12-11

round pin sticking out. At the other end, the end with the spring, there is a flat pin that fits into the slot (figure 12-12). The flat pin end also has a ratchet mechanism that keeps the shade in the position you set it at (figure 12-13).

Usually, a window shade doesn't require repairs, just adjustments. They are simple to perform:

1. The shade that doesn't want to go back up all the way needs more spring tension. First, pull the shade down about two revolutions. Then all you need do is remove the flat pin from its bracket and roll the shade back up by hand. When you get it all the way up, drop the pin back in the slot and try it. If it's not quite there, repeat the above.
2. To tame a shade that's so tense it wants to lift you up, decrease the tension. Take the flat pin out and roll the shade down by hand a couple of revolutions. Put it back in, and if it's still too tense try it again.

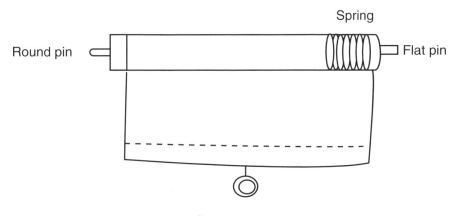

Round pin

Spring

Flat pin

figure 12-12

3. If the shade refuses to stay down, the ratchet mechanism is probably dirty. Remove the metal cap and clean the workings. Don't lubricate except with graphite.

4. If the shade wobbles, a pin is probably bent. Gently bend the pin back into shape.

5. If the entire shade falls out, the brackets are too far apart. Either bend them toward each other or move one of the brackets.

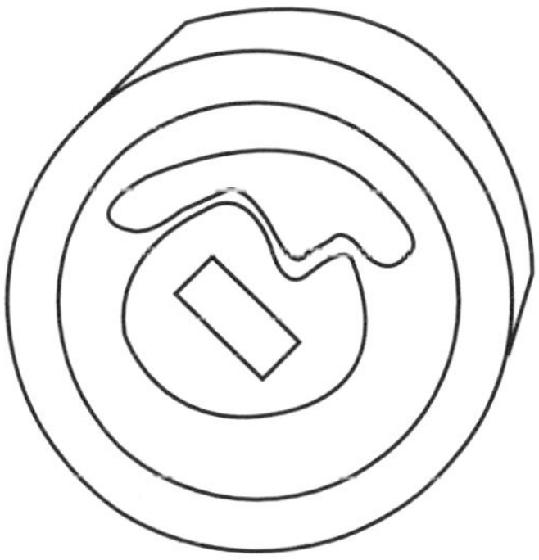

End of shade

figure 12-13

Blinds—Venetian blinds and mini-blinds are a lot alike. Repairs are easier than you think. The most common problems are with the cords. So, let's start with them. The cords often look like a maze, but if you lay the unit out on the floor face down, you can make a simple drawing of the route that the cords take (figure 12-14). The drawing will be your road map when installing new cords.

There are two cord systems . . . the lift cord and the tilt cord. Most blind repair kits come with cords for both systems. So, we'll replace both, starting with the lift cord:

1. The ends of the cords are knotted under the bottom of the tapes. Untie them and pull on the loop as if you were raising the blinds. This will pull the cords out.

2. Start feeding the new cord up through the bottom on the side next to the tilt cord. The cord goes on alternate sides of the ladder tape.

3. Bring it up over the pulley and along the top over to the mechanism on the other side.

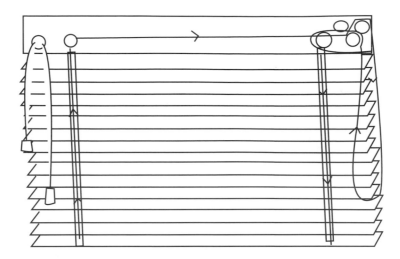

figure 12-14

4. Go under the first and over the second pulley.
5. Now bring the cord down through the lift cord locking device.
6. Go back to where you started and pull the cord until there is just enough sticking out from the bottom rail to let you tie a knot. Return to the other side, feed the cord over the second set of pulleys, and work it down through the other ladder tape.
7. When that's done, adjust the size of the loop, trim off the excess, and tie the other knot.
8. That's it except for the tilt cord. Just run it over the tilt pulley and back down. With this properly adjusted, add the pulls and you're finished.

The second problem area for blinds is the webbing or ladder tapes. If one or two of the small ladder pieces have come loose, use fabric glue, which is available at fabric stores. If the entire webbing set need replacing, here are the steps to new ladders:

1. Lay the blind unit on the floor.
2. Untie the knots of both ends of the cord and pull them up and out at the top.
3. This means the louvers or slats can all come out. Remove them.
4. A U-shaped hook holds the ladder tape to the top of the tilt bar. Pull it out and remove the ladder tape and hook the new one in place.
5. Insert the slats and run the cord through the ladders, knot the cord under the bottom rail, and take the rest of the day off.

Draperies—When you close the drapes do they close completely in the middle . . . or is there a 6-inch gap in the center? Does only one side move when you open the drapes? Adjusting the traverse rod is actually pretty easy once you have broken the code. Here are the steps:

1. If possible, lift the entire rod out of the brackets and lay it face down on the floor.
2. Pull the outer cord to bring the master slide all the way over to the wide-open position.
3. Look at the other slide and you'll see a loop of cord running through a pair of holes. Slightly below and in the center between the two holes is a V-shaped lug. The cord should not be hooked at this time.
4. While holding the cord tightly, manually move the other slide over to the other direction as far as it can go.
5. When this second slide is over as far as it should go, pull down on the cord running through the two holes and hook it over the lug.
6. With any luck at all, when the rod is back in place, both sides will move at the same time and at the same speed and there'll be no gap in the middle.

A CHEAP TRICK

If you'll be replacing the webbing because the once white material has turned yellowish, paint it with liquid white shoe polish. The blinds will look like new!

HANG IN THERE

About the only other drapery dilemma is that the drapes may be too heavy for the brackets to stay in place. Go back to what we learned in chapter 6 on hanging things.

Small Appliances 101

13

There is no way we could cover all of the small appliances that are in today's homes. It seems as if five new mechanical monsters are brought out every day. We've tried to zero in on those that are the most popular and hope the success you have with getting them back in running order will inspire you to tackle those we didn't include.

One really good idea is to save all that material you got when you bought the appliance. The owner's manual will usually have some troubleshooting suggestions. Many will have a toll free help line you can call.

ELECTRIC MOTORS

A simple, small motor powers many small appliances. Here are some maintenance steps that may keep your motor motoring:

1. Keep it clean. A build-up of dirt and dust should not be allowed.
2. Keep it properly lubricated. Check the owner's manual on where and when to oil.
3. Use the appliance only for things it is made to do. Don't push it into doing things it hasn't the strength to do.

A SAFETY TIP

Unplug any appliance before inspecting, dismantling, or repairing. Do not restore power until the repair is completed or while any wiring connections are exposed.

APPLIANCE CORDS

Another thing most appliances have in common is the appliance cord. If the machine isn't working, this is the first place to check. Go back to chapter 5 for details on checking and fixing or replacing electrical cords and plugs.

SINK DISPOSERS

Some people think this appliance will eat just about anything, so they feed their unit a bunch of stuff it can't digest. This can cause problems in the disposer, in the drain line, and at the water treatment plant. Here are some things you should never feed the disposer: glass, string, cloth, bones, paper, and seafood shells. Other things that are hard for the disposer to digest include stringy vegetables like celery or asparagus.

With a diet of garbage, it's little wonder that the disposer develops bad breath. Here is the cure:

1. Pack the unit with ice cubes, turn on the faucet, and hit the switch. This may make a loud racket, but as the cubes are slammed around they will be cleaning away food particles inside.
2. With the disposer off, put the stopper in place and fill up the sink with water. As you pull the plug, turn the unit on. This amount of water is a much greater volume than would come from the faucet alone.
3. Remove the splashguard and clean the underside of it.
4. Cut up a lemon wedge and let the disposer eat it for a nice citrus smell.

Take a look at the other most common problems and what to do about them:

Nothing happens—First, if the unit has a "reset" button, push it in and try again. Check to be sure there's not a tripped breaker or blown fuse. If it's a plug-in unit, unplug it and try a lamp in the outlet. Hit the switch. If the light doesn't come on, check out the outlet and the switch. There could be a small piece of grit that jams the impeller. Angle a broom handle down the throat of the disposer. If you can move it even a tiny bit, this may dislodge the object.

Disposer leaks—Check for a loose sink flange connection and tighten it. If it is leaking from some other source, you may have to call a service technician.

Very noisy—There is a foreign object inside or the impeller is broken. Remove the object. See if replacement parts are available if the impeller is broken.

VACUUM CLEANERS

A vital part of house cleaning is the vacuum cleaner. There are three basic types of home vacuums: the central system, the upright vacuum, and the canister vacuum. There is a cousin to the canister called the tank cleaner. These last two look different but operate the same.

The vacuum cleaner is a real workhorse. It's used and abused, but most just keep on sucking up all that dirt. If it starts losing its ability to vacuum items up, check the bag. If the bag is too full, it cuts back on the vacuum's airflow.

If it's a hose type unit, the hose could be clogged. Disconnect the hose, turn the unit on, and put your hand over the inlet. If you feel good suction, the hose is the culprit. Toothpicks, paperclips, pins and needles can get crossways and then start to snag thread and other debris to build up a clog. To clear it, poke a broom handle through the hose. Or, take the vacuum outside and put the hose into the outlet and blow it out. If the hose gets clogged regularly, it may be wearing out inside and as a result is more prone to catch items as they go through. You may have to spring for a new hose.

A common problem with an upright is a stretched belt. To replace a belt, remove the cover on the bottom. Notice how the belt is installed so that you get the new one in place the same way. You'll need to release the beater brush to slide the old belt off and install the new one.

Also, if the brushes get clogged, the vacuum is less efficient. A seam ripper from the sewing room will make quick work of removing hair and threads.

ELECTRIC CLOCKS

Most electric clocks are sealed, so if something goes wrong it's a job for the little old clock maker. However, there are some weird unscientific tricks that will solve some clock problems. When the clock starts to make a whirring noise, leave it plugged in but turn the clock upside down. Leave it there overnight. What happens is that guck that has collected on the gears will be redistributed by gravity and silence the problem. Another, even stranger solution is to put the clock in a *warm but not hot* oven. The warmth does the same thing. Just be sure it's not hot enough to melt your clock.

STEAM IRONS

If you've got a pressing engagement and the steam part doesn't work, there may be a simple repair. The most common cause is from mineral deposits that have separated out from the water and are clogging the steam ports in the sole plate or are causing blockage inside the iron. The steps to more steam are:

1. Empty all the water out.
2. Fill the reservoir with white vinegar.
3. Turn the dial to "steam."
4. As you know, the iron doesn't emit steam unless the iron is held horizontal with the plate facing down. If you held it that way for as long as it would take to steam all the vinegar out, your arm would fall off. Take your broiler pan from the oven with its slotted cover, set iron on top, and let it steam away. If the holes in the plate are still clogged, a pipe cleaner makes a good reaming tool after it has cooled.
5. Run water through a steam cycle after the cleaning to be sure all the vinegar is gone.

If the iron seems to drag a little bit during the pressing process, press over a sheet of waxed paper on which you have sprinkled salt. Silver polish or toothpaste and a damp rag will also clean the plate. Don't do this if the plate is Teflon coated, but press over a piece of aluminum foil.

COFFEE MAKERS

In most homes, this is an appliance that is used every morning. Follow the manufacturer's directions as to how much ground coffee to use. Then always use cold water. The results will be consistently great tasting coffee.

If the coffee does start to taste bad, there's probably a build-up of mineral deposits in the machine. A good way to clean the entire system is to pour in a pot of half cold water and half white vinegar without the coffee grounds. After this has brewed, empty the pot and run through a pot of plain water to get rid of the vinegar taste.

If you run out of filters and forgot to buy new ones, a paper towel will work almost as well.

Major Appliances 101

14

When a small appliance goes out, you can usually get by without it. There are other clocks in the house. Instant coffee may not taste as good but it does give you your daily caffeine fix. You can tidy up the floors with a broom. But if a major appliance goes out, you can have big problems. Like taking cold showers. Or, having six hundred dollars worth of food spoil and having to go out for every meal. You may not be able to fix all your appliance woes, but sometimes the big problems have a simple solution. So roll up your sleeves and get ready to go to work.

REFRIGERATORS

There are refrigerators that are twenty years old that are still on the job. Even though they have hundreds of parts, refrigerators are among the longest lasting of appliances. If you want yours to continue to be trouble free, here are several TLC steps to keep it working well:

> **A SAFETY TIP**
>
> Unplug, remove the fuse, or trip the circuit breaker for any appliance before inspecting, dismantling, or repairing. Do not restore power until the repair is completed or while any wiring connections are exposed.

1. Clean the condenser coils regularly. Some are located on the back of the refrigerator and others are underneath. A vacuum with a brush attachment does a good job. While you are vacuuming, remove dust from the compressor and the condenser fan, both of which are underneath.

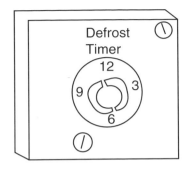

figure 14-1

2. Check the temperature in both the freezer and refrigerator. The freezer range should be between 0 and 5° F. The food compartment should be around 35° F. If these goals are not met, and everything is working right, it's just a matter of adjustment. There is a dial for each of these two areas.

3. Keep an eye on the frost buildup in the freezer compartment. A layer of frost will act as an insulator and cut down on efficiency. If the frosty freezer is supposed to be frost-free, locate the defrost timer unit (figure 14-1). Turn its dial until it clicks. It should start a defrost cycle.

4. If the freezer is not frost-free, you should manually defrost when a 1/4-inch layer of frost builds up.

Here are the most common refrigerator troubles and what to do about them:

Refrigerator is noisy—There are two or sometimes three fans. One is in the freezer. The others are underneath. Check for loose mountings, a bent blade, or whether lubrication is needed. The compressor is on rubber mounts that act as a sort of shock absorber. If these mounts are not properly anchored, tighten them up. Also, you should check to see if the unit is level. There should be leveling screws in the base. Lastly, there may be items on top of the unit that rattle from the vibration while the compressor is running.

Food storage area too warm—The food storage section in most home units gets its cool from the freezing compartment. The control dial for the refrigerator opens or closes a sort of door that controls the opening size of the air duct. If this doesn't correct the temperature, it may be that the linkage to the opening is broken and should be replaced. Or, the light stays on after the door is closed and is adding heat to the unit. Press the button with a finger and if the light stays on, replace the button switch. Or, the door is not sealing and warm air from the room is getting in. See the section below for "Changing a door gasket."

Excessive frost build-up—We just talked about defrosting, but another reason for this problem could be a faulty gasket on the freezer door. See the section below for "Changing a door gasket."

Water is leaking out under the unit—The defrost condensate system is clogged. Pour a few tablespoons of bleach into the condensate drain line. Or, the tube may not be aimed into the pan. Check to be sure the pan is in the proper location. Also check the icemaker connection.

Icemaker not working—The icemaker switch may be in the "off" position. More likely, there is no water getting into the icemaker. Follow the water line tube to where it is connected to the water supply, probably under the sink. At that point, there is a small shut off valve. Shut it off and disconnect it from where it enters the refrigerator. While holding the end over a pan, turn the water back on. If nothing comes out, the trouble is in the line. Look for kinks. If the line is OK, take the valve out and take it apart, looking for mineral deposits. There will be a small screen that catches any solids before they get into the valve. If it is clogged, that could be the problem. Soak all the parts in vinegar to dissolve minerals. The valve is controlled by a solenoid that may be faulty.

Icemaker turns out cloudy cubes—Water is loaded with minerals. Install an in-line filter. It's inexpensive and is a do-it-yourself project.

Cubes are too small—Inadequate water supply, which we just covered.

CHANGING A DOOR GASKET

Having a properly sealed door gasket is vital to the efficiency of a refrigerator or freezer. There are a couple of ways to check the gasket. One is to close the door on a dollar bill, leaving half of it sticking out. Tug on the bill. If it comes out easily, there's a gasket problem. Move the bill all the way around the door, testing all the way. The other way is to use a strong flashlight turned on and placed inside the refrigerator. Do this at night. Now turn off the lights in the room and closely eyeball the door all the way around. Light will point out the gaps. Do the same thing for the freezer. Food particles on the gasket could cause a less than tight seal, so clean it before you junk it.

If the decision is to replace the gasket, the procedure is simple:

1. Don't do anything until you have a proper replacement gasket in hand.
2. There are screws and retaining strips that hold the gasket in place but the gasket itself hides them. Lift the gasket at the top to remove the screws and the upper retaining strip.
3. Attach the new gasket at the top. The reason you don't remove all the strips and screws at once is because the door liner and shelves are also held in place by them. As you insert the screws, make sure they are in but don't tighten them all the way.
4. Any crimps from when the gasket was folded in packing can be worked out with heat from a handheld hair dryer.
5. When the gasket is in place, do the final tightening by starting with the center screw at the top. Next, go to the center screw at the bottom. Then do the center

screw on one side and then the other. As you install any other screw, the next one should be directly opposite it. This routine helps to avoid any warping in the door.

RANGES AND OVENS-GAS

The gas oven and range require little in the way of maintenance to keep on cooking. But here is a recipe of some things you can do to keep it at its best:

1. Clean the burners. Some burners can easily come out and can be soaked in detergent and water.
2. Clogs in a burner can be reamed out with a toothpick.
3. Make sure the range is level, or the cakes you bake are liable to be lopsided.
4. Newer ranges have continuous or self-cleaning ovens. If yours does, do not use any caustic or abrasive oven cleaner, but wipe up spills after the oven cools. If you have a "you-clean" system, do this whenever the oven is dirty.
5. The flame on a burner needs to be adjusted for best efficiency and better cooking. You can tell just by looking. The yellow flame has insufficient air. The blue flame that pulls away from the burner has too much air. The flame is proper when it is bright and steady and has a cone-shaped blue-green tip.

HOW DO YOU ADJUST THE FLAME?

There is an adjusting nut that lets you control the amount of gas. Clockwise increases and counterclockwise reduces (figures 14-2a-c). Opening or closing a sort of shutter called a mixer plate adjusts the air. The mixer plate is held in place by a screw. Loosen, adjust, and when the flame is right, lock the plate in place by tightening the screw.

Here are some common range and oven problems and how to solve them:

Burner doesn't light—Failure to light is often because the pilot light is out. Or, if you have an electronic ignition, there could be a lack of electricity. See if the clock or light are still working.

Surface burner makes a popping noise when it comes on—This happens because a lot of gas has come out before the pilot ignites it. This is probably caused by a pilot light that's too low. There is a pilot adjusting screw back where the pilot tube is supplied with gas. There is also the possibility that the burner is clogged close to the pilot light, so all the gas comes out further away from the pilot, and when there is finally enough gas to reach the pilot, it comes on with a small explosion.

Flame produces soot—This indicates that there is too much gas in the ratio.

Oven doesn't light—Same as above for burner, but with one other possibility. If the timer switch is not set on "manual" or "normal," the oven won't light.

Gas burner
air control

Lock screw

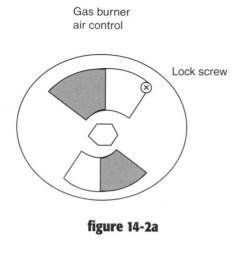

figure 14-2a

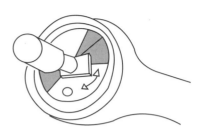

figure 14-2b

Clean burner

figure 14-2c

Baked food is burned—Oven temperature higher than called for. We'll address temperature in the box below. It also could be that the shelf is too low and thus the food is too close to the heat.

Baked goods are soggy—Oven temperature is lower than called for. We'll address temperature in the box below.

Oven does not maintain set temperature—We'll address temperature in the box below.

Pilot goes out—Adjust the pilot as discussed above.

RANGES AND OVENS-ELECTRIC

There are many similarities between gas and electric ranges. There are also some big differences.

PLAY IT SAFE

If your repair involves any steps that could lead to gas escaping, shut off the gas supply to the entire range. Also, remember that the gas range depends on electricity for the clock and light, so shut off the current when you'll be working on any electrical circuits.

OVEN TEMPERATURE

If the oven cannot maintain the desired temperature, you can end up with some cooking failures. Here's how to check the accuracy of the oven. Place an oven thermometer on a rack that is close to the middle of the oven. Turn the oven on and set it at 350° F. Leave it on for about 15 to 20 minutes. Check the thermometer. If the reading is more than 50° off of the setting, you should replace the thermostat. If the difference is less, you can recalibrate. To do this on some models, you remove the control knob and the calibration screw will be revealed. A quarter turn will make a change of about 25° F. Turn clockwise to lower the temperature and counterclockwise to raise. On other models, remove the knob and look at the back. There will be a moveable disc with a display that has a series of notches with a plus sign at one end and a minus sign at the other. When you loosen a setscrew, you can move the disc so a pointer points to a new notch. Each notch change will make about a 10° temperature change.

Let's start with a conventional electric range. The range operates on a 240/120-volt circuit. The heating elements require 240 volts and the accessories, such as the timer, clock, light, and convenience outlet run on 120 volts. Before making any tests or repairs to an electric range, be sure to trip the proper circuit breaker or breakers. Let's look at the most common problems, their causes, and what you can do about them:

Nothing heats and the light and clock don't work—As always, check the fuse, the breaker, and the power cord.

Surface burner is inoperable—Most ranges come with four burners, two each of the same size. Many burners are plugged into a terminal block. To remove, just pull it out. Others are wired in and removing two screws does the job. An easy way to test the burner is to switch the bad one with the other of the same size. If it doesn't heat there either, replace the burner. If it does heat, you need to check the wiring, the switch, and the terminal block.

Oven doesn't heat—The automatic timer may be set wrong. Move it to "manual" or "natural." With some, you must then advance the time-of-day clock 24 hours. The oven element can be bad. Some oven elements plug in and some are wired. Remove and test for continuity. If there is none, replace the element. If you have a double oven, do a switcheroo with another, same-sized element.

Oven light doesn't come on—Remove the bulb and get a duplicate replacement.

Broiler does not heat—Remove and test the element. Replace it if it is faulty.

Oven does not brown food—Another faulty element problem.

Oven does not maintain set temperature—Use the same procedure to test that we offered for the gas oven.

MICROWAVE OVENS

Maybe you remember when a lot of restaurants had little signs that proclaimed: "Warning! Microwave oven in use." Actually, about the only way a properly operating microwave oven can hurt you is if you drop it on your foot. **Or, if you try to make repairs and don't know what you're doing.** The reason we aren't suggesting that you make repairs is that a microwave oven has a high-voltage capacitor that stores power . . . even when the unit is unplugged. If touched, the jolt can physically knock you down and do great harm to you.

> **SCHOOL SUPPLY MUST**
>
> Invest in a couple of inexpensive test gadgets. One is called a continuity tester. The other is a volt-ohmmeter (see figures 5-6 and 5-7). These are great for quickly determining whether heating elements are good or not. You'll find other electrical uses for these testers.

We will give you some tips how best to use and clean your oven. Here goes:

1. Don't use a light, two-strand extension cord.
2. Don't run an empty unit for use as a timer. Many ovens have a timer setting that only runs the clock.
3. Don't use an abrasive cleaner to clean inside. Often a damp sponge will do. A mild detergent and water will get any tough spots.
4. Clean the door seal gasket often with a damp sponge.
5. Use only microwavable containers. When in doubt, here's a test:
   a. Put the dish in question in the microwave.
   b. Put a cup full of water onto the dish.
   c. Set the timer for 1 minute and 15 seconds,
   d. If the water is hot and the dish cool, it's OK.
6. Use no metal or aluminum foil.
7. Never use the microwave if the door doesn't close or is warped. Have it repaired.

Changing the microwave light—Unplug the unit before changing the bulb. It will be accessible only from the back. You'll see a small plate on the back, and by removing the left screw and loosening the other, the cover will swing down, exposing the bulb.

AUTOMATIC DISHWASHERS

The advent of the automatic dishwasher did away with the family dilemma of who was going to wash and who was going to dry. Not only does this appliance make family life easier, but also when things go wrong, most are easy to repair. Here are some fairly common problems:

> **SAFETY TIP**
>
> You'll be removing the access plate to work under the unit. Be sure the proper fuse is removed or the circuit breaker is flipped so there is no current to the dishwasher!

Nothing happens—Is there electrical power to the unit? Also, there is a switch in the dishwasher door. If this is not engaged, the unit will not start. The timer may also be suspect. Try this: turn the timer dial just a hair, and if nothing happens, the timer is the problem.

Doesn't fill—There are two controls for water. The first is a float switch that rises up as water comes in and, when it rises to the proper water level, it shuts off. It is inside the dishwasher, and most resemble a plastic cup turned upside down. Lift up on the cup and you should hear a click, which usually means the switch is OK.

The other is a solenoid valve that is in the water supply line. It is easy to spot because it has a pair of wires running to it. Shut off the hot water under the sink. Place a shallow pan under the switch, disconnect the wires, and remove the switch. Test it for continuity. There is often a screen that should catch mineral deposits. If clogged, soak it in vinegar and poke out the debris with a needle.

Over fills—The float valve isn't working. Test for continuity and look for any obstruction.

Dishes don't get clean—The most common cause is water that is not hot enough. See if the water heater setting is too low. Often the distance between the water heater and the dishwasher is far enough that you don't get hot water until the dishwasher is well into the wash cycle. Before starting the dishwasher, run water at the sink until hot. The heating element may not be doing its thing. Check it for continuity and replace it if faulty.

Another possible cause is that the spray arm(s) are clogged. A pipe cleaner will take care of that.

Won't drain—Check the drain hose to see if it has become kinked.

Lift up the screen in the bottom of the unit under the bottom spray arm. There may be food scraps or broken glass.

If you're really adventurous, remove the top of the pump and take the impellers out to look for clogs or broken fins.

Only partially drains and has food particles in remaining water—Drain hose going into disposer has low spot and when the pump stops, gravity lets water drain back into dishwasher. Loop hose up so it's higher than the inlet to the disposer. If need be, use a cup-hook and twist-tie to hold it in place.

Leaks around door—The door latch may be bent. Or, the door gasket may need to be replaced.

Leaks underneath—You'll have to look underneath to see whether there is a hose leak or a loose connection that needs tightening.

Detergent dispenser doesn't dispense—Often the use of detergent powder will end up caking and prevent the detergent dispenser from working. With the door open, flood the dispenser with vinegar. If the dispenser needs to be replaced, the door liner must be removed.

CLOTHES WASHERS

We've come a long way since the women-folk used to beat the clothing on the rocks down by the riverside. Not only have they done away with that, now the clothes are put in the machine, detergent is added, and then 30 minutes later, clothes are clean and spun almost dry. And neither rock nor river is in sight.

Even though it's a fairly complicated appliance, there are many problems you can take care of. Here are the most common:

Nothing happens—By now you know to make sure there is power. Check plug, cord, outlet, fuse, and circuit breaker. Also, there is a safety switch in the door. If it's faulty, it's usually because a wire is loose.

No water comes in—There are two hoses (hot and cold) that bring water in. Each has a screen to keep out mineral deposits. Turn off the faucets behind the washer and loosen the hoses where they enter the back of the unit. The screens can be cleaned with a small wire and by soaking in hot vinegar. The hoses are connected to the two inlet solenoid valves. The valves can be taken out and tested for continuity. If they are not functioning, it's probably because of mineral deposits. Soak the parts in hot vinegar and use an old toothbrush to clean with. Turn the timer just a tad and see if the water starts coming in.

Motor hums, but machine doesn't run—The washer is probably just overloaded.

Agitator isn't agitating—This cycle is belt driven and has an agitator cam bar that is supposed to shift into the agitate gear. If the belt is stretched, or if the gear didn't shift, you can replace the belt and lubricate the gears and cam bars. However, you must have the owner's manual for your particular washer. One type has a belt that simply loops around the pump, the motor, and a pulley. With the hoses disconnected, and unit unplugged, you can remove the back plate, turn the unit on its side, and belt replacement is a snap. In fact, if the belt is in good shape but just loose, you can loosen the motor mounting bolt and push the motor to tighten the belt. Other models have a very complicated belt arrangement that involves repositioning some of the bracing to get the belt off.

Water doesn't drain—The drain hose can be kinked, or the pump may be faulty. Check all the hoses and replace the pump if that's the problem.

Water leaks under the appliance—First, remember that water and electricity don't mix. In order to find out where the leak is, you have to move the unit away from the wall, remove the back cover, and stand in back on a wet floor. So, disconnect before you start the search.

Water backs up out of standpipe—This is a plumbing problem. Lift the drain hose from the standpipe and put it in a bucket to catch the water in the hose. Then check to see if there is a blockage by running a snake down the standpipe. The reason the clog may show up here—even though it may be farther down the drain line—is because suds slow down the flow and the pump pushes more water out than a faucet would. There may also be a problem with a partially clogged vent stack, as we discussed in chapter 4.

No spin cycle—Although different gears are involved, the non-spinning problem is much like that of the agitator.

Washer vibrates badly—The washer is overloaded or not level. There are leveling feet that can easily be adjusted

Belt squeals—It may be loose and, if so, can be tightened as we've discussed above. You can also try an application of belt dressing, available at an auto supply store.

Clothes get damaged—This can be from overloading the unit. Damage can also be caused by too much bleach. Another suggestion is . . . zip up your fly! An open zipper can chew up clothes. There may also be a snag spot on the agitator or other surfaces inside. Put your hand inside an old nylon stocking and rub over all the surfaces. If you hit a snag, light sanding should take car of it.

DRYERS

The clothes dryer can be gas or electric, but whichever it is, it sure beats taking a basket of wet clothes out to the clothesline on a cold day. With either type, the operation, and thus any problems, are about the same. Here are the most common hang-ups and some solutions:

Nothing happens—Even the gas dryer uses electricity, so no power means no go. The dryer also has a safety switch on the door, so test it and replace it if that's the problem.

Dryer runs but has no heat—If it is electric, the heating element, often coiled springs, can be broken. It should be replaced. The gas type may have a pilot light out, or the air mixture may be wrong. Reread the air adjustment steps earlier in this chapter on Gas Ranges.

Dryer heats but clothes still wet—The most common reason for this problem is that the exhaust system is clogged. Since the exhaust system is bound to expel lint along with the hot air, this is bound to happen. Start from the unit and work on up the duct. A shop vac with the hose in the exhaust port will usually remove the blockage. Try to ensure that there are no low places in the duct to prevent future clogs. Always clean the lint filter after each use.

Dryer drum fails to rotate—The belt runs around the drum and is kept tight by a pulley and tension spring. If the belt breaks, or if the spring no longer keeps the belt under the proper tension, the drum doesn't move. Either belt or spring is an easy replacement.

WATER HEATER MAINTENANCE

Whether the water heater is gas, oil, or electric, there are some maintenance steps that are common to all. Heat tends to cause minerals in water to separate out. These minerals can cause problems in a water heater. Therefore, it is a good idea to drain the tank from time to time to remove the sediment. It is done in a few easy steps:

1. Hook a garden hose to the drain valve located near the bottom of the tank (figure 14-3).
2. Run the hose outside.
3. Come back in and open the valve.
4. Now go back out and watch the water. You should see some sediment coming out.
5. When the water starts to run clean, come back in and shut off the drain.

The water heater has a T & P (temperature and pressure) relief valve (figure 14-4).

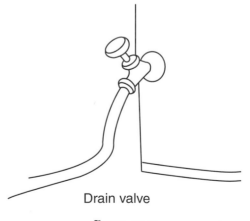

Drain valve

figure 14-3

It is a safety device so the tank doesn't explode if the temperature or pressure build up. It may be located high on the side or actually on top of the tank. Open this once a year to be sure it lets water out. If this valve ever pops open from steam or boiling water, shut down the unit—you have a problem.

The temperature setting is important, and many people set it too high. A good, economical, and safe setting is in the mid-range or around 120° F. Your automatic dishwasher has a heating element to get the water up to where it needs to be in the appliance.

Wrapping all accessible hot water pipes will let the water remain hot until it gets to where it is used.

If you live in an area that has water with a high degree of minerals, install an inline filter in the water supply line just before it goes into the water heater. The filter keeps out a lot of minerals and is inexpensive and easy to install. It can add years to the life of your water heater.

WATER HEATERS-GAS

Here are some problems common the gas water heaters:

No hot water—The pilot light must be on for the burners to light. You may need to replace the thermocouple. Skip over to chapter 17 under gas heating systems.

Not enough hot water—You could change the thermostat to provide hotter water. If the hot water lines are not insulated, and there is a long run, much of the heat is lost to the air. Wrap the pipes. Also, see Dip Tube on the next page.

Noisy hot water pipes—Sediment in the tank is the usual cause for the noise. Draining the tank as we've described above will probably silence the rumbling.

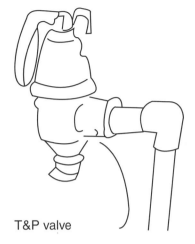

T&P valve

figure 14-4

> ### A WORD OF CAUTION
>
> If there is resistance to the opening of the valve, don't play King Kong. You might end up with the entire drain valve in your hand.

> ### TEACHER'S TIP
>
> Keep a barbeque mitt handy, as the hose and drain handle may become very hot.

Water leaks—A drip from the drain tap can be contained by the use of a hose cap. The T&P relief valve may be slightly open. Replace it.

Water has an odor—Water heaters have a sacrificial anode rod. This attracts lime and scale to prevent the corrosion or deterioration of the tank liner. When it has attracted too much stuff, it should be replaced. There will probably be a threaded cap on the top of the tank. When removed, the rod lifts out. Ask your local parts dealer if there is a special type for the water quality in your area.

WATER HEATERS-ELECTRIC

All of the same problems talked about under gas water heaters are found in electric heaters, except the heat source. Most electric water heaters have two heating elements. A couple of typical elements are shown in figure 14-5. However, there are many different elements. There is also a red reset button that often solves the problem when power is lost.

If the reset doesn't do the trick, there are several tests that can be made with inexpensive test equipment. Here are the testing steps:

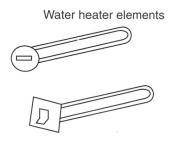

Water heater elements

figure 14-5

THE DIP TUBE AND A LAW OF PHYSICS

We know that heat rises and hot water does too. With any type of water heater, the water is heated and rises to the top of the tank where the hot water outlet is. To work properly, the cold water must come in near the bottom. A dip tube, a long pipe extending down from the cold water inlet, accomplishes this. If the dip tube disintegrates or comes loose, the water no longer goes to the bottom but mixes cold with hot near the top. This means the hot water doesn't last very long. You can check the dip tube by shutting off the water supply and loosening the inlet connection. This lets you remove the tube and examine it. With most units, this can be replaced. Then you can enjoy a hot shower again.

1. Shut off all current at the circuit breaker box.

2. Remove the two access panels on the side of the water heater. You may have to push insulation aside to get to these parts.

3. Test the high temperature cutoff with a continuity tester by fastening the clip and applying the probe to the two screws on the left-hand side of this part as shown in figure 14-6.

4. Be sure the reset button is pushed in. If the tester lights, remove it and reconnect to the two screws on the right side. If it doesn't light on both sides, replace the high-temperature cutoff.

5. To test the upper thermostat, use the continuity tester as shown in figure 14-7. If it fails to light, replace the upper thermostat.

6. To test the lower thermostat, hook up the tester as shown in figure 14-8. If it doesn't light the tester, replace the lower thermostat.

7. The first test on the heating elements should be a test for a short circuit. Attach the alligator clip to either element terminal and touch the probe to an element mounting bolt, as shown in figure 14-9. If the tester lights, there is a short and the element must be replaced.

8. To test the element for continuity, the clip and probe are

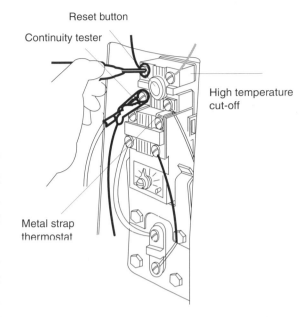

Reset button

Continuity tester

High temperature cut-off

Metal strap thermostat

figure 14-6

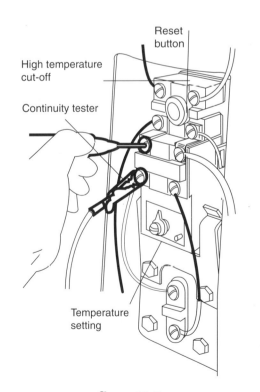

Reset button

High temperature cut-off

Continuity tester

Temperature setting

figure 14-7

applied to the two element terminals, as shown in figure 14-10.

If your water heater has only a single element, your tests are exactly the same, but all at one place.

To install a new element:

1. Be sure the current to the heater has been shut off at the entry box.
2. Shut off the water supply to the tank.
3. Open a hot water tap to start emptying the tank.
4. Hook a hose to the tap near the bottom and run it outside.
5. Open the tap. Remember that water needs air to drain, so open the T&P valve or a hot water faucet that is higher than the top of the tank.
6. Disconnect the wires from the element.
7. Unscrew the mounting bolts. This will also loosen the thermostat bracket. The thermostat will hang by its wires.

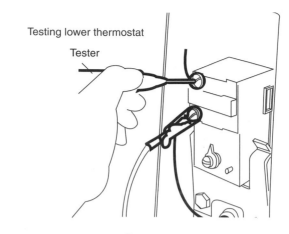

Testing lower thermostat

Tester

figure 14-8

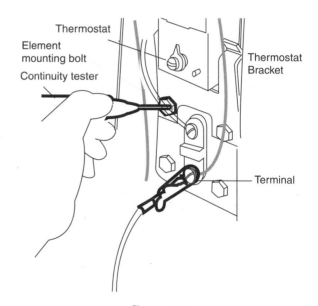

Thermostat

Element mounting bolt

Continuity tester

Thermostat Bracket

Terminal

figure 14-9

8. Pull the old element out of the tank and take it with you to get a replacement.
9. The new element should include a gasket but if not, get one.
10. Put the new one in and reinstall all of the parts.

11. Put any insulation back in place and reattach the access panel covers.

12. Close the drain tap and open the water supply valve. DO NOT restore electrical power until the tank is completely full. You'll know it is full when the open hot water faucet starts to run.

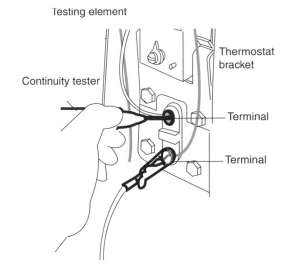

Testing element

Thermostat bracket

Continuity tester

Terminal

Terminal

figure 14-10

Painting 101

15

Painting is one do-it-yourself project that pays big dividends. Most of the cost of having the paint job done is in labor, and if you provide that labor you'll pocket big bucks. Also, the painting the outside of your home gives it protection from the elements, saving you even more moolah.

And we haven't even mentioned the main reason most people paint inside or out . . . beauty! A tasteful paint job outside can accentuate good parts of a home and minimize flaws. Inside color can completely change the look of a room or the whole house.

INTERIOR PAINTING

Once again, we're not going to help you pick out the color scheme. That is strictly a personal judgment call. However, we will suggest you buy high quality paint. Even though painting may turn out to be fun, you probably do not want to repaint next year. Poor quality paint often leads to that problem. Also, bargain paint will often require an extra coat to get the coverage you desire.

How can you tell quality? Unfortunately, cost is a good yardstick. Of course, even top quality paints go on sale. Keep in mind, though, that some very high priced paints are priced that way because you're paying for the designer's name on the can. His or her name doesn't guarantee quality.

Another selection factor is the sheen. There are several choices. The high gloss is very shiny and that or a semi-gloss is best for woodwork, particularly in kitchens and bathrooms where the woodwork may often need to be washed. For the walls and ceilings, a flat paint may do. However, eggshell has just a touch of gloss and it sure makes walls easier to clean. (Different paint manufacturers may have their own names for the various glosses.)

HOW MUCH TO BUY

It's all about doing the math. To figure out how many gallons for the ceiling, it's simple: width x length. That gives you the square footage. Look at the paint label for the estimated coverage and divide by this figure.

For walls, measure the length of all walls and multiply this by the height. Then you must subtract for doors, windows, and any other areas not to be painted. You can actually measure these or use the old painter's guesstimate of 20 square feet for each door and 15 square feet per window. Subtract these two numbers and divide by the square footage estimate from the label.

WHAT ABOUT TRIM PAINT?

You'll want to get higher luster enamel for the woodwork. Measure the linear feet of the molding, including baseboard and crown molding, if any. Then, the pros guess at the width by using half a foot and multiplying the total footage by .5.

To estimate the enamel for a door, use the same 20 foot guess. However, for a window, the glass doesn't figure in, so use 7.5 feet per window.

Now add door and window estimates to the woodwork square footage and divide by the label coverage figure. We're probably talking about less than a gallon, so look at quarts for the trim.

If the math has you confused, take all these figures to your friendly paint dealer for a second opinion.

While picking out the correct amount of the right paint is important, the key word in a successful paint job is:

PREPARATION

Here are the steps you must take getting ready to paint:

1. Patch all cracks and holes (see chapter 6). As you inspect for these problems, also be on the lookout for protruding nails. Drive them back in and spackle over the spot.
2. Remove all furniture, rugs, drapes, and pictures, if possible. If not, bring it all to the center of the room and protect it with drop cloths.

3. Scrape loose or flaking paint and feather the edges with sandpaper to remove sharp corners where the flakes were.

4. Clean all surfaces. It may be that just dusting will do. However, if there are grease spots or mildew, this stuff must be removed. Grease and oil from hands can be cleaned with mineral spirits paint thinner. Mildew can be removed with a mild bleach solution.

5. Paint does not adhere well to a glossy surface. A shine can be removed by sanding or by using a liquid deglosser. The latter method avoids work and dust.

6. Mask all the trim and everything else you don't want to paint. Cover the floor with drop cloths.

7. If you'll be painting the ceiling, loosen the light fixture and wrap it in a plastic bag. Remove the cover plates to wall outlets and electrical switches.

8. You should also protect yourself from the mess. Wear a cap to protect your hair. An even better head protector is a plastic shower cap. Wear safety goggles while painting the ceiling. Put a couple of patches of Saran wrap over the lenses to catch the drips. Wear a respirator if you are spray painting. Cut out holes in a trash bag for your head and arms and you have a paint-proof poncho to save your work clothes. A light coat of petroleum jelly on exposed skin will make paint splatters easier to wipe away. A stretched out pair of sweat socks can be pulled over your shoes. Of course, you'll look like a circus clown when the doorbell rings.

DO WE NEED A PRIMER?

If the room has already been painted and the paint is sound, you don't need a primer. If you removed any paint on the woodwork, all the bare spots should be primed. If you'll be painting over a dark color that may be hard to hide, a sealer/primer should be used.

Water spots on a ceiling will bleed through your new paint. A primer/sealer will prevent this problem. This type of coating is available in liquid or aerosol spray cans. For small areas, the spray is ideal because it dries fast and therefore lets you start the fun part sooner. The best primer is the one recommended on the label of your topcoat.

SAFETY

Many of the products you'll be using have hazardous contents. Some emit harmful fumes and vapors. Some are flammable, and a fire could start just from the fumes. Read the label for caution notices and then follow all the recommended practices they suggest. In the painting game, "adequate ventilation" means that you'd have no more of a build up of fumes and vapors than you would in using the product outside. Also be sure that paint products are properly and safely stored.

Many painting procedures require the use of a ladder. You'll learn more about ladder safety in chapter 22.

PAINT TOOLS

If you buy quality brushes, they'll give you a better chance at success, and if you care for them properly, they can actually last a lifetime. If the paint you'll be using is latex, use all-purpose brushes with synthetic bristles. Other coatings are better applied with natural bristled brushes. All better brushes will have flagged tips. (This is sort of like the split ends you try to avoid in your hair.) You'll probably get by with only three brushes for your interior paint job . . . a 3-inch straight edged brush for cutting-in (we'll explain that term in a sec.), a 2-inch trim brush, and a 1-inch tapered sash brush.

Rollers are the way to go for large areas like walls and ceilings. The roller covers come in different nap lengths . . . short, medium, and long. For the average room with light texture, the short nap roller is probably best. As you get into rougher texture, you'll probably get better, faster results from longer nap. The roller cover goes on a roller cage, and the handle should be one that accepts screw-in pole sections. That extra reach will cut down on your ladder time.

You'll either need a paint tray or a 5-gallon paint bucket with a paint screen.

PROCEDURE

There are other items you may wish to get, but for the first interior paint adventure, you're ready. Here's the sequence:

1. Start with the cutting-in for the ceiling. Cutting-in is the act of painting a band around the edges of the ceiling, wall, door or window with a 4-inch brush. This is an area that a roller can't properly get to. Then roll paint on the ceiling. As you paint, try to put your next stripe of paint against the wet edge of the previous stripe. This helps to avoid streaks.
2. The painting of crown molding follows this.
3. Next, cut-in the walls and around the doors, windows, and baseboards before rolling the wall. Never stop before completing a wall. When you come back, you'll be painting against a dry edge, and it will show.
4. The final steps are the doors, windows, and then the baseboard molding.

MIXING

It's important to keep the paint mixed before you start and as you paint. When you buy the paint, it will be machine mixed. When you're ready to paint, use a process called boxing. This requires an extra can. Pour about two-thirds of the gallon of paint into the spare can. Use the paint paddle to stir what's left in the original can, paying particular attention to any pigment that might have settled to the bottom. Now pour back the paint from the extra can, a little at a time and stirring as you go. Now pour back and forth between the two containers.

EXTERIOR PAINTING

Because of the size of an exterior paint project and the inaccessibility of many of the parts of the house to be painted, the thought of doing it yourself may be mind-boggling. It is time consuming, and if you hate ladder climbing, house painting may not be your cup of tea.

We mentioned at the introduction of this course that exterior painting is not just for added drive-up appeal, it's also a form of protection against the elements. So it has to be done! Your first decision is who is going to do it. Just as with interior painting, a big chunk of the cost of having it done is labor. Providing that labor yourself saves you big bucks. Let's assume you're game. What's next?

HOW MUCH TO BUY

While you still have to do the math, there are other considerations for outside painting. Whatever type of siding is on your home, there are apt to be edges that will require extra paint. So, take the square footage, figure the gallons required, and then add 20 percent.

PREPARATIONS

As with interior painting, the preparation work is a big key to success. Here are the steps to prep:

1. Pressure wash all surfaces. Rent the equipment and get the rental guy to run you through a quick course in operation and safety.
2. Scrape away all loose and flaking paint. A wire brush is also helpful with this chore.
3. Feather the edges to do away with sharp places on the remaining sound paint.

4. Replace damaged wood.
5. Prime all bare wood. We like to use an oil-based primer for exterior work even if the topcoat is to be latex.
6. Caulk around all doors and windows and any other exterior joints between different building materials.
7. Remove all mildew. If you just cover the fungus, it will grow right through the new paint.
8. Make sure all surfaces to be painted are clean and dry.

> **TEACHER'S TIP**
>
> You might want to consider renting scaffolding. Rather than trying to do it all from a ladder, scaffolding can make the job easier and safer. Most rental guys will deliver.

DOING THE ACTUAL JOB

With tarps down to cover walks, driveways, decks, and shrubs, get into your painting gear and get started. Here are steps that will help you get professional results:

1. Check the weather report. Avoid painting when there could be rain before the paint has time to dry. Moderate temperatures and low humidity will also help.
2. Work around the house so that you don't paint in direct sunshine. The heat causes the top layer to dry before the paint underneath does. Start on the shady side and try to move with the sun.
3. Mix the paint thoroughly at the beginning of and during the project.
4. Unless you have large areas of smooth surfaces, the roller is probably not going to be your choice. A four-inch brush will get the job done, slow but sure. You'll probably need a couple of smaller brushes for trim and window painting.
5. Once your ladder or scaffolding is set, paint all you can reach, top to bottom, before moving the stuff.
6. If a second coat is required, be sure to wait until the first coat is fully dry.

PAINTING METAL

Often the iron and steel items you'll be painting are rusted. Some folks think that covering the rust up is the end of that problem, but rust will continue to grow under the paint. You must remove all the rust using either a chemical rust remover or a wire-brush. A wire-brush attachment for your power drill expedites the job. Before you apply a topcoat, you should use a rust-preventive primer. Then you can use almost any type of paint made for metal.

Galvanized metal, such as gutters, needs painting for protection and often to make them blend in with the rest of the house. New galvanized objects don't accept paint very well. They require months of weathering. However, if you don't want to wait, clean and remove rust and etch the surface with vinegar. Then apply a zinc-based primer. When dry, apply any exterior paint, probably what you painted the rest of the house with.

Aluminum oxidizes, which prevents the metal from accepting paint. Remove any oxidation with steel wool and use a zinc-oxide primer. Actually, rather than painting, you may like what a shiny coat of paste wax will do.

For painting the outdoor grill, you must remove dirt, rust, and cooking grease. Then you must apply a heat resistant paint. The aerosol spray is the easiest way to go.

PAINTING BRICK AND CONCRETE BLOCK

You have to really hate the look of the brick to want to paint it. Once painted, it is next to impossible to get it off. If you've got your mind made up to do it, power wash the bricks, then roll on flat latex house paint.

Concrete block will need the same prep and will take the same type of paint as brick. Apply the paint with a long napped roller.

PAINTING A CONCRETE FLOOR

A garage floor can look a lot better with that nice concrete floor painted. First you must remove all oil and grease stains as well as any other dirt. Then you should acid wash the surface with 10 parts water to one part muriatic acid. Protect yourself from the acid and wear a respirator because of the dangerous fumes. We like the epoxy paint for it's staying power.

FAUX FINISHES

Faux finishes are fun and there are no rules. You can let your imagination run wild and create your own wild and wonderful finishes. The ones we've described really have to be seen to be appreciated. We suggest you get a sheet of gypsum board and experiment in the garage or basement. These treatments are as easy as one, two, three, faux.

Sponging—As you've already guessed, this technique uses a sponge to apply part of the paint. A sea sponge is better than the artificial kind. You start by using a roller to apply a base coat of semi-gloss wall paint. Next, you'll create your glaze coat. Glaze is a colorless milky looking liquid that dries to semi-transparency. You get a different effect when you add colorant to the glaze. A sort of norm is to add one part color to four parts glaze. Now, here comes the sponge. Dip the sponge into the glaze, blot the sponge onto a coffee filter and then dab the sponge against the wall, with a twist of the wrist. It's best to work diagonally across the wall rather than straight across or straight down. You can stop there, but a second sponge attack with a different colorant will make the effect more interesting.

Ragging—In this faux finish you take away rather than add as with sponging. You roll on a glaze over the base coat. Then you take an old T-shirt and roll it into a wrinkled cylinder. Start at the bottom of the wall and roll this cloth cylinder toward the top. As the rag fills with paint turn the whole thing inside out. When it finally is totally saturated with the glaze, start a new rag. Here again, using a second coat with a different colored glaze will add interest.

Pickling—This is a whitewashed look that starts with a thinned white paint that is brushed on and then wiped off. This is a faux finish used on cabinets, wood paneling, and even floors. The paint is pretty much wiped off the hard parts of the wood and is soaked into the soft parts. The thinned pickling coat is rolled or brushed on, then a clean rag is used to wipe it off. You have to work in small strips since the coating dries rather quickly. After the desired look is attained, protect the finish with a coat of polyurethane

Dragging—Like several of the other faux finishes, you start with a base coat and then apply a coat of glaze. The dragging is done with a long-bristled dry brush brought down the wall from top to bottom. After each stroke, use a coffee filter to remove the glaze.

Combing—This technique utilizes a metal paint-combing tool. These are available with a variety of spacing between teeth. This usually involves a base coat and when dry, a contrasting topcoat. While this second coat is still wet, the comb is raked through it. You can make a crosshatch pattern, a squiggly lined pattern, or whatever else grabs you. If you don't like the results, roll back over and try again.

BRUSH AND ROLLER CARE

The temptation when you are finished painting is go take a nap, have a drink, or otherwise get away from the work site. Not so fast! It's clean up time. Here are the basics of cleaning:

1. Clean all brushes and rollers as soon as the painting is done. For latex paint, use warm water and detergent. For oil-based paint, use paint thinner. Let the brush soak a few minutes before you start to work out the paint. Suspend the brush in the cleaner so the bristles don't rest on the bottom of the container. An "X" slit in the plastic lid of a coffee can will accomplish this.

2. Next, work the brush against the sides of the container to get the paint out.

3. Use your hand to squeeze the paint out.
4. Work the brush against a section of newspaper to absorb the cleaner and to check to see if all the paint is gone.
5. You may have to repeat all of these steps several times to get the brush clean. With latex paint, holding the brush under a faucet is good.
6. With either type, shake out the solvent or water when clean and use a brush comb to straighten the bristles. Hang the brush to let the bristles dry straight.
7. Rollers need to be scraped to remove excess paint. Most brush combs have a curved edge for use on rollers. The same solvent discussed above will work on rollers. A spin of the roller held down in a garbage can will sling out paint and cleaner.

PRESSURE WASHING

The rental of pressure washing equipment is popular these days. It's a quick way to clean the entire exterior of the house. The blast of water will also remove flaking paint much faster than you can scrape it off.

However, in the wrong hands, this much power can be dangerous. You must know how to aim the blast and how to control the force. Don't allow spectators during this procedure. Be sure to cover any vent openings, including gable vents, soffit vents, and crawl space vents. Do not spray directly on windows, or you're liable to end up with broken glass.

Be sure to wear your safety goggles.

If you're going to go this route, be sure you let the rental agent explain in detail the operating and safety instructions.

SPRAY PAINTING

You may be wondering why we haven't mentioned spray painting. In the hands of a novice you can cover more than you had planned . . . like the neighbor's house, his newly restored Rolls Royce, and maybe his cat. That may be the reason that some communities have outlawed the use of paint sprayers outdoors. Even on a relatively still day, the fine mist can travel for blocks. Also, until you really get the hang of it, you can apply more paint than is needed and end up with sags and drips.

If you are going to rent a spray rig, dilute the coating and experiment with the consistency until you get it right. Then, practice maintaining a constant distance while moving the gun back and forth. Practice starting and stopping the unit and be sure you know how to adjust the nozzle and how to control the spray pattern.

In other words, Practice, Practice, Practice!

Wallpaper 101

16

Wallpapering is a very popular way to completely change the look of a room . . . or maybe the whole house. It is also a very popular do-it-yourself project.

Newer wall coverings are washable, pre-pasted, fade resistant, and strippable. Being strippable won't mean much right now. But in four years when your spouse decides the old wallpaper has got to go, you'll love the fact that entire strips can often be peeled off without the mess of steaming, soaking, scraping, and cursing.

The first step in wallpapering is the one that takes up the most time and is one we can't help you with . . . the selection of the pattern. All we can contribute is to wish you "Good luck!" Hanging the wallpaper is the easy part, once you get the hang of it! Here are the steps:

1. Do the math. Figure out how many rolls are required. Wallpaper comes in various widths. However, regardless of width, most rolls deliver 36 square feet. But the yield is less because of waste and other factors—in the end, you probably only get 30 square feet. The best way to order the correct amount is to measure the perimeter of the room, then the room's height, and multiply the two figures. Then measure the openings, windows, and doors, and subtract these. Write all that down and then measure again. Take this into your wallpaper dealer and let them tell you how many rolls to buy. They will sell you enough so you'll have a little left over for repairs later on. The dealer will also make sure you get the proper adhesive and sizing for your project. In addition, you'll need a paste brush, a water box, (for pre-pasted paper,) a seam roller, and a smoothing brush. See some of these tools in figure 16-1.

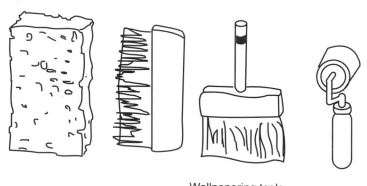

Wallpapering tools

figure 16-1

2. The unpapered wall will usually have texturing. This must be sanded to remove bumps. It doesn't have to be smooth as glass. A fast way to do this is to cover a scrap of 2 x 4 lumber with window screen wire, grab the "tool" with both hands and rake it across the wall to smooth the surface down flat.

3. Patch and seal any cracks or holes.

4. Apply sizing to the entire wall.

5. Remove the plates from wall outlets and switches. It's a good idea to shut off the current to these outlets since wet paste is a conductor of electricity.

6. Select the most inconspicuous corner in the room and measure out from the wall the width of a roll less 1 inch.

7. Lower a plumb bob and strike a chalk line.

8. Cut your first strip so it's about 4 inches longer than the height of the wall. Before you cut though, hold the roll up to the wall and move it up and down to see where the pattern will look the best. Figure the repeat and add to the length to allow for matching.

9. If you are using pre-pasted type wallpaper, put the strip into the water, following the manufacturer's suggestions as to water temperature and length of soaking. If you're using the type where you brush on the paste, you need a long table. This could be an actual table or a sheet of plywood or a door over saw horses. A paint roller is a faster applicator than the paste brush.

> **FACT OF LIFE**
>
> Never buy only a few rolls at a time. This could mean the rolls might not be from the same dye-lot. The difference in color would be minor until your job is finished and then the difference would be monumental!

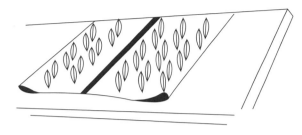

figure 16-2

10. Next, cover the top half and "book" it. "Booking" is a step where you fold the strip over, paste against paste, as shown in figure 16-2. Do the bottom half and book it. This allows you to carry the pasted strip without getting paste all over you.

11. Unfold the top half and position the edge against the chalk line, leaving a couple of inches sticking up at the ceiling.

12. Smooth from that edge over to the corner, using your hand and the smoothing brush. Check to be sure that this edge is still exactly on the chalk line. The paste will allow you to slide it back if it's not in place.

13. When you get back to the corner, the extra inch makes the turn and is pasted to the other wall.

14. Unfold the bottom half and smooth it in place.

15. Use the smoothing brush to poke the paper into the corner.

16. See if the pattern matches before cutting the next strip. In matching patterns, check to see how much waste there will be by holding the roll up to see where the top should be cut off. If there is significant waste, open another roll and see whether you can minimize the waste by alternating rolls.

17. When the second strip is ready to be hung, unfold the top half and slide it up against the edge of the first panel. If the first panel is plumb, all subsequent strips will be as well.

18. As you work around the room, don't skip over any places. Keep going until you've covered all around the room.

19. With the next strip in place, go back to the previous strip and trim it top and bottom using a wallpaper trim knife. This special knife has a long blade that you snap off when the exposed section of blade gets dull. A dull blade will tear the wet paper.

20. Roll the seams as soon as you install the next panel.

21. When you come to a window or door, use your utility knife to make a 45-degree cut into the obstacle to relieve the pressure on the paper. Smooth the paper right up to the molding or trim and cut off the excess by placing a straight edge against the molding and cutting the excess off. Run the paper on out at the top and bottom of windows. This can be a good place to try to use some of the waste that you may have accumulated by now.

22. On inside corners, cut the length first, matching the pattern if needed. Then measure at the top, middle, and bottom, from the last piece of paper to the corner. Take the widest measurement, add 1 inch, and then cut the paper to that width. Save the cut-off piece. Hang the paper, continuing around the corner with the spare inch or so. Measure the width of the cut-off piece and mark another plumb line to that width. Hang this strip against the plumb line and smooth it down. It should overlap the previous piece.

23. When you have gone completely around the room, let your final strip overlap the 1-inch wide strip at the corner. Make a cut top to bottom going through both layers. When you peel away the cut off parts of both strips, you'll have an exact match.

WHAT ABOUT PAPERING ELECTRICAL PLATES?

It's optional! If you want to do it, however, here are the simple steps:

1. Reinstall the plate over the outlet.

2. Take a scrap of the paper and cover the plate, moving the paper around until you match the pattern. Tape it to the wall.

3. Carefully feel the outline of the plate and poke a hole with a needle at each corner.

4. Remove the plate and the scrap and draw an outline of the plate on the back of the paper.

5. Trim the scrap so there is about a 1/2-inch border around the plate.

6. Snip off the corners at the needle holes.

7. Apply vinyl wallpaper adhesive to the face of the plate and smooth the paper in place.

8. Fold over the edges and tape them to the back of the plate.

9. Cut out for the switch or outlets and poke holes with an ice pick for the screw holes.

Done right, you may have a problem finding these wall outlets.

WHAT ABOUT PAPERING THE CEILING?

This is an option. However, while papering walls is fun, doing a ceiling is torture. You basically need a helper to handle those long strips while going all the way across the ceiling. Scaffolding has to be used. Sometimes gravity becomes your enemy and when you get to the end of a strip, the other end is peeling loose.

To make matters even worse, ceiling papers often make the room seem smaller. However, if you are bound and determined to embark on this trip to hell, you will use the same general principles we talked about for walls.

Another negative: If you do decide both walls and ceilings are to be covered, you should do the ceiling first. By the time the ceiling is covered, many folks are so tired of it all, they hire somebody else to do the fun part.

CAN YOU PAPER OVER OLD PAPER?

Actually, you can paper over almost anything. A friend in Chicago (we're not making this up) applied wallpaper over every bit of a toilet, including inside the bowl. Several coats of marine varnish later, he had a one of a kind serviceable toilet. So, certainly you can apply paper over existing paper. There are some possible pitfalls:

1. Sometimes the moisture from the wet paste will soak through the old paper and make the old paste let go.
2. Often the pattern on the old paper will become visible through the new covering.
3. The seams of the old paper can show through the new panels.

Having said all that, we know many will want to gamble that these things won't happen, and so they'll go ahead with putting new paper over old. To find out if the old covering is solidly attached, use this test. Apply water to the surface on a spot about the size of a dinner plate. If the paper does not come loose, maybe that pitfall isn't a problem. If the old pattern is bright enough to show through, apply a coat of shellac or a sealer/primer. To make sure the seams don't become visible, tape and bed the wallpaper seams as you would drywall joints.

Before starting your new papering, roll on a coat of sizing.

HOW ABOUT PAPER OVER PANELING OR CONCRETE BLOCK?

The secret is **lining paper.** Available in different thicknesses, it is made to hide minor irregularities. Lining paper is usually applied horizontally.

REMOVING WALLPAPER

If you do have to remove old wall covering, here are some things that may help. Assume that it will just peel right off. Go up to a corner and pick at it. You may find that it strips right off . . . but probably not.

If not, water or steam will soften up the old paste. Use very hot water to which you've added a cap of liquid detergent, and apply this to the surface with a paint roller. If the paper is vinyl, the water will not soak through. There is a tool called a Paper Tiger which, when rolled across the surface, uses a series of needle points to poke holes in the paper. Now the water can get to the paste. You can rent a steamer, and after poking the holes, the hot steam will soften up the adhesive.

Be sure to shut off the electrical current to switches and wall outlets during this part of the job.

> **TEACHER'S TIP**
>
> Removing wallpaper is never going to be easy, but this solution may help. Mix one part liquid fabric softener to 2 parts hot water. Roll this over the surface. After 10–15 minutes, your scraper will find the paper easier to remove.

Even after the paste becomes soft, you'll probably have to scrape the old paper off in tiny pieces. This is a tedious and messy project at best!

WALLPAPER SPOTS AND GOOFS

For the kitchen and bath, you should get washable wall coverings. That way, a damp sponge and detergent will remove most spots. Here are some common spots that can spoil your wallpaper:

1. **Handprints** around light switches will come clean with a paste made of cornstarch and water. Brush it on and it will absorb the oil from skin. Or, try using an art gum eraser.
2. **Grease spots** as well as airborne grease from cooking can be removed by using a powder puff to apply talcum powder to the walls. Dust the talc off and then repeat until all the grease is gone.
3. **Spots of unknown origin** can often be removed by rolling bits of rye bread into a ball and then rubbing them over the spot.
4. **Loose seams** can be corrected by lifting the edge and squirting white glue under the edges. Press both sides down. Wipe away the excess glue that is squeezed out and then use a seam roller to make it right again (figure 16-3).
5. **Shrunken paper** may leave a slight gap between strips. Mix acrylic artist's paint to match the wallpaper and use a tiny artist's brush to cover the gap.
6. **Bubbles** happen when the paste lets go or where there is too much paste. You can cut an "X" in the center of the bubble (figure 16-4). If there is wet paste inside, use your hand to move the paste toward the center of the bubble and use

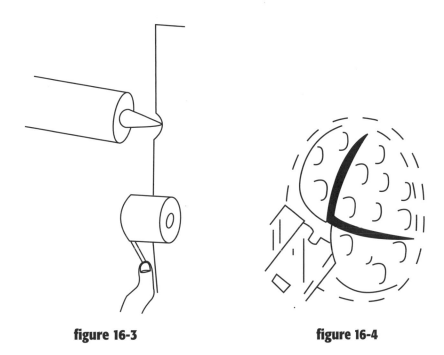

figure 16-3   **figure 16-4**

a damp sponge to wipe it away. If the paste just lets go, scrape away the old paste. Apply white glue and press the flaps back in place. Secure the flaps with the seam roller.

7. **Patching** is the best way to take care of torn places. Take a scrap (you did save some, didn't you?) and match the pattern. Tape the scrap in place and use a sharp knife to cut through both layers. Remove the scrap and wet the edges around the torn place. Let it soak for a few minutes and use the point of the blade to peel away the old paper with the torn spot. Apply paste to the patch and carefully align it to make the pattern match. You should have a perfect patch.

With all this knowledge, you should be able to hang in there with the best of paperhangers!

Heating and Cooling 101

17

God takes care of the climate outside, but it's your responsibility to take charge of the climate inside your home. Only you can determine your comfort level. Of course, you couldn't do it without your heating and cooling systems, but if you can keep these mechanical monsters running properly and safely, you are in control.

We will cover the various systems, try to let you do the maintenance, adjustments, and repairs that you should be able to do yourself, and hopefully let you know when it's time to call a pro. First of all, we believe that your heating system, no matter what type, should have a yearly inspection. The pro who does this should make sure the system is running properly, efficiently, and safely.

Don't be sucked in by a special cheap price for a seasonal inspection. The so-called pro who comes out is not going to make the trip for $19.95 or some other low-ball figure. The company would lose money at that price. Therefore, he has been instructed by management to "find" something wrong that costs four or five hundred dollars to fix. Find a reputable company that charges a reasonable fee for an inspection and will put in writing all the things that are wrong.

HEATING SYSTEMS

The most popular heating systems today are the ducted type. Most are the forced air types that use a blower fan to send the heated air through a series of supply ducts going to registers in each room. Return air ducts pull air back through a filter and then through the furnace. The furnace can be either natural gas, electric, or oil burning. With any of these, there are some common elements . . . filters, flues, ducts, thermostats, blower fans, fan motors, room registers, and cold air returns. So, before we get specific on the type of heater, lets address these common components:

Filters—Since the house is heated by circulating warm air, this air stirs up dust. When this dust is pulled back through the heater, it can cause problems that reduce the capacity of the heater, and can even shut it down. That is why the filter needs to be clean. If you use the very inexpensive "throw away" filters, they should be replaced each month during the heating season. If you have reusable filters, clean them monthly. Most technicians do not recommend the lifetime electrostatic filters. However, the electronic filters are good but fairly expensive.

The filter will have an arrow pointing in the direction of airflow. That's the only trick to correctly changing the filter.

Flues—The flue carries away combustion gases. It should be checked for any obstructions, such as bird nests. It should have a cap over the top on the roof. All the joints should be properly connected. Electric heating doesn't require a flue.

Ductwork—If the ducts become disconnected or if leaks occur, you could be warming the attic at a big waste of energy.

Thermostat—This is the brain center of the heating system. Keep it clean, as dust can impair the accuracy. Use a small, very soft brush. Then blow away the dust with your breath. Never use a vacuum cleaner. If yours is the type with contact points, clean by sliding a hundred-dollar bill (Actually our tests show a one-dollar bill works almost as well!) back and forth on the metal surfaces. Most thermostats also work best when level. It's a good idea to give the thermostat a lie detector test. Tape an accurate thermometer to the wall next to the thermostat (figure 17-1). Make sure there is no outside influence, such as air blowing from a register, heat from a TV set, etc. Wait about fifteen minutes for the thermometer to stabilize, then compare. If they differ more than a degree or so, most thermostats can be recalibrated. That said, now might be a good time to replace the old thermostat with a new automatic setback type that can save energy dollars.

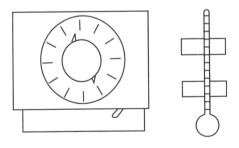

figure 17-1

Blower fans—Most heater fans are of the squirrel cage variety (figure 17-2). With all these blades, too much dust accumulates and not enough air is circulated. Here are the steps in cleaning:

1. Turn off electrical current to the unit.
2. Remove the access panel covering the fan. The fan is usually attached to a track by screws.
3. Remove the screws and the fan should slide out.
4. Each blade should be brushed with a toothbrush, preferably one you'll not be using in your mouth.
5. Vacuum up the loosened dust all around the fan.
6. When put back in place, make sure the fan is properly anchored to the track.

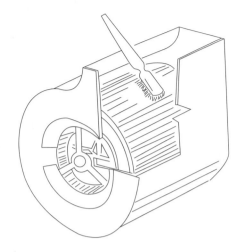

figure 17-2

Fan motor—Some motors for heaters are direct drive while others are belt driven. Whatever type of heater you have, look for oil ports or cups. They have flip-up lids and should be given a few drops of oil at the beginning of heating season. To be sure of oil requirements, check your owner's manual. If your fan is belt driven, the belt shouldn't be tight, but loose enough to depress about an inch.

Room registers—Remove and clean at the beginning of heating season.

Cold air returns—Clean when you vacuum the floors.

NATURAL GAS AND LP GAS

Where it is available, natural gas heat is usually economical and clean burning. When properly maintained, a gas furnace is fairly reliable. Here are some common problems:

Pilot light out—If your furnace has a pilot, it is accompanied by a safety device called a thermal couple.

Lighting the pilot is usually simple. Turn the gas valve to "Off" for five minutes. Then turn the knob to "Pilot" and hold a lighted match to the pilot while pressing down on the red reset button for about thirty seconds. When the time is up, release the button and the pilot should stay lit. Then turn the knob to "On." If it doesn't work the first time, give it a couple more tries.

Newer heating units ignite the gas with a spark from a glow bar. If this malfunctions, the bar must be replaced. It's usually best to have this professionally done.

Some problems that could occur include:

THE THERMOCOUPLE (figure 17-3).

This is a sensing device that tells the gas valve that it is OK to supply gas to the burners because the pilot is "on" and will ignite the gas. The pilot flame bathes the sensing tube. If the flame isn't hitting the top half-inch of the tube, the thermocouple assumes the pilot is out and tells the gas valve to shut down. Either reposition the tip of the tube or adjust the pilot flame. The flame should be mostly blue with yellow tips. There is usually an adjustment screw on the gas valve. If the thermocouple malfunctions, you can get a replacement at a home center, and it is an easy replacement to make. You'll also run into this when we talk about gas water heaters. In buying a replacement, be sure the tube is long enough to reach from the pilot to the gas valve.

Burner doesn't come on—Could be caused by a thermostat malfunctioning or turned too low. The pilot light could be out. Check for a tripped circuit breaker or blown fuse. Many units have a safety switch that shuts off the unit if an access panel is loose or open.

There is a delay in the heater coming on followed by a booming noise—This usually means that the burner is clogged and the ignition doesn't happen until enough gas is released to finally reach the pilot flame. Clean the burners using a wire brush. Vacuum up the debris.

Not enough heat—Check the ductwork. Most of your heat may be going to the attic. Or, the filter may be clogged, choking the airflow.

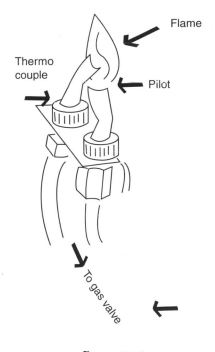

figure 17-3

Unit cycles off and on—Filter is clogged, or fan and limit switch is out of adjustment. This switch is usually on the face of the unit. Most have two sets of dials. The right hand dial controls the fan. When the heat builds up to a certain temperature, it calls for the fan to come on. Then, after the burners shut down, this switch keeps the fan blowing until the air inside the unit drops to a preset point. There should be about a 25-degree span. A good setting would be for it to come on at around 110° F and go off at 85° F. The right-hand dial may be preset so that the burners shut off if the heat becomes excessive inside the heat exchanger.

Blower fan stays on even after air is cooled—Another sign the fan and limit switch is out of adjustment.

ELECTRIC

Even though electric heat is 100 percent efficient and is the cleanest form of residential furnace, it's a fairly expensive way to heat a home. Since there is nothing being burned, there is no problem with combustion gases, so there is no flue and no heat exchanger.

There may be internal fuses that blow. Be sure that you shut off the current to the furnace before replacing a fuse.

For filters, thermostat, blower fan, and ductwork problems, refer to the section on gas furnaces.

OIL FURNACE

Although much like the gas furnace, the oil furnace has some other components. You should clean or change the oil filter at least at the beginning of the heating season. Also, there is a pump strainer that needs to be cleaned annually. Soak it in kerosene and replace the gasket at that time.

STEAM

The steam boiler heats water until it creates steam. This steam then rises and goes to the various radiators throughout the house. The hot steam heats the metal radiators. They in turn radiate heat to the air in the room. As the steam cools, it turns back into water and returns to the boiler to go through the cycle again.

There are two versions of steam heat: one-pipe and two-pipe. The steam and water travel in opposite directions in the same pipe in a one-pipe system. The other type has a supply pipe and a return pipe.

Even though steam heat works on the natural laws of physics that steam rises and water flows downhill, there are a few things you should do to ensure continued operation. The unit must have the proper water level. There is a sight glass that should be checked monthly with the boiler "off." There is a steam gauge that tells the pressure. If it gets into the danger zone, shut down the boiler and call in a pro.

Here are some common problems:

No heat—If there isn't any water, or if the burners are not on, there will be no heat. Also, the trouble could be from a tripped circuit breaker or a blown fuse.

Not enough heat—If you have furniture in the way, or have covered over the ugly radiator, you may be blocking the free flow of heat. Rust or lime and scale buildup may constrict pipes, so you should occasionally flush the system. Check your owner's manual for flushing instructions for your particular system. And don't just flush once and refill. Keep doing it until the water coming out is clear.

Water level regularly too low—There is obviously a leak. If the leak is in a pipe, go to chapter 4 to see how to handle leaking pipes. If the leak is in the boiler, get a pro to handle the repair.

Water in sight gauge is rusty—The unit may need to be flushed or it may just be that the sight gauge needs cleaning. Here's how to clean it:

1. Turn off the boiler main switch.
2. Allow the boiler to cool down.
3. Turn the valves above and below the gauge by turning clockwise.
4. Loosen the nut at each end of the tube.
5. The glass lifts up and out.
6. When clean, insert in the lower valve first, making sure the washers are in place before tightening the nuts.
7. Open up both valves and turn the boiler back on.

Banging in pipes—This probably means that water is trapped in the return line or in a one-pipe radiator. Everything must slope downward toward the boiler. Use a level on radiator and if it doesn't slope, use shims to lift the legs on the end away from the pipe. Also use the level on all return pipes. Sometimes you can use pipe straps to reestablish the slant. Also, make sure the valves on radiators are fully opened.

HOT WATER

The hot water heating system is much like steam heating, except that newer installations have convectors rather than radiators. Many people will end up replacing the radiators with convector units. They are more attractive, take up less space, and heat better. Convectors are available as upright consoles or as baseboard units.

Another difference from steam is that hot water heat uses a pump called a circulator to deliver the heated water and bring it back to the boiler. Really old systems are gravity operated and do not use a pump. Another feature not found in a steam system is the expansion tank. This tank is charged with air that prevents the water from boiling even though the temperature may be well above the 212° F boiling mark.

Many of the problems common to steam heating are found in the hot water systems. Sometimes a noise problem can be attributed to the pump. Be sure to follow the suggested maintenance procedures for your particular hot water heating system as found in the owner's manual, and you should have very few problems.

FIREPLACE

As a source of heat, the wood-burning fireplace isn't all that great. As a source of enjoyment, it's hard to beat a romantic crackling fire and proverbial jug of wine, bearskin rug, and thou.

To be sure the fireplace isn't a fire hazard and is as efficient and trouble-free as possible, follow these fireplace rules:

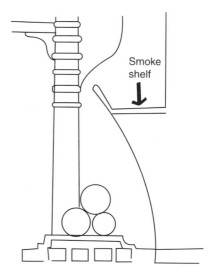

figure 17-4a

1. Inspect the flue each fall. Open the damper, shine a flashlight up the chimney, and use a hand mirror to get a better view of what's up there. Look for any creosote build up on the chimney walls. Also, be sure no bird nests are in the chimney.
2. With a gloved hand, reach around the damper to the smoke shelf (figures 17-4a-b) and remove any debris that is there.
3. Look at the bricks inside the fireplace. Any missing mortar or cracked bricks should be repaired. The gap could act like a tiny chimney and bring the flame inside the walls, where it could start a fire. Use only special fireplace cement that outlasts regular mortar. If bricks need to be replaced, use fireplace bricks.
4. Have a fireplace screen that will prevent embers from popping out. Glass doors will save energy because they prevent the updrafts from sucking heated air out of the house.

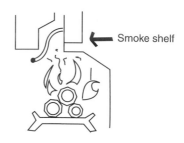

figure 17-4b

5. Do not burn treated lumber. It throws off harmful chemicals when burned. Pine burns too fast, and the smoke carries creosote up the chimney.

6. Install a chimney cap on top of the chimney to prevent flying cinders, to keep rain—as well as birds and pests—from coming down the chimney, and to prevent down drafts from smoking up the house.

7. Be sure the damper is open before lighting the fire.

> **TEACHER'S TIP**
>
> A child's little red wagon is a good way to bring in a load of firewood without getting your clothes dirty.

Do you know exactly what a cord of wood is? Firewood has become very expensive and since it is sold by the cord, you should be getting a full cord. A cord should measure 128 cubic feet. Measure the length of the stack and multiply it by the width and then the height. If it's close to 128, enjoy!

Stack the firewood off the ground to keep it from getting damp. You can make a dandy rack with some concrete blocks and a few 2 x 4s (figure 17-5).

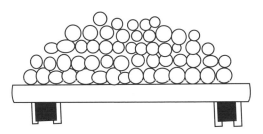

Concrete blocks & 2 x 4s keep logs off ground

figure 17-5

AIR CONDITIONERS (CENTRAL)

Almost a hundred years ago, when a chap named Willis H. Carrier got hot under the collar, he invented the forerunner of air conditioning as we know it today. Unfortunately, most of us don't really know it today.

It's really a pretty simple concept, based on the fact that when a gas expands, its temperature is lowered. Conversely, when a gas is compressed, it gets hotter. Your central air system has a compressor unit outside that compresses Freon gas, causing it to heat up. A fan blows across the fins of the condenser, dissipating this heat. The gas is then piped inside to evaporator coils where it expands and therefore cools. The blower fan pulls in air from the house and sends it across these cold coils, and the cooled air is sent out into the house. At the same time, moisture in the air condenses and forms a frost on the coils. The gas is then piped back outside.

As you can see, all the hot stuff happens outside and the cool stuff inside.

There are a number of things you can do to keep bad things from happening, and some bad things that you can repair. We've already talked about filters and thermostats earlier in this chapter.

There is also a regular chore that needs to be done to the outside unit. The fan outside pulls air through those fins. If they are clogged, the airflow is lessened and this can cause compressor problems. Look for vines growing up onto the unit, grass clippings, pet hair, or any other debris. It's best to trip the circuit breaker while turning the hose on the fins.

The fan in the outside unit should be oiled per the owner's manual instructions. If a blade gets loose or the fan comes loose, it can result in a bent blade. Don't try straightening the blade. Opt for a new fan blade assembly. Other common problems include:

Unit is leaking water—There is no water involved in air conditioning except the moisture taken from the air that condenses on the evaporator coils and turns to frost. When the thermostat sees that the temperature goal has been reached, the compressor shuts off and the frost on the coils begins to melt. This water drips into a pan and is drained away. However, if the drain hole in the pan or the drainpipe becomes clogged, the water finds another way out . . . namely, all over your floors or ceilings depending on where the unit is located. The clog is often a fungal growth, and if you can get liquid laundry bleach to that plug, the bleach will eat up the problem. You will probably have to remove an access panel. The evaporator somewhat resembles a car radiator and the drip pan is directly under it. The pan may be dirty, but cleaning it will allow you to find the drain hole. Poke a small piece of coat hanger wire in to see if the problem is there. A pipe will come off of this and will usually have an open standpipe. Using a funnel, you can pour bleach down the line. If that doesn't work, compressed air may blast out the clog.

Now that you've found this unit, it's a good time to clean the air-intake side of it. A suede brush does a good job here. This should be done annually. Some problems that may occur include:

Nothing is happening—Check the power switch, fuses, and circuit breaker switches. Also, make sure the thermostat is set low enough to call for cooling.

Fan blowing but no cold air coming out—Sometimes two breakers control the unit. If the one going to the compressor is tripped, the fan could be on but no cold will be coming out. Some outside units have a reset button that may have popped out. The unit could be low on Freon, and this should be checked by a pro.

Unit cycles off and on too often—Check airflow outside, as well as the filter and blower inside.

Some rooms not cool enough—Try to balance the system by partially closing registers to cooler rooms. Also consider an in-line fan that replaces the register in a too-warm room. It can pull more air in.

AIR CONDITIONERS (ROOM)

If you're moving into an older home that has no air conditioning, room units may cost a lot less than adding a central unit. Since you can shut the unit off when you are not in the room, it may save energy dollars. This fairly compact little unit has all the elements of a central system, except for ductwork. A single motor operates two separate fans that expel heat out the back and blow cold air out the front. The same fan that is blowing cold air out gets the cold air from the room, and in addition to cooling it, dehumidifies it. The fan that is blowing to the outside is often a slinger fan that disperses the condensate water. By changing a setting, the unit can also ventilate the room with fresh air from outside.

These are commonly called window units because the window is the easiest place to install them. Here are the basic installation steps:

1. Select a unit that includes mounting hardware, expandable curtain assembly (takes up the gap between the unit and the window and frame), and mounting frame (supports the weight of the unit outside).
2. Install the curtain unit to the window frame.
3. Remove the air conditioner from its casing.
4. Slide the casing into the opening from inside the house and screw it to the sash and sill. Put the mounting frame together and attach it as per instructions that come with the unit.
5. Use a level to ensure that the unit slopes down toward the outside so that the condensate can drain and be dispersed. There should be a leveling screw with the mounting frame.
6. Slide the air conditioner in place and make sure it is sealed and weatherstripped.

ROOM UNIT MAINTENANCE

Routine maintenance for a room unit is a piece of cake (figure 17-6). Here is the recipe:

1. Clean the air filter at the start of the cooling season and once a month thereafter. Wash it with detergent and water and then let it dry before putting it back in place.

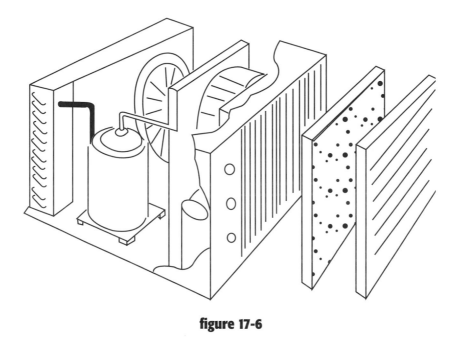

figure 17-6

2. Give the fan motor a few drops of oil in line with the instructions in the owner's manual.
3. The fins on the outside must be clean and not crimped. Clean with detergent and water and use a fin comb to correct fin crimps.
4. Remove the facing and vacuum the evaporator coils to rid them of dust.
5. Pour bleach into the drain system and see that it lets the condensate flow down toward the outside.

If the above preventive maintenance fails, here are some common failures:

Nothing happens—Test the wall outlet and inspect the cord and plug. Check for a blown fuse or tripped circuit breaker switch.

Fan works but blows warm air—It could be a compressor malfunction. Is the compressor still under warranty?

Not enough cold air—Check the blower fan for dirt or lack of lubrication. Insufficient airflow can be from the need to clean the fan or filter.

Cooling is off and on—There may be blockage from drapes or furniture. Or, the condenser coils need to be vacuumed.

Noisy operation—Check for a bent or damaged fan blade. Or, the setscrew holding the blower fan on the shaft is loose. The entire unit could be loose in the mounting frame.

Water is dripping inside the house—Reposition the unit for a greater slope to the outside. Be sure the setscrew on the slinger fan is securely holding the fan in place.

HEAT PUMPS

Many people think that a heat pump is some sort of home heater. Well, it is . . . but it is so much more, because it is also an air conditioner. You see, in the summer time, the heat pump removes heat from the house and expels it by pumping the heat outside. In winter, the process is reversed in that the heat pump takes heat from the outside air and brings it inside.

The problem here is that most of us find it hard to realize that even though it may be freezing cold outside, there is still heat involved. Believe us. We're not just making that up. The secret is in the fact that the refrigerant is circulated outside and has a temperature of minus 20° F, 52° F colder than freezing, and can indeed pick up heat. It costs a lot less to move the heat in from the cold than to fire up a furnace or run electricity through resistant heating elements.

However, this only works to its full advantage in moderate climates. If it is really cold, the heat pump needs some help, often in the form of electric heat that can run the meter at a high rate of speed. There are also dual-fuel systems that get that extra heat from a gas furnace.

The system we've talked about gets heat from the air, but there are other sources, namely from the ground or from water. Both ground and water temperatures are more constant. These systems, called geothermal heat pumps, are much more expensive to install . . . but do the math because they are very efficient.

The heat pump needs much the same maintenance as the central air conditioning system. Here some common symptoms and causes:

Frequent cycling—This is often caused by oversized equipment. Let's hope it's just a thermostat that needs adjustment or replacement.

Frequent fuse blows or breaker trips—Check for undersized wiring to the supplemental heating. It could be a fire hazard.

Excessive vibration—See if the unit is securely anchored to the slab.

Compressor runs but heat is insufficient—Supplemental heating system is malfunctioning.

Compressor runs but cooling is insufficient—Check for blocked ducts or registers. Inspect ductwork in the attic for leaks. Refrigerant may be low.

If its time for a new heating and cooling system, at least see if a heat pump is right for your area.

VENTILATION

Many folks think ventilation is just a means of cooling the house in the summertime. But cooling is just one feature of ventilation. A more important function of ventilation is to get rid of excess humidity. And moisture is probably a home's worst enemy. Proper ventilation fights the moisture problem year round. Here are the places where ventilation should be addressed:

1. Of course, the attic is a prime target for ventilation. Since heat rises, the attic can be subject to intense heat in the summer. This warm air also transports humidity to the attic, and that can cause problems. The best attic ventilation for most homes would be a ridge vent along the top and soffit vents down below. If the roof doesn't have a long ridgeline, a powered vent with a thermostat and a humidistat can rid the attic of heat and moisture.
2. A brick veneer home will have weep holes in the bottom course of the brick. These are just places where the vertical mortar joint between bricks is not filled. Often the homeowner thinks this was a bricklayer's goof and fills the spaces. Don't make this mistake! These weep holes add ventilation within the walls and offer an escape for moisture.
3. Bathrooms often have excess moisture and require vent fans to exhaust the steam from showers. Let the fan run for 10 to 15 minutes after a shower. These fans should exhaust to the outside if at all possible.
4. The airborne grease from cooking also has moisture. The vent fan over the range can usually handle this problem. However, the filter must be cleaned regularly.
5. Crawl spaces should be kept open to allow for cross ventilation except in the coldest of times.
6. The basement often suffers from lack of ventilation, and an exhaust fan may be the only answer.

HUMIDITY

In the winter, proper humidity makes us seem warmer at a lower temperature. In the summer, excess humidity may make it feel like it is hotter than it really is. Too much humidity can cause mold and mildew. But a too dry house is also bad for some wood furniture.

The air conditioner dehumidifies the house, but if it's not doing the job you can buy or rent dehumidifiers that are portable and plug into a wall outlet.

In the wintertime, you may wish to use a portable plug-in humidifier. Or, a humidifier unit can be added to the duct system.

Having the proper humidity is not just a comfort thing; it may also be important to your health.

18

Energy Saving 101

Did you ever stop to think that when you became an adult, left home, and went out on your own, in effect, you would make a lifetime obligation with the utility companies? Even if you live in a house and have paid off your mortgage, you still have those utility bills every month. To make matters even worse, these bills seem to have a continuing upward spiral.

That's why this course may be the most important one in your curriculum. If you use the knowledge gained here, it can more than pay for your tuition. While you can't control the utility rates, you can control the amount of energy you use by controlling the amount of energy you waste. Take what you learn here to heart and you can also take it to the bank.

First, let us take a look at how your energy dollar is spent. As you can see from the pie chart (figure 18-1), about 50 percent goes for heating and cooling. Since that's the biggest expenditure, it also represents the biggest opportunity for savings. Let's look at what causes waste in heating and cooling and what we can do about it.

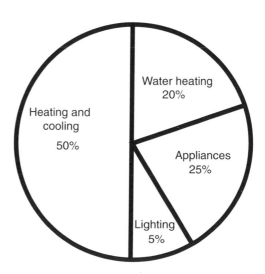

How the average energy dollar is spent

figure 18-1

INSULATION

Whether you live in a moderate climate, a warm climate, or a cold climate, upgrading your insulation will usually pay off. Insulation is measured in R-values. The "R" stands for resistance to heat transfer. The greater the R-value, the better the insulation. The recommended R-values for a home vary with the climate. Contact your local utility company to see what the suggested R-values are for the attic, walls, and floors.

ATTIC

The easiest place for the homeowner to check insulation is the attic, and the good news is that's also the easiest place to add insulation. The best news is that the attic is usually the place where having the proper insulation pays off most in energy savings.

To determine the R-value of your current attic insulation, measure the height of it and then refer to the chart below, which tells you the approximate R-value per inch for the most common types of residential insulation. If you can't identify your existing insulation, take a small sample in to a dealer.

Material-Approximate R-value per inch

Material	R-value
Vermiculite	2.08
Perlite	2.70
Fiberglass	3.33
Rock wool	3.33
Polystyrene	4.00
Cellulose	3.70
Urethane foam	5.30

Once you know what you have and how much, you need to figure out how much more you need to attain your goal. You don't have to use the same type as the existing insulation. The best insulation is the one that reaches that goal for the least money. If you'll be doing it yourself, another big determining factor is the type that will be the easiest to install.

For the attic, batts and blankets are a popular addition. They come in fiberglass or rock wool, and may be faced or not. The facing is a vapor barrier, and when adding batts or blankets over existing insulation, you should use unfaced materials. If unfaced batts are not available, you can slit the facing all over with a utility knife so that moisture doesn't get trapped within the insulation. Batts and blankets also come in standard widths that will fit between attic joists.

Batts and blankets can easily be cut to fit. We've had good luck using a hand-powered hedge trimmer. Another way is to place a 2 x 4 across the material at the intended cut line (figure 18-2). Push down firmly and use the 2 x 4 as a straightedge. Cut with a utility knife.

Loose fill is another way to go. This includes fiberglass, rock wool, cellulose, perlite, or vermiculite. Loose fill type is either poured or blown in. If poured, it goes right on top of existing material and can then be raked off for leveling.

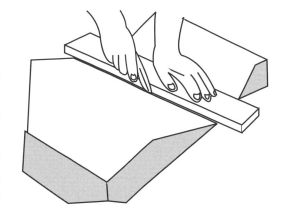

figure 18-2

Blowing the stuff allows you to get material back into the far reaches of a low attic. Some home centers loan or rent blowing machines if you buy the material from them.

Here are things to keep in mind with any type of attic insulation upgrade:

1. Place wide boards crossways over the joists to use as walkways.
2. Some materials are irritants to the skin, so cover your arms and legs and wear gloves and safety goggles. If you do get any fiberglass on your skin, pat the area with the sticky side of duct tape.
3. Wear a hard hat. There are often nails sticking through the roof decking that can stab you in the head.
4. Airborne particles are harmful to the lungs, so wear a mask.
5. Take care not to cover any vents including those in the soffits.
6. Don't cover any recessed lighting cans as this could cause overheating.

WALLS

Adding insulation within existing walls is not easy. First of all, if insulation was installed as the house was being built, there is usually no room for more insulation. If there is no insulation, or if the walls have loose fill that you believe may have settled down, you must cut holes in the walls every 16 inches so that insulation can be blown into each wall cavity between studs. Additionally, holes must be cut under all windows. After cutting holes at the top of the wall, drop a string with a weight down the hole to see if there are fire stops—2 x 4s nailed horizontally between studs. Holes must be cut below these and any other obstructions. In a two-story house, additional holes must be cut at the top of each floor.

With a brick veneer exterior, a single brick is removed at the top of each cavity and then replaced when the insulation is installed.

These holes can be inside or out. The key is to determine how best to close and hide the holes. If the drywall is cut inside, decorative molding makes a nice cover as well as an attractive addition to the house.

Before tackling this job yourself, you might wish to get an estimate from a pro. The cost might be less than you'd think, and you might wish to avoid a rather involved project.

FLOORS

If you have an unheated crawl space or unheated basement with exposed joists, insulating the floors is fairly easy. Get batts or blankets that are the proper width to fit between joists. Get the kind with vapor barrier facing. In fact, those with aluminum foil facing will reflect heat back into the room. Remember the vapor barrier always goes on the side next to the heated space, in this case, facing up.

There are several ways to keep the insulation from coming loose. One is to staple widths of chicken wire at right angles to the joists, leaving open strips so you can slide the batts in place. Also, there are special wires that snap in place between joists and are friction-fit.

In most cases, floor insulation doesn't make a big difference, but every little bit helps. It may also make your feet feel warmer in the winter.

BASEMENT INSULATION

If yours is a heated basement, you'll do well to at least insulate the walls. A heated basement doesn't necessarily mean it's finished, it could just house the heating system and maybe the utility room. Even though most of the basement may be underground, where temperatures remain more constant, the insulation will usually pay off.

Be sure to solve any moisture problems before tackling this job.

The easiest way to insulate these walls is probably with rigid foam. You do need to install furring strips on the wall about two feet apart and with a strip at the top and bottom. Furring strips are strips of wood attached to a masonry wall to provide a nailing surface. The rigid foam can easily be cut to fit between the furring. Use the adhesive recommended by the foam manufacturer to attach the panels to the wall.

Next, you should install a vapor barrier by stapling polyethylene sheeting to the furring.

Because many rigid foam insulation products are combustible, you'll probably be required by code to cover the walls with drywall nailed to the furring.

An alternate method for insulation is to erect a stud wall and staple fiberglass batts between the studs.

With either method, you should cut pieces of batts to poke into the cavities formed at the band joist above the basement walls.

INSULATING A SLAB

The application of rigid foam insulation to the edge of the slab as well as exposed parts of the basement will help the slab to be insulated. You should dig down to just below the frost line. The foam is attached using mastic recommended by the insulation manufacturer. Because this material should not be exposed to the elements, it should be covered over with stucco, plaster, siding, or whatever is code approved.

INSULATION DURING CONSTRUCTION

This is the time when you can make the biggest gains in energy savings. For one thing, you can opt for 2 x 6 exterior stud wall, which allows for more room for insulation. This can make a lasting difference in utility bills. This also makes for stronger construction, and the extra cost is minimal. The extra thickness also makes for a quieter house as far as keeping out exterior noises.

For even better insulation, look into sprayed-in polyurethane foam insulation. It not only offers better R-values, it expands and fills in every little nook and cranny. This virtually eliminates air infiltration, which we'll discuss later in this chapter. It's even better at acoustical control than ordinary batts or blankets. With this added protection, your home may require reduced heating and cooling equipment, saving you more money. Unlike the old formaldehyde foam, the urethane products are environmentally safe, emitting no toxic or ozone depleting chemicals.

RADIANT BARRIER

One of the best-kept secrets in the energy saving world is the radiant barrier. Properly installed, this can save utility dollars both summer and winter. You see, radiant energy from the sun travels through the air in waves and only when it strikes an object does it actually produce heat.

In the summertime, radiant heat attacks your home when it hits the roof. From there it will heat everything inside the attic, including the insulation, to extreme levels during the day. This heat is trapped and can continue to emit heat into the home long after the sun has gone down. Radiant barriers can block more than 50 percent of the radiant energy from entering your home, keeping it cooler and more comfortable.

In the winter, the very expensive heat you have created will radiate from insulation and building materials and be lost to the cold outside. A radiant barrier can reflect more than 50 percent of this radiant energy back, cutting down on heat loss.

There are three basic types of radiant barrier being used in residential buildings. They are all effective.

The least expensive is an aluminum foil that is stapled to the rafters. Over time, dust settles on the surfaces, taking away some of its reflective qualities. Staples have a way of cutting through the foil to let it sag. We have also heard from a few people that this installation has caused problems with their TV reception.

When a home is being built, radiant barrier decking can be installed to rafters instead of conventional decking. This is nailed to the rafters with the reflective barrier facing down.

For retrofitting, there is a special paint called Radiance that can be applied between the rafters. It can be brushed, rolled, or sprayed on the roof decking. One coat does the job.

FREE SAVINGS

There is one very easy way to save lots of energy with no expenditure. This involves proper management of the thermostat. Back in the days of cheap energy, somebody decided that 72° F was ideal. And it is pretty comfortable to your body, but not to your pocketbook. Your body can get used to more economical settings.

In the winter, try 70° until you get used to it. Then drop back to 68°. To help you get used to the cooler temperature, wear warmer clothes. At least wear sleeves and maybe a sweater or light jacket. At night when you're in bed, turn the setting down even lower. Likewise, when everyone is off to school or work, move the setting back to 65° or less. If you're away on a winter trip, set it back to 55°.

There's an old wives tale that says that the energy saved is eaten up when you have to reheat the house upon getting up/getting home. Don't you believe it.

In the summer, you can be comfortable once your body gets used to 78° F. To help, use fans. The flow of air across your body will let you feel just as comfortable as if your thermostat was set at 72°. Lowering the thermostat can up your utility cost about 9 percent and the lower it goes, the more it costs.

Look at the chart (figure 18-3) to see what difference a few degrees can make . . . and these savings cost you nothing.

THERMOSTAT MAINTENANCE

Rarely does a thermostat fail completely. Instead, it may not be properly calibrated so it turns on or off at the wrong temperature. To find out if this is your problem, give your thermostat a lie detector test. Here's how:

1. Tape a known-accurate thermometer to the wall a few inches to the side of the thermostat. Be sure the bulb does not touch the wall.
2. Wait about fifteen minutes for the thermometer to stabilize.
3. Compare the reading to the reading of the arrow on the thermostat.

If there is a difference of more than a degree or two, it may be worth calibrating it. Since there are so many different types, you should consult your owner's manual. If you no longer have that, see if the manufacturer has an 800 number.

Another option is to learn what each erroneous setting means in real temperature and compensate.

Another maintenance step is to check for cleanliness. If your thermostat is the type with a glass vial that contains mercury, dust on the vial can throw the action off. Remove the faceplate that is usually snapped on and held with a friction catch. Remove the dust by first using a soft-bristled artist's brush and then blowing the loosened dust away with your breath. Do not use a vacuum cleaner.

If the thermostat is not controlling the heating and cooling unit, check for loose or corroded wires. Also, if it's the mercury vial type, make certain the unit is level. There will be markings that allow you to use a plumb bob to get it level.

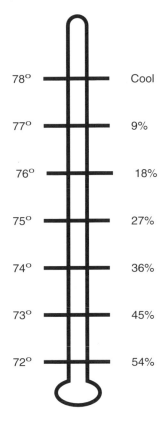

Each degree cooler ups your air conditioner costs...

78°	Cool
77°	9%
76°	18%
75°	27%
74°	36%
73°	45%
72°	54%

Energy monitor

figure 18-3

PROGRAMMABLE THERMOSTATS

A good way to remember to set back the thermostat when you'll be in bed or gone for the day is with an automatic electronic programmable thermostat. Some can even be set for the different lifestyle we have on weekends. Once set, the thermostat doesn't forget. Changing out the conventional thermostat is an easy do-it-yourself project. Even though you're nearly always dealing with low voltage, shut off electric current to the unit to be sure you don't get even a tingle. Then, once the old thermostat is removed, you can connect the wires coming from the wall to the new unit, using the directions that came with it.

Properly set, the electronic thermostat will soon pay for itself in energy savings.

AIR INFILTRATION

According to studies we've seen, between 25 and 40 percent of the heat loss and heat gain in the average home is from air leakage in the shell of the home. There are literally dozens of places for hidden air leaks. Usually finding these gaps is more difficult than filling them.

EXTERIOR LEAKS

Here are the places to look and what to do:

1. Door frames and window frames should be caulked.
2. Any joint where differing building materials meet should be caulked, for example,where the siding meets the foundation. Or, where the siding butts up to the exterior part of the chimney.
3. You should caulk around exterior wall outlets.
4. Dryer and range vents should be caulked, and you should make sure the dampers in each of these systems open and close properly.

INTERIOR LEAKS

1. Doors should be checked by having one person with a hand held hair dryer move around the edges on the outside while a helper inside follows with a lit candle. Flickers mean leaks. Leaks around the door's edges require weatherstripping. For leaks coming under the door, check the threshold. If the threshold is in good condition but air still comes in around it, there is an add-on called a door sweep that has a flexible vinyl piece attached to a metal strip. The metal part has holes and screws that are used to attach the unit to the bottom edge of the inside face of the door. The flexible piece sticks up and, when the door is closed, it seals against the threshold.
2. Windows can also be checked using the hair dryer, and appropriate weatherstripping can be added.
3. Electrical wall units can account for about 20 percent of all air infiltration that occurs in the average home. There are very inexpensive foam gaskets that

can be installed behind wall outlets and switch plates to block
the flow of air (figure 18-4).

4. Holes where plumbing pipe comes
in through the walls can be made
air tight with a shot of expanding
foam that comes in aerosol cans.

5. The fireplace is not only an ineffi-
cient way to heat, it is a mam-
moth source of airflow. In the
winter when the fireplace is being
used, the updraft it creates will
also suck up lots of heated air
from other parts of the house. A
glass fire screen can help to pre-

Foam gaskets under outlet and switch plates

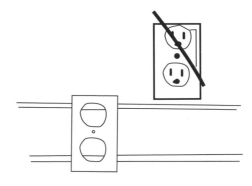

figure 18-4

vent that. However, the fire needs combustion air to burn and therefore you
need an outdoor air intake vent installed in the back of the firebox, providing
the fireplace is on an exterior wall.

FIGHTING LEAKS DURING CONSTRUCTION

The well-built energy efficient house eliminates having to fight air infiltration later
on. Here are some things to shoot for:

1. Seal between the sole plate and the foundation using a good caulk.
2. Seal all corners where exterior walls meet.
3. Seal between studs and window and doorframes.
4. Use a house wrap.

WINDOWS

Having windows is essentially like having a wall full of holes as far as energy efficiency is concerned. In our heating bill, we pay a high price for the view windows
provide us. We've already talked about solving air infiltration problems. But did you
know a single pane of glass allows for a lot of heat transfer right through the glass?
What can we do? Here are a couple of ways to stop the flow of dollars blowing in
the wind.

STORM WINDOWS

The addition of a second pane of glass outside your primary window cuts the heat transfer by 50 percent. Even using the cheapest storm window on the market, this still holds true. In fact, it doesn't even have to be glass. There is a kit with clear, thin, plastic sheeting that is held by a track over the window inside the house. The heat from a hair dryer causes the plastic to shrink, making it super tight. It's practically invisible and still cuts the heat transfer.

The reason for buying better windows is because they are longer lasting and often look better. Since the frames of many storm windows are metal and many primary windows have metal frames, you must be sure the installation doesn't end up with metal touching metal. Metal is a good conductor and this would mean energy loss through conduction.

THERMAL WINDOWS

If you are building a new home, it will certainly pay you to check out energy efficient windows that are multi-glazed. Most are double paned but some are triple paned. The double-paned jobs give you that 50 percent less heat loss while the triple panes up lessen the heat loss by about 70 percent. Installation is just about the same as with any other windows, so the only extra cost is in the window itself. Whereas, if you plan to retrofit an older home with these better windows, you have the problem of removing the old windows. While this doesn't present an impossible task, it can be a challenge. Having it done by a pro usually takes only a day or two of installing. Don't worry about having big holes in your home for several days. The pros pop the new windows in as soon as the old ones are removed.

These windows have two panes of glass joined and sealed together with just a small space in between. With some, there is an inert gas in the cavity. Others have a desiccant that keeps the moisture level inside at a constant low level. If the seal holding the two panes together is cracked, air gets into the cavity and you'll see fog or condensation in between panes. It is important that you get a window that carries a good warranty against this kind of failure. If it happens out of warranty, there are companies in most areas that make and install after-market replacements.

LIGHTING

How many times have you heard your Mama say, "Turn off the lights!" as you leave a room? This is good advice. However, when you learn that a light burning constantly may represent only a penny or two of your energy dollar, you may say, "Why bother?" At the end of the year, it can mount up. Operating under the theory that "every little bit helps," we're going to tell you some ways to save on lighting. Here are some common sense ideas that you should try:

1. Always heed your Mama's advice. Of course it's easy to remember to turn off lights in rooms often used. Check on those lights in the basement, attic, closets, and other infrequently used areas that could be left on for days.
2. Use the proper size bulb for the lighting task at hand. If a 60-watt bulb will do, don't waste the extra energy consumed by a 100-watt bulb.
3. Convert your lamps to 3-way bulbs, using the least wattage needed.
4. Dimmer switches can save energy as well as act as mood lighting.
5. As we learned in chapter 5 on electricity, fluorescent lighting costs less than incandescent, so change when you can.
6. Clean both bulbs and fixtures. A layer of dust can give you a dim outlook that may mean you have to turn on more lights.
7. Daylight is free, so open blinds, shades, and drapes, and make sure the window glass is clean.
8. Reflective light is also free, so use light or white colors on walls and ceilings when practical.
9. A timer or an electronic eye should control security lights. That way you don't forget to turn them off each morning.

Never cut back on light to the point where your eyes will be strained or where the lack of sufficient light becomes a safety or security hazard.

WATER SAVING

Yes, we know that water is not part of the energy program. However, if we have you in a saving mode, water is a precious commodity and shouldn't be wasted. Here are some common sense ways to save water:

1. Repair all dripping faucets and running toilets immediately. (Check back to chapter 4 for plumbing repairs.)
2. Showers can get you clean while using quite a bit less water than a tub bath. However, not if you take long showers. Limit your shower to the time it takes for lather up, wash down, and rinse off.
3. Install water saver showerheads. They can be inexpensive and easy to install. While they may take a little while to get used to, water use can be reduced by 50 percent and still produce an invigorating spray.

4. Turn off the water while brushing your teeth. Wet the toothbrush and then use a glass of water to rinse with.

5. When shaving, lather up and then turn the water off until rinsing off your face.

6. Remember that the toilet is not a wastebasket. So don't flush each time you drop in a tissue, cigarette butt, dead bug, or bit of trash.

7. Don't run the dishwasher or clothes washer until you have a full load.

8. When washing the car, use a bucket of water with the cleaner. Then rinse it off with a hose.

9. Check your sprinkler system to be sure you're not watering the streets or sidewalks.

10. Water plants and lawn only when there is a need, not automatically every day on a regular schedule. Also, water early in the day when evaporation rates are at the lowest.

11. Wash vegetables in a pan of water rather than under the sink faucet.

12. And finally, shower with a friend!

FACT OR FICTION?

Some communities have sent civic groups out to sell bricks to be placed in the toilet as a water saver. The idea is that with each flush, the amount of water displaced by the brick is water saved. One fallacy in this idea is that when the toilet is flushed, water starts to come back into the tank before the tank completely empties. So, much of the water displaced wasn't going to run out anyway. Plus, some bricks start to disintegrate after prolonged contact with the water, and the particles may damage the toilet and waste water.

19

Storage 101

Most people, despite their best efforts, tend to collect lots of stuff as they get older. In any household, each member of the family has his or her own stuff and then the family has their collective stuff. And we never seem to have enough stuff since we're always buying more. Our big problem has become: where do we put our stuff? What we hope to do in this section is make better use of existing spaces. With your new space program, you can more than double your storage area without adding on to your home.

WHERE TO LOOK

Here is a potpourri of ideas on where to find unused space to store some of your stuff.

Under beds—There is space under almost every bed. Flat items can just slide under, or you could build rollout bins or a drawer system. You can buy chests made for this purpose.

Window seat—Not only does this add a functional piece of furniture, but the seat can also be hinged to make a good-sized storage chest. You could even line it with cedar to store woolens in spring and summer.

Under sinks—A rollout double decked shelf unit could use the space next to the trap and drain line. This would work under kitchen or bath sinks.

Above utility room appliances—Install cabinets or shelves in this otherwise unused space.

Next to fireplace—Bookshelves look very much at home on either side of the fireplace.

Under eaves—Even though there isn't headroom, there is room for low cabinets.

Garage—See chapter 21, "Workshops."

In furr-downs—Often kitchen cabinets are boxed in from the top of the cabinet to the ceiling. By cutting into this cavity and adding doors, you will have discovered lots of new space.

Under stairs—By cutting into the wall under a stairway, you can make a new closet. It may require a door with an angled top and be very low space at one end, but it's new space. Another stairway storage idea is to make pull out drawers on the risers (figure 19-1).

Kitchen countertops—The space between the lower and the upper cabinets could be partially used for an appliance garage.

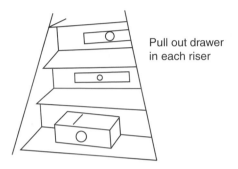

Pull out drawer in each riser

figure 19-1

SHELVES

There are many shelf systems available that attach to walls. It is easy to install them wherever they would be appropriate. Many have tracks that allow for adjustable shelves. Remember that books are very heavy, so you should either install screws into studs or use heavy-duty hardware, like molly bolts or toggle bolts.

Some places to consider might include over a door, a second shelf in all closets, or on any blank wall. A combination shelf and coat rack might go in the entry hall.

Free standing shelf units come in a wide variety of sizes, and unfinished furniture shops have very economical prices.

Wire frame closet organizer systems are very popular and quite easy to install, and they don't have to be used just inside closets.

BETWEEN THE STUDS STORAGE

Most homes today are of hollow wall construction, which means the space between the studs is being wasted. This narrow space is deep enough to become a pantry for canned and packaged goods. Building a cabinet in this void is very simple, or you can buy medicine chests that fit. You could add such a cabinet in a kitchen, utility room, or bathroom. Here are the steps in capturing this extra space:

1. Use a stud finder to locate adjacent studs. Try to avoid spaces with plumbing pipes or electrical wiring.

2. Decide on the height of the cabinet and drill holes at all four corners. You can make it floor to ceiling or any height in between.

3. Use a keyhole saw to cut out the opening in the gypsum board. The edge of the gypsum board should be flush with the studs.

4. Cut 2 x 4 cross blocks to be toenailed to the studs at the top and bottom of the cabinet (figure 19-2).

5. Shelves can be made of 3/8-inch plywood and finished on the edges with stick-on veneer. Glue blocks on the sides for the shelves to rest on.

6. Apply trim mold all around the opening.

7. Use 3/4-inch plywood for the door. Use a magnetic catch to hold the door closed. Add a decorative knob and hang the door with hinges. Finish the door and molding to blend in with the decor of the room.

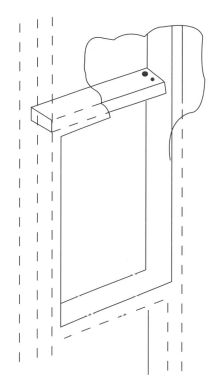

figure 19-2

8. If you want the cabinet to look more finished inside, give all the surfaces a coat of paint. Now you're ready to start stocking your mini-pantry.

MORE SPACE FROM EXISTING CLOSETS

By being better organized, most home closets can hold an estimated 30 percent more stuff. The first change to consider is if all the closet poles are up high. This means shirts, jackets, and skirts have a lot of unused space halfway down. By adding a second pole at a lower level the closet space for hanging garments is greatly increased. Or, build a drawer unit under the short items.

A hanging shoe bag on the closet door or a wire closet organizer unit that hangs from the door can hold lots of accessories. Shoes can also be hung from doorstops screwed on the inside of a closet door (figure 19-3).

Usually there is room for a second shelf above the poles. Even if the stored items up there are beyond reach, it could hold rarely worn or seasonal items.

Often a stand alone or built-in shelf or drawer unit can fit against the back wall of a walk-in closet.

CREATING A CEDAR CLOSET

The aroma of cedar is pleasing to us humans but acts as a repellent to moths that would like to devour your cashmeres. It's fairly easy to convert a regular closet into a cedar-lined

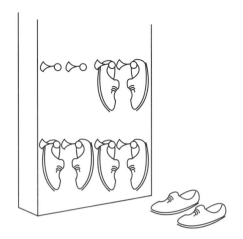

figure 19-3

space. Your local home center or hardware store will have fairly thin tongue and groove cedar planks. They can be easily cut into proper lengths and used to line the walls of the closet. We used a stapler that nailed brads to attach the boards. Once the entire closet is lined, there is still work to do. You need to weather-strip the closet door and also add a door sweep to the bottom of the door. This way all the cedar odor is kept inside. Incidentally, the cedar odor doesn't kill moths, just repels them. Make sure the clothes you store have been washed or dry-cleaned to kill any moth eggs. The cedar odor will help keep a new family of moths from getting in.

GARAGE STORAGE

Many of the storage ideas we discuss in chapter 21, "Workshops," can be adapted for general storage.

ATTIC STORAGE

The average attic has a lot of unused space to offer for storage. Overall, it may not be the greatest for storing your stuff. First, you need to have good access to the attic, which usually means a disappearing stairway. This is a do-it-yourself project for a moderately handy person.

Then you will probably need to floor at least part of the attic where things are to be stored. This can easily be done using 4 x 8 sheets of plywood or particleboard. However, the opening for the stairway may require that the sheets be cut in half to be able to get them into the attic. Next, you must realize that anything stored up there may be subjected to extreme heat and cold. Keep that in mind when selecting things to go to the attic.

FOR EXTRA CREDIT

As a last resort, you can always solve your space problems by getting rid of stuff you don't need. Join the great American pastime of holding a garage sale. Extra credit and extra cash . . . to buy more stuff! Or, donate your things to your favorite charity.

Pests and Messes 101

20

WHAT'S BUGGING YOU?

Evidence shows that some insects have been around longer than humans have. There are tons of different types of bugs, and there's no way you'll ever completely get rid of them. What we can do is try to control them and keep them out of our homes. Many of the pests we have are there because we invited them. It's been estimated that roaches, rats, mice, and squirrels eat more pet food than our pets do. To make it even more inviting, we usually have the pet's water dish right next to the food. Remember that we want to zap the pests . . . not people or pets. So always keep safety in mind. Here are some common sense safety tips:

1. Be sure the insecticide or bait you're using is made for the control of the bug that's bugging you.
2. Read the label! We know that is a foreign concept for many of you, but it really pays here.
3. Avoid contact with insecticides and wash your skin after any contact.
4. Do not inhale any spray or fumes. Avoid spraying into the wind, as this could carry the spray back to you.
5. Keep these materials away from foodstuffs and don't spray kitchen surfaces where food is prepared.
6. If you smoke, don't do so while using insecticides and wash your hands before lighting up after the attack on the bugs.
7. Remove pet dishes before spraying.

8. Use only the amount recommended. Too much is wasteful and could be dangerous.
9. If mixing is required, be sure to have adequate ventilation.
10. With any aerosol, avoid spraying near a flame.
11. With foggers, vacate the area for the time suggested on the label. Some foggers will also set off your smoke alarm.
12. Do not use pest strips in the nursery or sick room.
13. After treating, keep kids and pets off the lawn for the prescribed time.
14. Store insecticides in a safe place away from heat and out of the reach of kids. Don't reuse insecticide containers.
15. If you feel any ill effects, head for the ER, taking the insecticide with you.

ROACHES

Roaches are after food and water. Make sure you take care of any water leaks and keep the areas dry. You should also see to it that foods are stored away from pests. They like to forage at night or in the dark. The females produce an egg casing that contains the eggs. The entire life cycle can take as little as two months, so they can overrun your home if you don't get them under control. The growth regulator insecticides work well on these pests.

Here is our favorite boric acid recipe:

4 parts boric acid powder
2 parts of either flour or sugar
1 part cocoa

Put this out in bottle caps or other small containers under the sink, behind appliances, and other places where kids and pets can't get.

As a matter of fact, boric acid powder by itself does a good job of controlling roaches. Put it where they will walk through it and then clean it off their feet. A thin layer of it is better than a thick covering. The small, compact bait traps are super easy to use and will work well if placed in the right spots. Clean and sanitary conditions will make the biggest difference. Keep after them, and you can win the battle.

ANTS

There are many species of ants. Most ants live in highly structured colonies. There will be one queen and hundreds of workers or soldiers. Ant baits take a while to work but persistence will pay off. If your ants are outside, you can use a wide variety of insecticides. In fact, boric acid powder is also good for getting rid of ants. Mix equals parts of boric acid and flour.

Here's a trick for treating the mound outside. Apply the insecticide, whether liquid, dust, or powder in rings. Start about three feet away from the main entrance. Move in about six inches for each subsequent ring. As the workers go in and out, they will track in the deadly stuff and gradually kill off the colony, including the queen.

Indoors, you must be more careful, as they are usually in kitchens or baths where food and water are present. Keep your kitchen clean and use baits to kill the colony.

Carpenter ants are a very destructive breed. They will live in your walls, often in wet wood around windows. They don't actually eat the wood as termites do. They hollow it out to be able to house the colony. You can often locate the colony by seeing where there are small mounds of sawdust. Rather than tearing into a wall to access the colony, use a granular product that they will take back to the colony and that will kill the queen.

Fire ants are normally found in the South, but bug experts believe they will spread to all parts of the country in years to come. They inflict a lot of pain on their victims, and have have been known to take down small animals.

They are tough to control but there are several effective products on the market made specifically to eliminate fire ants. Treat all the mounds on your property at the same time. Unfortunately, even when you rid your yard of them, they will move back in from a neighbor's untreated yard. Fire ants also like the hum of electrical sources for some reason and can settle in air conditioner compressor units, pool motors, and the like.

SILVERFISH

Silverfish are sneaky little devils and can go undetected for years because they never show their faces except at night. They will eat your clothing, upholstery, wallpaper, books, and other things. There are several effective products that will help control silverfish. Additionally, you should remove all the cushions and vacuum your upholstery, even down where you'll find loose change.

SPIDERS

Spiders for the most part are considered beneficial insects because they eat other bugs. They often create webs on the outside of windows since the light at night attracts their food. Keep webs knocked down from the areas where you don't want them and the spiders will move elsewhere.

Brown recluse spiders are venomous and can cause serious harm to their victims. They like to stay in dark, humid areas. Black widow spiders are also venomous. Most spiders can bite you but few will cause the kind of damage that these two will. You should see a doctor immediately if bitten by either of these, or if you have a severe reaction to any insect bite. If spiders are not in the way, leave them to do their job and be thankful that they like to eat other bugs.

MOSQUITOES

Mosquitoes thrive and multiply in moist areas. Make sure you don't have any standing water around your home . . . bird-baths, potted plant containers, clogged gutters, old tires, and other debris that collect and hold rain water. Foggers and sprays work best to control an area where you find a high concentration of the biting pests. Repellants will send them packing. Pre-treat the area before entertaining outdoors, and you should be okay. Mosquitoes can carry many dangerous diseases, including the most recent West Nile virus, and should be avoided. Their peak biting times are at dawn and dusk, but they can get you any time.

HOUSEFLIES

Houseflies carry diseases that can make you sick if you eat food that they have contaminated. They can be controlled by sprays and by hanging insecticide strips. These should not be used where food is stored. Flies don't like cooler temperatures and can be kept outside if you close up all of the windows and doors. Be sure your screens are in good shape.

TERMITES

Termites feed on wood and can be extremely damaging to your home. Some do-it-yourself products are available, but professionals have the tools and know-how to properly treat the average home much better than you can do yourself. Termites are hard to detect, and you could suffer quite a bit of damage before you ever know they are around. Have the home inspected annually. There are things you can do to prevent an easy termite entry.

1. Pick up any scrap lumber under the house if you have a crawl space.
2. Cut back shrubs and other vegetation that's right against the house.
3. Don't stack firewood directly on the ground nor right next to the house.

4. If you see swarms of flying ants in the springtime, call for a termite inspection. Figure 20-1 shows the difference between flying ants and termites.

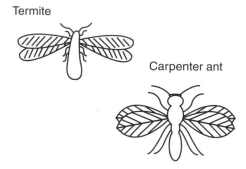

Termite

Carpenter ant

figure 20-1

WASPS

Wasps are relatively harmless unless provoked. Keep wasp nests knocked down when possible. The long-distance sprays made for these pests generally work pretty well. The best time of the day to spray is at dusk when most of the insects are back at the nest. Make sure you have a clear path for your getaway and then spray them and run. Plan to stay out of the area for a little while until they are all dead or gone. The wasps you hit with the spray will die, and the survivors will not come back to the contaminated nest.

> **TEACHER'S TIP**
>
> If you are unlucky enough to be stung by a wasp, pour straight vinegar over the sting and it will give you instant relief.

BEES

Bees also tend to be harmless unless provoked. They are also beneficial to the ecology. If you have a hive on your property, try to locate a beekeeper. He or she will be able remove the entire colony to set them up in a new hive that he can tend. If you cannot locate a bee person, contact your county agent. Also, fire departments usually know of beekeepers.

Carpenter bees like to drill into wood to lay their eggs. They will go into wood that is softer, and once inside they will cause the tunnel to take a 90-degree turn. Behind this turn is where the egg is hidden. First, use a wasp and hornet mist to spray into the hole. This will make sure the bee is gone. Then stick a stiff wire up into the hole and destroy the eggs. Plug the holes with putty and prime and paint all bare wood. A general insecticide sprayed in the area will prevent them from coming back to the site.

RODENTS

MICE

Mice like to come indoors when it is cold, hot, or if they don't have a good food supply outdoors. They can squeeze in through the tiniest cracks, so make sure your home is sealed up tightly. If you find where they are getting in, close up the area and block it with wire, steel wool, or other means covered with caulk, wood, or weather-stripping. Traps work best. Poisons can also be used, but don't blame us if they eat it and die inside your home. Also, take great precautions when using this stuff to make sure that neither pets nor kids will get into them.

RATS

Rats are not just big mice. They carry diseases. They cause fires by chewing the insulation off electrical wiring. They've been known to sharpen their teeth on plastic pipe, eventually causing a leak. They are generally nesting when they are in your home.

There are two ways to get rid of them . . . traps and poison. Here's a trick to play on them. They will be wary of traps at first. Put about half a dozen traps in the attic. Bait them, but do not set them. Check the traps each morning and if any bait is gone, replace it. After a week, bait and set all the traps and don't be surprised if you catch one in each trap. The poisons available to homeowners are all about the same. They are called anti-coagulates. After the rat eats it, he gets very thirsty. If you haven't left any water supply out, he'll go outside for water and not die in the house.

Once rid of them, seal them out and you should be fine. If you use poisons, make sure they are placed where no pets or children will accidentally get into them.

SQUIRRELS

Squirrels are equally damaging once inside your home. They are usually just sleeping and nesting when they are in your attic. They sleep at night and forage during the day. You can apply a repellent during the day that may make them go elsewhere for their next night's sleep. There are traps that do not harm the animal. When caught, the critter can be carried to the country and let loose. Some communities have such traps they loan to citizens and some will also pick up the trap and the animal.

OTHER RODENTS

Opossums, raccoons, and skunks are rodents that also forage for food at night. During the day, they like to stay in protected areas—for example, under your house—so keep these areas blocked off to them. Keep garbage containers closed up tightly and your yard cleaned up. These animals also respond to repellents.

BIRDS

Our feathered friends are beneficial because they feed on insects in your yard. Don't park under a tree, and you won't think of them as pests.

There are a few things you can do to gently persuade them to perch elsewhere, though. Covering ledges with some screening can make it more comfortable for them to light in another place. Plastic birds of prey like owls or hawks can be placed in the area. This can deter them from hanging around the area. These plastic birds will need to be repositioned every few days to make them look more real.

DEER

These only bother your garden and landscaping. Fencing is about the best and maybe the only way to keep deer out of your yard. Here's our home recipe for a deer repellent that really works to protect young trees: Start with 3 quarts warm water. Add a well-beaten egg, and mix in a teaspoon of tobacco juice (make by soaking chewing tobacco in water). Stir it well and then brush the mix on the trunk of the tree as high as you can reach. Another repellent is to scatter human hair around the garden. Get your barber to save it for you.

MILDEW

Not all the pesky problems around the house are from critters. There is an airborne spoor that is floating around inside most homes that is just waiting to find a proper place to land, to eat, and to grow. We're talking about mildew. It needs a dark, moist place the live. One of mildew's favorite dishes is soap scum. It will soon take over a large part of your home.

Quick now class, what room did you think of when we described the life of mildew?

Right! The bathroom. Once mildew gets started, you will see how ugly it looks. Soon you'll smell its unpleasant odor. If you don't get rid of it now, it will grow.

Fortunately, mildew is easy to kill. Here's how:

1. Fill a plastic spray bottle with liquid laundry bleach.
2. Squirt this on the mildew spot.
3. After a few minutes the magic should make the mildew disappear. If not, spray again and use an old toothbrush to scrub with.
4. Rinse with plain water.

Now that the mildew is gone, you should figure out the cause and eliminate that. In a bathroom, you'll always have the possibility of excess moisture. One option is an exhaust fan after each shower. Leave it on long enough to get all the moisture out. If the excess humidity is from a water leak, fix it. Maybe the house is too tightly buttoned up and without proper ventilation. See the scoop on ventilation on page 156.

CAUTION

Don't let the bleach get on carpets or fabrics as it can take the color out. CAUTION #2: Have plenty of ventilation.

Mildew can also get started on the exterior parts of the house. Here is a great mildew remover recipe:

3 quarts of warm water
1 quart of liquid laundry bleach
1/4 cup of any powdered detergent
2/3 cup of TSP (trisodium phosphate)

Mix it well and then apply with a stiff broom. Leave on for about 15 minutes. Then rinse completely and dilute so there's no harm to landscaping.

To prevent future mildew, use paint with mildewcide on your next paint job. Be sure trees and shrubs are trimmed back so that they don't hold moisture against the house and allow free circulation of air.

Hopefully, there is now nothing left to bug you!

Workshop 101

21

We firmly believe that every household should have some sort of workshop. In most cases, there is the problem of space. How much space you need usually depends on just how involved you expect to get with this do-it-yourself game. If all you want to do is cope with home emergencies until the repair-pro can arrive, you don't need much room. Part of a closet will do. On the other hand, many shops take up the entire basement. In selecting the space for your shop, here are some deciding factors.

1. Think about access. You should be able to get large materials in and large finished projects out. We've all smiled at the do-it-yourselfer who builds a boat in the basement and must completely dismantle it before heading for the lake.

2. Inaccessibility is also important. We're talking security against theft. Tools can cost a lot and thieves like to steal them. The shop can also be dangerous to children, so it and the tools inside should be inaccessible to them.

3. Also, you need enough space to work with large materials. Eventually you'll be working with a 4 x 8 sheet of plywood.

4. Bench space is also a necessity. If your shop ends up in a closet, you may need to have a foldout workbench.

5. You'll need several electrical outlets. Also with heavy-duty tools, you may need additional wiring. Be sure all electrical work complies with the local electrical code.

6. Ventilation is a big factor because many projects involve chemicals that release hazardous fumes and vapors. Woodworking also means sawdust. In addition to natural ventilation, most shops do better with an exhaust fan.

7. To maintain peace in the family, consider the noise factor. Some shop tools make a lot of noise.

8. Consider the climate. Heat and humidity can leave you with discomfort. Also, humidity can damage your tools and maybe some wood projects.

PICK YOUR SPOT

You may not have much choice because of the limits of your house. However, the most popular selections are the garage, the basement, or a separate out building. Here are some thoughts on each:

GARAGE—An attached garage is a good or bad choice because:

- It's very convenient to get to. This can also be bad because it's easy access for children.
- The big garage door makes it easy to bring in big items.
- Sweep up is easy.
- Usually, you do have to move the car or cars out when you're working, but a garage floor provides plenty of room.
- With the door open you have a bonus in natural light.
- The ventilation is pretty good.
- Security against tool theft is as good as it is against car theft.
- The garage is usually already wired for electricity, even if you have to add to it.
- Most garages have room alongside the car for a bench. There may also be closet and cabinet space already in place.
- Most garages are not heated or cooled, but fans and heaters can be added.

BASEMENT—Here are the pluses and minuses for the basement:

- Many are already heated if they are also used to house the furnace, or also act as the utility room.
- Manhandling large materials down a stairway isn't fun. The same goes for big power tools.
- There is usually not much natural light.
- Sound is usually fairly well contained.
- Many basements are dank and must have humidity control.
- Your family may sometime wish to convert the basement, including your workshop, into a den or playroom.
- Most basements are already wired.
- There's usually enough room for a big workbench and lots of large power tools.

A SEPARATE OUTBUILDING—It's sounds great to have a separate building away from the house, and pre-fab buildings can easily be moved onto your property. But wait:

- Dashing out to the shop in the pouring rain can put a damper on your do-it-yourself projects.
- Running wiring and maybe plumbing to the shop can be costly.
- Being away from the house might make the tools inside more appealing to a burglar.
- Heating and cooling would be another expense.

IF YOU'RE BUILDING

Since the garage pluses are many, why not build a bigger garage and dedicate one bay to your shop? If you have two cars in the family, build a three-car garage. Also have your bench and special cabinets built in. Provide many wall outlets for the shop area.

ONCE YOU'VE PICKED THE SPOT

Whether your shop is big or small, plan ahead before you start. We've already mentioned lots of things to consider. Now let's get more specific. Here are some things to do and to consider in your planning:

1. Make a to-scale layout drawing. Add cut outs of the workbench, all the power tools, a trash bin, and any other things your shop will include. Move these miniatures of the items around until you decide on the best layout. Be sure there is room around the tools for the materials you'll be using. Keep in mind that you'll have one other thing in the shop . . . you! Provide room for you to work.
2. A stationary workbench is good. However, if there isn't enough room around it, go for a bench that can be rolled into a larger work area.
3. Pegboard walls are great for small tool storage that keeps the tools at hand yet up off the bench.
4. You must have light over each stationary or bench-type power tool, as well as over the entire workbench.
5. Plan for storage brackets or bins for long materials such as lumber and pipes.
6. Often the floors in the shop are concrete, and this is hard on the feet. Plan for mats or rug scraps.

7. Since many shop chores can be done while sitting, include a comfortable stool in your plan.

So much for the basics! You might also consider running plumbing to the shop with a clean-up sink. An extension phone will be handy, as will an intercom station to keep in touch. The radio can also keep you company as you work away.

The planning you do can make for a safer, more comfortable, more convenient and more productive shop. At any rate, plan on having fun in your shop!

WORKING SAFELY

One way to have fun in your shop, as well as when you are performing all these home fix-it projects we talk about, is to keep safety in mind. There are lots of ways to get hurt. Here is a list of some common sense safety tips:

1. Always wear whatever safety gear is needed for the project at hand.
2. Make sure cutting tools are sharp. With a dull tool you may have to give it extra muscle and lose control.
3. Be sure handles and grips are properly attached
4. Oil or grease on the tool may mean you can't get a safe grip.
5. Use each tool only for the task the tool is made for. Don't try to force it to do things it cannot do.
6. Wear safety goggles when using a striking tool. Avoid glancing blows and never hit the face of another striking tool.
7. When using a wrench against strong resistance, push with an open palm. If there is a slip, you won't skin your knuckles.
8. Always clamp your work if there's a danger of it slipping
9. Some power tools make lots of noise. Don't forget hearing protection.
10. When using a power tool, don't carry the tool by the cord or yank on the cord to disconnect.
11. Wear proper apparel when using bench-type or stationary tools. Avoid loose or baggy sleeves, ties, jewelry, or anything that could get caught in a moving part.
12. Be sure the switch is off when you plug in a tool and that adjusting keys are not still in place in the tool.
13. Always work with proper lighting conditions and don't overreach or get off balance.
14. You don't need an audience when working with power tools.

LADDER SAFETY

Many of the projects a homeowner tackles mean getting up to where the work is. That means using a ladder. The two basic types of ladders are the stepladder and the straight ladder. The extension ladder is a cousin to the straight ladder.

Stepladders are made of wood, aluminum, or vinyl clad aluminum. A big advantage to an aluminum ladder is that it is much lighter weight and thus easier to handle. Vinyl clad ladders have an advantage of being a nonconductor when working on electricity. Here are a few safety hints:

1. Always inspect any ladder before using it.
2. When opening a stepladder, make sure the bracing mechanism is locked.
3. Never step on the top shelf. If you must do that to get to the work, you need to get a taller ladder.
4. Never paint a ladder, as the coating may hide splits or other problems.
5. Keep the steps clean for better footing.

Straight and extension ladders are used to get to really high work. They should be handled with care. Here are some handling tips:

1. If you haven't used the ladder for some time, lay it flat on the ground and walk on each rung. If one is faulty, you can't get hurt falling from ground level.
2. Visually inspect the ladder from top to bottom.
3. Do not extend the ladder until you have it in a vertical position and at the place it'll be used.
4. Be mindful of all power lines. Don't use the ladder when there is lightning in the area.
5. When positioning the ladder, walk it up hand over hand. This gives you more control with less effort.
6. As you pull the rope to extend the ladder, be sure that the locking mechanism on both sides is properly in place.
7. The proper angle is important. It is easy to get it right because the feet should be away from the wall one fourth of its length. Be sure the feet are on solid, level ground. To be sure the ladder can't scoot out from under you, use sandbags or anchor the base with a 2 x 4 and a stake (figure 21-1).
8. As you climb, use both hands. You can hoist your tools and materials up with a bucket and a rope.

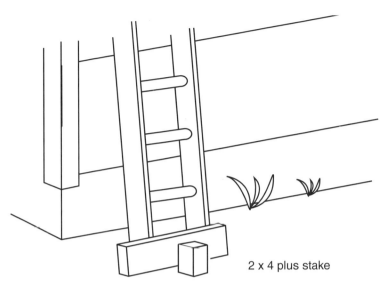

2 x 4 plus stake

figure 21-1

9. As you work, always keep your hips within the space between the side rails so you won't overreach.

10. Be sure the rungs are clean, dry, and mud free, and always wear slip proof shoes.

This is a very timely topic because our next course is on roofs.

Roofing 101

22

Not only does the roof of your home have a lot to do with the overall look of the house, it protects the structure from water damage. Whether the roof has wooden shingles, cedar shakes, asphalt shingles, slate, built-up, metal, or thatch, it can develop leaks. A tiny leak can eventually cause thousands of dollars in damage.

With that bit of knowledge comes two realities:

1. Maintain your roof to prevent the leak.
2. Fix the leak as soon as possible.

ROOF MAINTENANCE

These few simple steps may keep your roof from letting you down:

1. Give your roof an inspection at least twice a year. In the springtime, look for any damage Jack Frost may have caused. In the fall, look for any flaws that could go bad during the winter.

2. You should avoid walking on any type of roof any more than you have to. (We know what you're thinking: How can you inspect the roof without walking on it?) A ladder leaning against the edge of the roof lets you have a pretty good view of things. A good pair of binoculars will bring everything closer. Here are the places to look and what to look for:

    a. The ridges are more likely than other parts of a roof to fail. Look for loose or cracked ridge shingles. Replacement asphalt ridge shingles are often made from regular shingles. Examine yours to see. Wood ridge shingles can be purchased in bundles from a lumberyard or home center.

b. Over the broad expanse of the roof, look for splits as well as missing shingles.

c. With an asphalt roof, look for curled edges, blisters, or places where the granules have left the surface balding. Check in the gutters for an accumulation of the granules.

d. Valleys are another common trouble spot. If the valleys are galvanized metal, be on the lookout for rust spots or split places.

e. All flashing must be inspected as the metal can have problems that lead to leaks.

f. Make sure the gutters and down spouts are free of leaves and debris. A dammed up gutter can cause water to back up under the shingles.

REPAIRS

One of the most frustrating roof repairs is when you repair the wrong place! It happens more often than you'd think. Often you see the wet spot on the ceiling inside the house and patch the roof directly above this place. However, water can come in at one spot and then run down a rafter to drip off five or six feet away from the actual leak (figure 22-1).

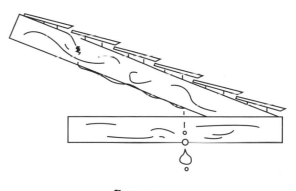

figure 22-1

One of the best things you can do is to get into the attic while it is raining and spot the exact spot where water is entering. From inside, drive a nail up through the roof. Then, when the roof is dry and safe to work on, find the nail and make the repair.

TEMPORARY REPAIRS

While you are in the attic, there are some things you can do to minimize the water damage. First, get a bucket or other large container to catch the water. You may need more than one container and may have to empty these water catchers from time to time.

You can try using asphalt roofing cement to plug up the hole. It's hard to do with water running through, but apply a thick layer and work it into the hole.

Another temporary repair involves a scrap of plywood coated with roofing compound. This is applied against the hole. Then wedge a pre-cut 2 x 4 against the patch and the attic floor to hold the patch firmly in place.

ASPHALT SHINGLE REPAIR

Minor holes, including the one from the nail you drove up to mark the spot, can be easily repaired using asphalt roofing compound in a caulking gun cartridge. This product can also take care of splits and glue down curled corners or edges.

This same type compound from a large container, using a putty knife, can handle bigger patching problems.

REPLACEMENT

First, you must remove the old damaged shingle or shingles. You can often pull the shingles out, ripping them where the nails are. You can remove the remaining nails with a flat prybar. Or, saw through the shank of the nail with a hacksaw blade not in the frame.

Cover over all nail holes with roofing compound.

If there are several shingles to be replaced, start with the lower shingles and work your way up. These lower replacements should be nailed in place. Top all the nail heads with roofing compound.

The last replacement piece must be slipped into place under the existing shingle above. Gently lift up this existing shingle. This top replacement shingle can more easily be inserted if it is trimmed off an inch or so along the top edge. In addition to nailing the last shingle, you'll do well to apply a wide bead of roofing compound along the top of the underside before sliding it in place.

Exposed nail heads are called "face nailing." You should avoid this. However, sometimes it has to happen. Cover all exposed heads with the black stuff. If your roof is a light color, use clear silicone sealant instead.

Curled up edges can allow the shingles to lift up with a strong wind. This can eventually lead to the shingles being blown off. A blob of roofing compound about the size of a half-dollar under the edges and pressed firmly in place prevents this problem.

TEACHER'S TIP

Asphalt shingles are much more flexible and thus less likely to crack when warm, so pick a summer day for this repair. If the job has to be in cooler times, warm the new shingles with a heating pad before installing them.

WOOD SHINGLE REPAIR

The most common wood or cedar shake problem is the split shingle. Replacement is best but often you can slide a piece of metal flashing under the split. Then drive in a nail on each side of the split (face nailing is pretty much unavoidable here) and cover the gap with roofing compound. Also, cover the nail heads.

REPLACING WOOD SHINGLES

Remove any damaged shingles by splitting them with a chisel and hammer. Use the hacksaw blade to cut off the nail heads under good shingles. If the damage involves more than one course, start your replacement at the lowest point and work up. Nail the new shingles on the lower courses, leaving space along the sides for expansion. The top course must be held in place by compound and then slid into place. Tapping the protruding end with a hammer will help move the shingle into alignment. We recommend face nailing here and then covering nail heads with compound.

THE AGING PROCESS

Sure, you're proud of your roof repairs. However, new wood shingles and shakes stick out like a sore thumb. Not to worry. After a few months, or maybe years, the weathering process will minimize the difference. If you'd rather not wait, here's an instant aging tip. Dissolve a small box of baking soda into two quarts of warm water. Brush this mix on the replacement shingles and place them outside in the sun for a few hours. Rinse and let dry. If they don't look old enough, repeat the process.

METAL ROOF REPAIR

There are several types of metal roofing used on homes. Aluminum shingles are made to look a lot like shakes, and carry a long warranty. Copper roofs, long forgotten, are making a comeback. Except for aluminum roofing, other metal roof problems can be soldered. All metal roof flaws can be solved with roofing compound but this may not be the most attractive approach.

BUILT-UP ROOF REPAIR

This type of roofing is used on nearly flat roofs and is composed of layers of roofing felt coated with hot asphalt and then topped with pea gravel. For home use, this type roof might be found on carports, over patios, and on homes with low-pitched roofs.

It's often easy to spot leaks in this type of roof because they usually show up on ceilings directly below the problem. Repairs don't have to be a thing of beauty because the roof is not usually seen unless you're above it.

If you see cracks in the roofing, our old friend asphalt roofing compound can usually solve the problem. Sometimes exposure to the heat from the sun can cause the top layer to blister. Sweep away the gravel over the area and slit the raised area. Use roofing compound to cover the slit and also force the cement into the slit. Lay down a bed of compound at least a couple of inches beyond the slit and apply a patch of roofing felt pushed into this bed of compound. Nail the patch in place using galvanized roofing nails. Then cover the entire patch with another bed of compound. Sweep the gravel back in place and your fix is done.

SAFETY ON THE ROOF

Unless you can fly, you should exercise caution where roof work is involved. Here are some common sense safety tips reminders:

1. Never walk on a wet roof.
2. Leave the roof repair to someone else if you're afraid of heights.
3. Don't get on the roof when there is a wind blowing. A gust can throw you off balance.
4. If you're taking medicine or have been drinking, wait for a sober, drug-free day.
5. Don't be on the roof during an electrical storm.
6. Look out for power lines!
7. Wear non-slip rubber soled shoes.
8. Be sure not to walk on rotting decking or other unsafe material.

Since you'll probably use a ladder to get up to the roof, review the ladder safety section in the previous chapter.

Gutters and Downspouts 101

23

Not having a system to adequately control rain water can cause loss of soil, cut trenches in the flower beds, wash away landscape plants, and cause moisture problems under your house that can undermine the integrity of your foundation. The most common way to control precipitation run-off is with gutters and downspouts.

CARE AND CLEANING

Unfortunately, most homeowners tend to forget about the guttering system. The gutters don't require a lot of attention, but the system must stay clean or the water can't flow down to the downspouts—and that can cause problems. Here are the simple steps in cleaning conventional gutters:

1. Use a ladder tall enough to allow you to see and reach into the gutters. Rather than lean over to clean the gutters, move the ladder. If you'll always keep your hips inside the side rails, you'll not have to overreach.

2. If you clean with your hands, always wear gloves. A whiskbroom does a good job of raking out leaves (figure 23-1). Also, many people use a leaf blower to blast out the leaves for 10 or 12 feet at a time.

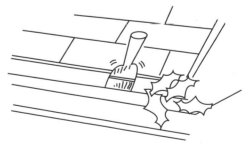

figure 23-1

3. After cleaning, go to a high end of the gutter and flush it out with a blast of water from the garden hose.

4. If a downspout is clogged, try flushing it out by poking the garden hose down into the cavity. Be prepared to get wet if the stream doesn't blast through the clog. Next, try a plumber's snake to remove the problem.

As you clean, be on the lookout for holes, rust spots, or joints that need caulking. Also check to be sure the gutter is angled down for proper run-off.

NO MORE LEAF PROBLEMS

Screen products are made to snap into place atop the gutter to prevent leaves from getting in. Sometimes these screens get covered with leaves that won't allow the water to get in, defeating the purpose of the gutters. There are new systems with names like Gutter Guard and Gutter Helmet, which cover the gutters completely and yet let the rain water flow over and follow the contour of the curved surface into the gutter (figure 23-2).

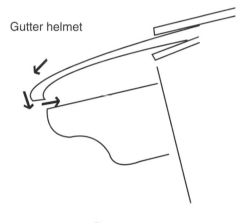

Gutter helmet

figure 23-2

SAGGING GUTTERS

This is usually the result of a loose hanger. There are several types of hangers, and you should get a replacement to match. One type uses a long spike that is driven through a tube and into the fascia. Sometime you can squirt caulk into the wood before driving the spike back in. If the holes are reamed out and won't hold, add a new unit alongside the old one. As a rule of thumb, the gutter should slope down about 1/4-inch per 10 feet.

HOLES

If a hole is the result of rust, you need to get rid of the remaining rust. A wire brush works well. Once the rust is removed, you can cut metal flashing to fit over the hole. Lay a bead of asphalt roofing compound around the edges of the hole and press the metal patch in place. Then coat the entire patch with the same stuff. Rust spots that have not yet become a hole can often be stopped in their tracks. Brush away the rust and then apply a thin coat of roofing compound.

LOOSE SECTIONS

Many gutter installations have connectors to join sections together. If there are leaks around any of these areas, caulk inside and out. Use the black stuff inside and a clear silicone outside. The elbows used in the downspouts are often friction-fitted. If they keep coming loose, use pop rivets to secure the connections.

INSTALLING GUTTERS

If you don't mind spending some time on a ladder, and if you have a willing helper, installing a gutter system may be your cup of tea. The systems available at home centers are all modular and, once you figure out what you need, it's then just a matter of cutting, putting it all together, and hanging it. Here are the steps:

1. Start with a sketch of the roof. This will let you figure out the number of sections you need. Most come in 10-foot sections. The different connection parts include inside and outside corners, end caps (they come for right and left ends), connectors, drop outlets, hangers, and a strainer, all shown in figure 23-3.

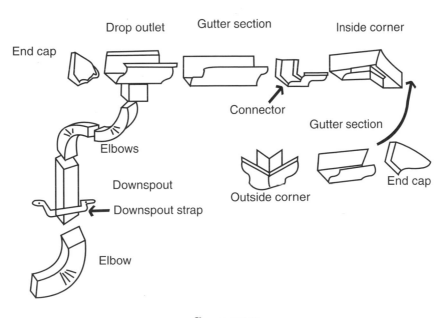

figure 23-3

2. Downspouts are also in 10-foot sections and elbows are used to complete the spout. Straps attach the downspouts to the side of the house. A spout should be installed for every 35 feet of guttering.

3. It's a good idea to lay the pieces out on the ground all the way around the house to let you make sure you have everything you need.

4. Snap a chalk line on the fascia to attain the slant of about a 1/4-inch per 10 feet.

5. Start with the end farthest from the downspout. Install an end cap using the manufacturer's suggested caulk.

6. Depending on the type of hanger used, drill any holes needed before installing any section.

7. Use a support hanger about every 3 feet.

8. Most sections and other components are joined with slip connectors that are caulked to fasten.

9. Use a support hanger on each side of a corner piece.

10. Cutting sections can be done with a fine-toothed hacksaw blade with a 4 x 4 block of wood as support. Otherwise the gutter can get bent out of shape.

11. Use a strap near the top and bottom of the spout. Nail these in place, using masonry nails if the wall is brick or concrete.

If the gutters are not prefinished and are galvanized, you have to wait several months for the metal to weather. Ask your paint dealer how long to wait, taking into account your local climate. When it's time, use a zinc-based primer before putting on your topcoat. The paint is not only for beauty but also protects the metal from rust, even though in theory, galvanized metal doesn't rust.

> **TEACHER'S TIP**
>
> You can cheat on weathering by using a rag and white vinegar to go over all the surfaces. But waiting is best.

Q: If the metal can rust, what about the inside of the downspout where you can't paint?

A: But you can paint if you know the trick. Drop a string with a weight on the end down the spout. Remove the weight and tie the string to a sponge that must be compressed to fit into the spout. Now pour some paint down the spout from the top. As you pull the string slowly up the spout, the sponge coats the inside surface.

AN ALTERNATIVE TO GUTTERS

We have discovered a newly designed product that handles roof water. It's called the Rainhandler. It has a series of blades that resemble mini-blind slats (figure 23-4).

As water runs off the roof and hits the curved blades, it is thrown outward so it hits the ground like rainfall. There are no downspouts to worry about. There is no gutter to catch leaves. There is no worry about the slant, so it makes for an easier installation for the do-it-your-selfer. The units are easily cut and the material is lightweight so you don't need a helper.

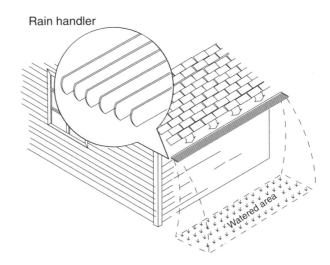

Rain handler

Watered area

figure 23-4

THE SUPER SAGE SAYS

"Controlling rain water is a good thing, so this is one time when it is good to have your mind in the gutter."

24

The Garage 101

Many garages throughout the country are used as a catch-all for junk that you don't have room for in the house. Soon, your two-car garage has room for only one automobile. It's only a hop, skip, and jump, plus a new bicycle, before there's no longer room for one car . . . even if it's only a Yugo. While our curriculum in this class is on home fix-it, we'll tell you how to fix up the garage too! We'll help you to better organize your attached junk room to turn it from a Sanford & Son rerun back into a garage. The key word for the garage transformation is WALLS.

WALLS

The more things you can hang on the walls, the fewer things will be taking up floor space.

Exposed studs may not look all that good, but the cavity between studs spells opportunity. See figure 24-1 for ideas and read on for more help.

The space above the hood of the car (if you could get a car in) can become a space bonanza (figure 24 -2) .

Peg board with all the various hook designs can hold everything from hand

figure 24-1

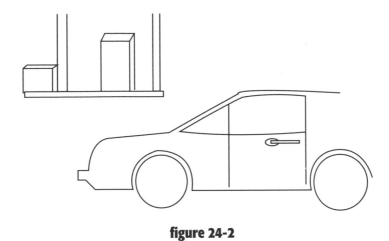

figure 24-2

tools to snow tires on the wall. (Go back to chapter 21 for peg board installation and use.)

The taller ceilings in most garages offer room for floor to ceiling skinny cabinets or deep cabinets or shelves on the upper walls. A trip to the salvage yard for building materials or a visit to a few garage sales might let you score some old cabinets you could hang on a garage wall.

Exposed ceiling joists are great for suspended racks and shelves.

That bike that's always in the way could hang from a big hook in the ceiling.

PARKING SPACES

Big items like a mower or bike that have to be parked in the garage will always be out of the way of the car(s) if you paint white lines to indicate their space.

GARAGE DOORS

Sometimes a garage door will get cranky . . . usually when it's raining or on the coldest day of the year. The most popular type today is the overhead door that comes in hinged sections. Each section is hinged to the adjacent section in several places. The hinges on each end each have a roller that rides in a track when the door is being opened or closed. This means there are dozens of fasteners that can come loose from vibration. Check all the fasteners from time to time to be sure they are all tight.

A loose bracket holding the track may keep the door from staying plumb. This puts a bind on the rollers, causing poor operation.

Another reason for a garage door being out of sorts is dirt in the tracks or sticking due to lack of lubrication.

Grease in the track will collect dirt and gum up the works. A lightweight spray lube and a rag will let you clean the tracks.

Lubricate the rollers and hinges with a lightweight oil. Open and close the door several times to help distribute the lubrication.

If yours is a wooden door, you must keep it sealed against moisture. If you see peeling paint, remove that, prime the bare spot, and repaint. The moisture that gets into the wood, not only can cause rot, it can also add considerable weight to the door. Maybe you don't need that much of a workout?

AUTOMATIC OPENERS

The remote control garage door opener is a wonderful convenience. If you don't have one, you should know that they are easy to install and are not all that expensive anymore. Many manufacturers have an 800 number to help if there is a problem during the installation.

If the door is hard to open and close manually, don't expect your new opener to solve that problem.

Not only is there the convenience factor, there is the matter of greater security. However when it stops working properly, it becomes a pain. You must keep your owner's manual because all that we've seen have a very complete troubleshooter's guide that applies just to your system. But here are some quick checks to make.

1. Most problems with an automatic opener are the fault of the door itself. Pull the emergency release cord that allows you to operate the door manually. Raise and lower the door very slowly. Be alert for any places where there is a drag.

2. If the door doesn't work from the remote control, try the push button. If that works, you probably have a dead battery. It's a good idea to replace the battery on an annual basis.

3. If the remote works, but the push button doesn't, check the wiring between the switch and the unit.

4. All newer doors have an electric eye safety control system. If the plane between the two components is broken, like if a child, pet, or your new Rolls is in the line of fire, the opener doesn't operate. One of the units could be out of line or there could be something that is in the way.

5. If the door doesn't open or close all the way, check the height and sensitivity settings as per the manual.

6. If the door opens on its own, this may be a phantom signal from a neighbor's opener on the same circuit. Change your code. (See you owner's manual.)

7. If the opener is inoperable, and you have to manually open and close it, you can still be safe at night. Install a c-clamp in the track and snugly down against a roller. As long as the clamp is there, the door can't be raised.

WEATHERIZING THE GARAGE

If yours is an attached garage, the heat in the summer and the cold in the winter may be affecting your energy bills. Even if the wall between the living quarters and the garage is well insulated, you'll be experiencing some heat gain or heat loss because of the garage. You've already learned what to do about the door between these two areas. Here are some things to do for the garage:

> **TEACHER'S TIP**
>
> Now that you're able to again park a car in the garage, maybe you'd like to always stop before ramming into the wall and yet be far enough in so the automatic door will close. Park the car in the exact spot you want it. Then suspend a sponge rubber ball on a string from the ceiling so the ball rests against the windshield in front of the driver's face. Drive into the ball and the car will always be in the ideal spot.

1. Get a weather-stripping kit made especially for garages. It will contain pieces for the bottom of the door as well as both sides.
2. Adjust all the hinges to close any gaps between panels.
3. If there are windows and/or doors to the outside, be sure they are properly weather stripped and caulked.
4. An exhaust fan can take away a lot of heat build up in the summer.

If the garage is tight for space and you bang the door against the wall when you get in or out, glue a strip of carpet scrap on the wall where the door touches . . . no more dings!

Masonry 101 **25**

CONCRETE AND BRICK

Masonry is used in home building for several reasons, not the least of which are strength and beauty. This course will teach you how to fix the things that make your home's masonry become not so strong and not so beautiful.

CONCRETE

Most concrete fixing chores require mixing. Since the repair projects are small, you won't need to worry about the proper amounts of cement powder, gravel, and sand. These dry ingredients are already in the bag of ready-mix. It is critical that you add the proper amount of water and mix it in properly. This is an important part of the success of your repair job. Here are a few simple steps:

1. Try to figure out how much concrete you'll need. There aren't too many ways to use an extra cubic yard of slush that will soon be hard as a rock.
2. The bag will tell you how much water to use. Measure this out ahead of time rather than guessing. Add the water in a little at a time. When you first start mixing, it will seem to need more water.
3. Mixing can be done in a wheelbarrow or even on a plastic sheet on a driveway. A hoe is the proper tool for mixing.
4. You are not finished mixing until every grain of sand and every bit of gravel is coated with the gray mix.

Cracks in concrete are pretty much a fact of life. But once there is the smallest of hairline cracks, there's a better than average chance it will grow into something resembling the Grand Canyon. Patching can stop the crack's growth.

HAIRLINE CRACKS

The main goal here is to just seal up the crack to prevent moisture from getting into and expanding the crack. Rather than getting a bag of mix, there are pre-mixed patching compounds that are chemical instead of cement based. They contain no aggregate (rocks or gravel). The only tool you need is your index finger in a rubber glove (figure 25-1).

figure 25-1

There are also patching compounds in a cartridge for use with a caulking gun that can be used for slightly larger cracks (figure 25-2).

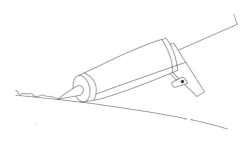

figure 25-2

MAJOR CRACKS

This fix-it project is a little more complicated if done right. Here are the steps:

1. The crack needs to be "undercut." This means it is wider underneath than on the surface (figure 25-3). Use a cold chisel and a short handled sledgehammer to undercut. (Wear safety goggles and gloves.)

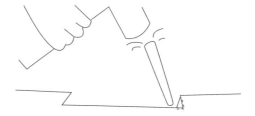

figure 25-3

2. Clean away all the dust and debris. Wash out the cavity, leaving it wet but with no standing water.

3. Brush the surfaces with concrete bonding adhesive. This is a white liquid that bonds the old to the new in concrete work.

4. Fill the crack with one of the patching compounds mentioned above or with "sand-mix," a dry mix that contains no aggregate. A putty knife or small trowel will let you push the mix firmly in place and smooth off the surface.

HOLES IN CONCRETE

Sometimes the surface on a big concrete slab like a driveway or patio will start to crumble. These holes become great bird baths for sparrows but can soon become mature potholes . . . not a good thing for cars or people. Often when patches are made, they don't last. Here's how to do it right:

1. Brush and wash out all the dust and debris and leave the cavity wet but with no standing water.
2. Use a pre-mix called sand mix (contains no rocks).
3. Now comes the secret ingredient, concrete bonding adhesive. You see, new concrete does not adhere well to old, hence the cause for the frequent failure we mentioned. Brush this liquid on all the surfaces to be patched. You can also pour bonding adhesive into the mix of new concrete, using less water to compensate for the added liquid.
4. Scoop the mix into the cavity and level it with a 2 x 4.
5. When the sheen starts to disappear, smooth it with a trowel or a metal float.
6. Cover the patch with a tarp or plastic sheet for six days while the concrete cures. If it is drying out too fast, uncover it and mist it lightly with the garden hose.

CHIPPED CONCRETE EDGES

This problem occurs on curbs, walks, and on concrete steps. Once this starts, particularly on steps, foot traffic will make it worse. Not only does it look bad, there can be a safety issue. Once you know how to provide forms for the repair, the project is easy. Here are the steps for fixing steps:

1. Undercut the edge, as shown in figures 25-4. Use a circular saw with a masonry blade for a long undercut. Wear safety goggles and a breathing mask. Sweep and wash away the dust and debris.

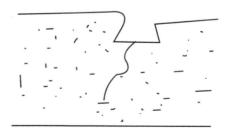

Undercut crack in concrete

figure 25-4

2. Cut a board the width of the step and at least as high as the step. Use bricks or a cinder block to hold the form in place (figure 25-5).
3. Brush the area with bonding adhesive and use a sand mix. Apply and smooth the patch with a trowel or float.
4. Be sure to go though the six-day curing process as described above.

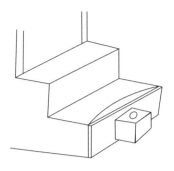

figure 25-5

SPOTS ON CONCRETE

Since a concrete driveway and garage floor are constantly being run over by cars, there are often spills that may look worse than cracks and holes. You may be amazed at how easily many spots can be removed.

OIL AND GREASE SPOTS

You'll want to get after these as soon as possible, but even old spots can be removed. Here's the routine:

1. Wipe up the excess with a paper towel.
2. Saturate the spot with paint thinner. This gives it more liquidity.
3. Cover it with a layer of something that will absorb. We use cat litter, but baking soda, cornmeal, dry Portland cement powder, or sawdust will all work as well.

> **TEACHER'S TIP**
>
> Fix the car or you'll be doing these chores every week or so!

4. Leave the spot until the next day and, when you sweep it up, the spot is usually gone. Repeat the process for a really stubborn spill.

Sometime the oil or grease has all been lifted out, but has left a stain. These and other stains in concrete can usually be removed by pouring on liquid laundry bleach straight from the jug.

RUST STAINS

This is another memento from the family car, often from the radiator. Some stuff called oxalic acid is a great rust remover. Rather than tracking down a chemical company that carries this, head for the supermarket. Two cleaning products containing oxalic acid are Zud and Barkeeper's Friend. Wet the spot, sprinkle the cleanser on, and then scrub with a stiff wet brush. Some folks make a paste with the cleanser and water and let that sit for a while before brushing.

BRICKS

There were two reasons why the third little pig built his home of brick. First, he knew that a brick structure would be strong and long lasting. But he also knew that it would be a thing of beauty. He was right, his house was the talk of the neighborhood.

Most brick homes today are of the brick veneer variety, so the brick is pretty much for looks rather than strength. Most of the time, the brick is long lasting but occasionally something happens. You'll soon see how easily the brick problems can be solved by you.

REPLACING A DAMAGED BRICK

Sometimes a car hits the wall or a stray golf ball leaves the fairway. Or, maybe settling under the house causes a brick to crack. You can extract the bad brick and put in a new one. Here's how:

> **A BRICK TRICK**
>
> Rather than chiseling all the mortar, use a power drill with a masonry bit to drill a series of holes all around the brick. Now the chisel has an easy job with what's left of the mortar.

1. Your first problem may be in finding a matching replacement brick. It usually doesn't have to match exactly. If you strike out, maybe you can remove a brick from an obscure part of the house where the unmatched brick won't make any difference.

2. Remove the bad brick. This means you must remove all the mortar holding it in place.

3. Remove all of the remaining mortar from the cavity with a wire brush. Then hose the cavity out.

4. Put the new brick in a bucket of water. A wet brick doesn't suck all the moisture from the new mortar. Also dampen the new cavity and the bricks around it, but leave no standing water.

5. You can buy a small bag of mortar mix that requires only that you add water. When properly mixed, spread a little of the mortar on a folded-over paper towel. The towel will absorb a lot of the moisture from the mix, so you can see just about the shade of gray it will be when dry. If it's too light, add a little lampblack

to darken. If too dark, rub blackboard chalk across a cheese grater from the kitchen to create white dust to lighten the mortar.

6. Now lay in a bed of mortar on the floor of the cavity.

7. Remove the brick from the bucket, shake it off, butter the two ends and the top with mortar, and ease it into place using a trowel to push in any mortar that didn't go in with the brick.

8. Wipe away any excess mortar. Before the new mortar joints set up, rake them to make them match the rest of the wall.

TUCKPOINTING

This ridiculous term means the replacement of mortar joints. Sometimes mortar starts to crumble and needs to be replaced. From what we learned in replacing a brick, you should be able to solve this problem . . . but now you also know what the procedure is called.

CLEANING BRICK

Usually brick walls can be cleaned with a garden hose. If there is some stubborn dirt, use a hose-end sprayer with detergent in the receptacle. However, if the surfaces are really dirty and maybe even have mildew patches, here is a magic formula:

Start with three gallons of warm water.
Add a quart of liquid laundry bleach.
Stir in a cup of powdered detergent.
Mix in 2/3 cup of TSP.

TSP stands for trisodium phosphate (not a brand name), available at paint stores. Apply this mix to the exterior brick wall with a stiff broom. Leave it on for 15 to 30 minutes, then hose it off, using lots of water to dilute the mix and protect your lawn and landscape.

ANOTHER EXTRA CREDIT PROJECT

Now that you're a brick expert, how would you like to make a patio from bricks but with none of that messy mortar. Skip over to chapter 26 and see how easy this project is!

Decks, Patios, and Porches 101

26

Outdoor living is in vogue these days. A deck or patio is a very popular addition to the backyard. And their cousin, the porch, is often on the front of the house. In many families, these additions are outdoor living spaces. Because they are outside, they are subjected to the elements, and so there are times when repairs are needed. We'll cover the most common woes and then give you some pointers on actually building a deck or patio. It can be a fun project that may include the whole family.

DECK PROBLEMS

Most decks are built of either pressure treated lumber or wood that is resistant to rot and insects. So those things don't usually present problems.

NAIL HEADS

One common problem is nails that have popped up. The best thing to do is to pull the nails and replace them with deck screws or spiral nails. These fasteners are less likely to ever come out.

WARPING

Another deck malady is the warped board. Replacement is one way to solve this. However, in many cases you can just pry up the warped board. Flip it over and reinstall it with the same success.

GREASE SPOTS

Since we often cook on the grill on a deck, the surface can end up with grease spots. Often detergent and water will remove these stains. If not, saturate the spot with mineral spirits paint thinner and then cover the area with cat litter or some other absorbent material. Wait overnight before sweeping up the mess.

MILDEW

If you start to see black mold growing, use half-and-half bleach and water solution and a scrub brush to get rid of the mildew.

OOZING SAP

Use a rag and mineral spirits paint thinner to remove sap from the surface. It may come back after a while.

TURNING GRAY

Weathering of wood will fade it to silver gray. Some people like this look, but if you're not one of them, there are deck-wash products that are easy to apply and will restore the wood to a like-new appearance. Another approach to this situation is to use an exterior deck stain. Get one that is labeled "water repellent."

PATIO PROBLEMS

Patios are made from a number of different masonry surfaces, which are all long lasting. However, Mother Nature does have an effect on these surfaces. For cracks, holes, and surface damage, go to chapter 25, page 204. Later in this chapter, we'll tell you how to make your own mortarless patio from brick. We'll also tell how to repair problems with this type surface.

EFFLORESCENCE

This shows up on masonry surfaces as a sort of salty looking white substance. It is actually salts that are leaching up through the patio. Use a solution of one part muriatic acid and ten parts water to scrub away the efflorescence. Wear protective gloves and goggles and have plenty of ventilation, as muriatic acid throws off some violent fumes.

GREASE SPOTS

Use the same technique as described above under "deck problems."

PORCH PROBLEMS

Most porches are not add-ons but were built when the house was being constructed. If the porch is concrete, it was probably a separate pour from the rest of the foundation. If there are heaving or shifting problems, cracks may occur and should be filled promptly. (See page 203.)

If the porch has a wooden floor, it is probably painted. Because of foot traffic and maybe even a rocking chair, the paint may wear off. Inspect the floor regularly and repaint when needed.

Many porches will have railings and these should be inspected regularly to be sure they are securely attached. Metal railings should be protected by paint to prevent rust. If rust appears, use a rust removal product and completely remove the rust before repainting. Apply a rust-preventive primer on all the bare spots and let it dry before putting on the topcoat.

PORCH COLUMNS

Moisture can work its way under porch columns and cause rot. If you can get after it soon enough, you can dig out any rotted wood and replace it with wood filler or an automobile body repair compound. Either of these can be sanded and painted. You must completely remove all the rotted material and treat the remaining column area with a preservative.

If a column or post has to be replaced, you will need temporary support to hold up the roof while the old post is removed. Either brace the roof with a 4 x 4 or rent an adjustable jack-post.

LET'S BUILD A DECK

Our next class project is fun and is the easiest way we've found to build a deck. Before we tell you about the easy way, let's see what goes into building a conventional deck (figure 26-1). The ledger can be a 2 x 4 on up to a 2 x 10, depending on the size of the deck. It is attached to the side of the house. The ledger can be attached using lag bolts or bolts and masonry anchors, depending on the house material to which it's attached.

To prevent water damage to the ledger, coat the side next to the house with wood preservative and caulk the top seam. Flashing is also used to protect a ledger.

If the joists rest directly on the ledger, add that width plus the thickness of the deck material to determine the finished height of the deck. Keep in mind that the finished deck should end up being approximately level with the floor coming out of the house, if a door is involved. Either a step-up or step-down can result in falls.

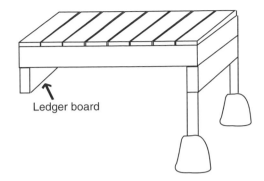

Ledger board

figure 26-1

A beam that is resting across posts that are atop concrete piers will hold the other end of the deck. The joists span from the ledger to the beam. The decking material is then attached to the joists. Spacing between boards is important. The thickness of a 16d nail is a good spacer gauge. Use ring-shank nails or deck screws to avoid nail head pop-ups. Aluminum or stainless steel nails will prevent discoloration on redwood.

PROTECTION

Even if you used pressure treated lumber, the wood will last longer if treated with a water seal. Wait about thirty days for the wood to dry out and apply the seal. Using a pump-up sprayer will make this job a snap. The seal will help fight against splitting and warping. You can tell when the sealer needs to be reapplied by pouring water on the surface. If it beads up, it's still OK. If it readily soaks in, give it a new coat.

THE EASY DECK

The hardest part of building a conventional deck is digging holes for the concrete piers and mixing the concrete. Dek-Block piers (figure 26-2) do away with those hassles and a few others. As you can see, the deck blocks have slots that hold 2 x 6 pieces. There is also space for a 4 x 4 post for a raised deck or to compensate for a sloping surface (figure 26-3). These blocks are designed to be placed directly on the ground, so level the area where the pier goes.

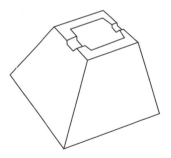

figure 26-2

Let's say we'll build a simple 8 x 8 deck. Here are the easy steps:

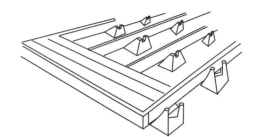

figure 26-3

1. You need 12 piers laid out as in figure 26-4.
2. Next you put the four joists in place in the slots, parallel to each other. These are 2 x 6s.
3. Make sure the joists are all level with each other.
4. Attach a 2 x 6 at each end to close the open ends.
5. Lay out the 2 x 6 deck boards at right angles to the joists.

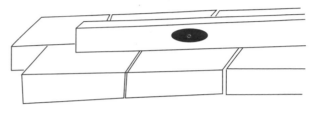

figure 26-4

6. Use the 16d nail between each board as a spacer. Adjust the spacing so that the deck boards at each end of the deck have the same overlap as the finish boards at each end.
7. Use deck screws to attach the deck boards, installing two at each joist.
8. Drag out the deck chairs and the grill and enjoy!

If it sounds simple, that's because it is!

BUILDING A BRICK PATIO

Our patio project is almost as easy as the deck we just finished. It's made of brick, but without the messy, labor-intensive use of mortar. There is a small matter of digging. True, it's hard work, but that will look good on your resume. After you decide the size you want your patio to be, here are the steps:

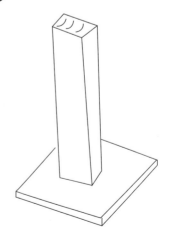

1. Dig down the thickness of the brick plus an extra 3 inches. The extra depth is for a bed of sand.
2. Pour in the sand and level it off to about 3 inches.
3. Tamp it down well. (Make a tamper from a 2 x 4 and a foot square scrap of plywood as in figure 26-5.)

figure 26-5

4. It helps to have some sort of border around the entire patio to prevent the bricks at the edges from sliding away. This can be from 2 x 4s of pressure treated wood or flexible edging material from the garden shop. Make the border so it will be level with the top of the bricks (figure 26-6).

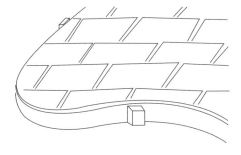

figure 26-6

5. Select bricks graded SW (severe weathering) for longer life.

6. Lay the bricks on top of the sand in any pattern you like but don't leave any space between bricks. As you go, make sure they are level. If one is not, level it by adding or removing a little sand under it.

7. With the bricks all down and level, sprinkle dry sand all over the top of your patio. Use a broom to sweep the sand back and forth. Even though the bricks are butted together, a little of the sand will go into the tiny cracks.

8. Using a garden hose with the nozzle set to a fine mist, wet down the entire surface.

9. Let it dry and repeat this several times.

One of the nice things about this patio is the ease of repair. If a brick or an area sinks, pry up the brick(s) involved, add more sand, and replace.

This same technique can make a great brick walkway in your yard.

PLANNING NEW OUTDOOR LIVING

A little planning ahead of time can make your outdoor living project turn out better. First, think about what you'll use this outdoor room for. How big should it be? Will you need enough space for outdoor parties or just outdoor grilling for the family? Would you rather have a small deck for intimate cocktails with your spouse? Would you like to use the deck or patio for sun bathing? Should there be a kid's play area on or near your new addition? Are there any zoning conditions that would limit the size?

Next, look at the existing elements of the yard. Where are the trees, flowerbeds, and shrubs? Are there sheds or other outbuildings? Is there anything else that would restrict the reach of your patio or deck?

Once you decide the size of the project, plot out the yard and house and see where the deck or patio will fit.

A sloping lot may dictate the height of your addition and may even allow you to take advantage of this feature to install a multilevel installation.

Also consider the orientation of the property as relates to the sun. You may wish to change the size or location of the project to take advantage of sun or shade. Remember that the amount of sun or shade varies with the seasons.

After you have laid out the project on paper, you should check with the building inspector's office to see if you need a permit and if the design complies with local codes and restrictions. Often the basic deck or patio needs no permit, but if you start adding extras like plumbing and electrical, it may call for one.

Once you have your dream plan, you'll be happy to know that many building supply outfits and home centers have computer packages that can take your plans and quickly give you a list of all the materials you'll need.

Such outdoor projects are often great do-it-yourself endeavors for the whole family.

> **TEACHER'S TIP**
>
> How about a pre-patio party to sort of test-drive the size of the intended patio? Stake off the area, put some patio furniture in place and invite a bunch of friends over. This way you'll know whether the new addition can handle the crowd. Enjoy!

Fences 101

27

E recting a fence is certainly a popular do-it-yourself project. It is a great way to improve your property. Fences can keep children and pets from straying. They can also keep stray animals and strangers from entering your property. A solid fence also gives you some privacy and may block out an ugly view or dampen the noise from a freeway. To some people, the fence marks the boundary of their property.

There are literally dozens of styles, sizes, and materials for fence building. The reason you are building the fence may dictate the fence you decide on. You wouldn't want a 3-foot high picket fence to keep a 150-pound Great Dane corralled.

Wood is the most popular fence building material. Because the fence is out in the elements, you may wish to use pressure treated lumber. You should at least go for wood that is resistant to rot and insect damage. The wood should later be treated with a water seal or other appropriate sealer.

Before we get into fence repair, we want to show you how to build a fence. The fence-building example may not be exactly what you would want but you'll learn many things that will apply to the construction of any fence.

BUILDING A FENCE

Probably the most common fence is a 6 or 8-foot tall wooden privacy fence. Before starting your plan, check with the local building inspection department to find out if there is a height limit and if there are any restrictions on the materials you want to use or the style you'll employ. Also, there may be a restriction on how close to your property line the fence can be. It's much better to find out these things now rather than waiting until you have to rip your new fence down and rebuild it to comply. Look at the survey done on the house at the time you purchased it.

Your next step is to plan your fence.

The posts for our 6-foot high fence will be no more than 8 feet apart. Measure the entire length from corner post to corner post and divide it so the distance between posts will be more or less equal. After all, you don't want four sections that are 8 feet long and one section that measures only 2 feet.

After you have drawn out your fence on a diagram of your property, decide where you want a gate or gates. Also be sure your gates are wide enough to let you move a mower or wheelbarrow in and out.

Your first construction effort will be a set of temporary layout aids called batter boards. You'll need a pair for each section of fence. Place them a couple of feet beyond where the terminal posts will be. Each batter board can be made from a pair 2-foot long 2 x 4 stakes driven into the ground about a foot deep and about 18 inches apart. Nail on a 1 x 4 cross piece that is perfectly level (figure 27-1). These batter boards are used to run a very taut line of mason's twine to indicate the perfectly straight line. When the twine lines are set for all sections of fence, you're ready to pick out the locations for postholes.

YOU CAN DIG IT!

There are several ways to dig postholes . . . none of which are all that much fun! First, of course, there is the shovel. Not only is this hard work, it often renders an

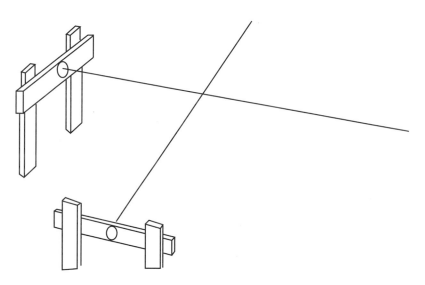

figure 27-1

uneven hole. Then there's the clamshell digger (figure 27-2), and the bladed scoop type of clamshell digger (figure 27-3). If you just have a few holes to dig, either one of these will get the job done—eventually. If your fence involves ten posts or more, rent a power posthole digger. There are gasoline powered two-man types that will do a quicker job than the one-man models. From experience, the two-man tool starts to get heavier with each hole, and after twenty holes you'll wonder if you'll be able to lift it out. Also, in clay soil, the tool develops considerable torque and the side handle will beat up your body, leaving a series of bruises along one side. You can always farm out this part of the job to a pro.

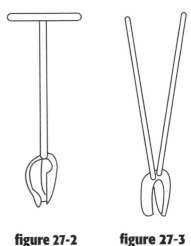

figure 27-2   **figure 27-3**

WHAT SIZE HOLES?

For a 6-foot high fence, the hole should be 2 feet deep with an extra 2 inches for a bed of gravel. For a 4-foot high fence, dig to a depth of 18 inches. If you dig a hole too deep (heaven forbid!), add enough gravel in the hole to bring the post up even with the rest.

For end posts and others set in concrete, the diameter of the hole should be about 12 inches. If you live in an area with very stable soil, you may backfill around the post with earth and gravel. The diameter here should be about 8 inches.

> **WORDS OF WISDOM**
>
> We recommend that all the posts be set in concrete. This means an extra bag of pre-mix per post, but the additional cost is small and you'll have a much more stable fence.

As if you haven't done enough digging, there is one extra step you can take to make the post even more stable. Take a shovel, and angle it into the hole to widen it at the bottom. This flared shape adds stability (figure 27-4).

KEEPING POSTED

The wooden post is the most likely part of a fence to go bad. Posts are below ground and moisture can attack them in many ways. That's why many fence builders have gone to metal posts, even though the rest of the fence is wood. Posts sometimes develop a lean, and this could put undue stress on the rest of the fence and might even mean that the fence could fall down. Plus, a leaning fence is not a thing of beauty. If none of the rest of the lumber is pressure treated, go the slight extra cost for treated posts.

Once all the holes are drilled, drop in the posts and brace them with outriggers, angled and staked, to hold them plumb and in place (figure 27-5).

When pouring the concrete around the post, poke it to get rid of any air pockets. Bring the level up above the ground and use a trowel to taper it down away from the post (figure 27-6). Set only one post at a time, doing the two end posts first.

After all the posts are set, you should wait at least 24 hours for the concrete to set. If the posts are random heights and need to be cut off, strike a chalk line and go for it. This is also the time to install the rails, or stringers as they are often called. Most 6-foot fences can get by with two rails. A taller fence will often have three or even four rails.

The top rail can be nailed on top of the posts. Lower rails will then need to be toenailed (figure 27-7). Or, all rails may be nailed to the sides of the posts.

FILLING IN THE INFILL

Now you have a skeleton of your fence. Next come the fence boards, which are called "infill." Here you have lots of choices. The boards can be in a straight line, pointed, dog-eared, scalloped, and many other designs (figure 27-8). Many people cap off the fence with a 2 x 6

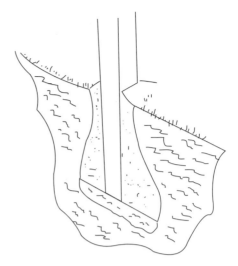

figure 27-4

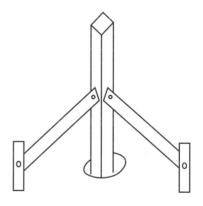

figure 27-5

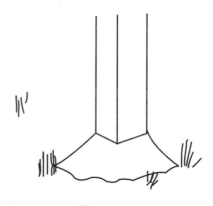

figure 27-6

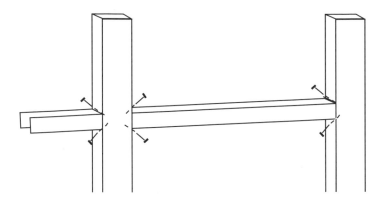

figure 27-7

board nailed to the top rail. The boards can be nailed to both sides of the rails, either vertical or horizontal, in a shadow box effect.

Another neat addition is to top off the fence with framed latticework inside continuous 2 x 4 frames to give the fence taller look (figure 27-9).

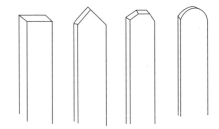

figure 27-8

MAKING A GATE

The gate, in most cases, is just a moveable section of fence. The gate doesn't have to be of the same design as the fence. However, since it does get a workout, it must be sturdy.

Thought should be given as to which way the gate is to open. There are no hard and fast rules, so it is pretty much a judgment call.

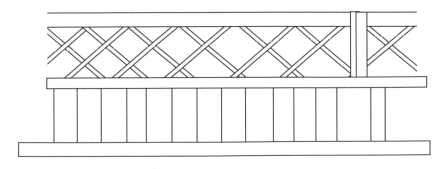

figure 27-9

Gates don't have to match the rest of the fence but that is usually an easy way to go. Once you've decided on the design, follow these steps to building a simple gate:

1. Measure the distance between gate posts or between one gate post and whatever else the gate will be attached to.
2. Subtract 3/4-inch from this measurement to allow for gate swing.
3. Make a simple frame of this width from 2 x 4s. The height will probably be best if it's even with the rest of the fence.
4. Diagonal bracing is important. It can be a 2 x 4 brace or a wire and turnbuckle brace. These are easy to install, and your home center will have them. The turnbuckle is good for later on if the gate starts to sag. A couple of quick turns will remove the sag. Whichever bracing is used, it should angle down toward the hinge side (figure 27-10).
5. The same infill material used on the fence is nailed to the frame.
6. Install the hinges, using fasteners as long as possible without the points sticking out.
7. Install the latch.

Hopefully your gate will be swinging as long as you do.

TEACHER'S TIP

Often when nailing boards very near the end, the wood will split. Avoid this by turning the nail upside down and tapping the point a few times with a hammer to blunt it.

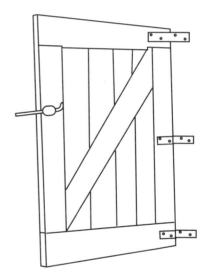

figure 27-10

28

Picking Out a Pro

CONGRATULATIONS! YOU ARE A GRADUATE DO-IT-YOURSELFER!

We know that some homeowners will not tackle all the projects we've talked about during the course. If you decide you want the help of a contractor, repair guy, or tradesman, we want you to get the best available. How do you do that? Here are some tips:

1. Ask your friends and neighbors if they have had work like yours done recently. They could give you a run down.
2. Ask your hardware or paint dealer if they can recommend someone who does the kind of work you need done.
3. As you drive around, look at houses where work is being done. Most will have a sign in the yard.Check the pickup trucks for a sign as well. If you start to see that one company is doing a lot of work, it may be a good sign. It's not a bad idea to call on the homeowner to see if they are satisfied.
4. Once you have several prospects, contact them and ask for references of recent work as well as work done a few years ago. As you check these references , here are things to ask:
   a. Was the work done to your satisfaction?
   b. Were there any surprises?
   c. Was the price as estimated?
   d. Was the work done on time?
   e. Were the workmen people you felt comfortable having in your home?
   f. Did they clean up after the job?

5. Ask the contractor for a run down of what insurance he has.

6. If a license is required, be sure he has one and that it is up to date.

7. Find out how long he has been in business.

8. Check his standing with the Better Business Bureau, but don't make that your only checkpoint as many people do.

9. Ask for banking references. After all you don't want the guy to go bankrupt in the middle of your job.

As a matter of fact, the tradesman who leaves his card in you door is probably not a good prospect because a good tradesman is too busy to walk the streets.

If this is a small job, you probably won't require competitive bids. If it's a major big bucks project, get at least three bids. Be sure you give the bidders the same information so that you are comparing apples to apples.

> **WARNING**
>
> Don't fall for the guy who knocks on your door and wants to top your asphalt drive, or seal and treat your roof. He may claim he just finished a job in the area and has enough materials left over to do your house. Rather than have to dump the leftovers, he'll "be giving you a great price." The roof sealer may be mostly water and the asphalt may be mostly drained motor oil. All he'll be giving you is the shaft.

Once you have decided on your dream contractor, be sure to have a contract drawn up that spells out all the details of the project. Specify the materials and products to be used. Include a payment schedule. Completion dates for various phases should be outlined. It's a good idea to indicate how disputes will be handled.

If you've picked out the right company, they should willingly give you the information you ask for, and at the end of the job both parties should be happy.

Glossary

IF YOU'RE GOING TO BE A GRADUATE DO-IT-YOURSELFER, YOU NOT ONLY HAVE TO WALK THE WALK . . . YOU MUST TALK THE TALK!

Hopefully, this section will help you to translate most of the mysterious language you hear at the home center, hardware store, and from tradesmen.

ADJUSTABLE WRENCH—The jaws on this tool are adjustable so it can do the work of many wrenches. It is also called the Crescent wrench, which is the name of the company that makes a line of such tools.

ALLEN WRENCH—A wrench for hexagonal nuts or screws often used as setscrews. The simplest set would be L-shaped while the better ones have a handle for easier use.

AMPS—The term used for the unit of electrical current going through a circuit at any given time.

BALUSTERS—The upright pieces that help to hold up the hand rail on a stairway or the cap-rail of a deck.

BAR CLAMP—This type clamp uses a bar to span wide areas.

BAT—As in brickbat, refers to a piece of a brick.

BATT—A term for a section of fiberglass and other insulation that is 15 or 23 inches wide to fit between studs and joists and usually 4 to 8 feet long.

BATTEN—The narrow strip often used to cover seams between panels.

BEAM—A horizontal support member.

BEARING WALL—Also called load bearing. These are walls that hold up the structure above. Removal is a "No-No" without solving the load problem in another fashion.

BLIND NAILING—When a nail is installed so as not to be seen on the surface.

BOXING—A process of mixing paint by pouring back and forth between two containers. This helps to preserve the color throughout the project.

BOX WRENCH—A wrench where the business end is a closed circle that fits over a nut. The notched surface inside the circle gives the tool a better grip.

BRAD—Really small nails for really small nailing chores. (Also the name of the pool boy.)

BRIDGING—Can be metal or wood members that are installed between floor joists to add rigidity. Bridging is often a solution to squeaking floors.

Btu—British Thermal Unit. The standard of measure that indicates the amount of heat it takes to raise the temperature of 1 pound of water 1° F.

BUTT HINGE—A two-leaf flat hinge most commonly used for doors. One leaf is attached to the door edge and the other to the jamb. These edges are usually mortised to accept the hinge leaf.

C-CLAMP—Just look at one and you'll know how they got their name.

CANTILEVER—Part of a structure that extends beyond the foundation or other support.

CASING—The trim around a door or window.

CHALK LINE—A container with a reel of string and colored powder. When the string is pulled out coated with chalk, it can mark a straight line by pulling the string tight and snapping it.

CHALKING—A powdery surface developed on some exterior paints that provides a cleaning effect as rain washes it away. Often this process creates problems on the surfaces below.

CHISEL—A wood cutting tool used in shaving and trimming.

CIRCUIT—A system of wiring that travels from the entry box to various fixtures and then completes the circuit back to the box.

CIRCUIT BREAKER—A safety device that automatically shuts off the current when there is a short or overload.

CIRCUIT TESTER—A tool used to check that electrical current is present.

CIRCULAR SAW—A power saw with a circular blade, often called Skilsaw after one of the early manufacturers.

CLAW HAMMER—A carpenter's hammer with a curved claw that is used for removing nails.

CLOSET AUGER—The tool often used to remove clogs from a toilet.

COLD CHISEL—A chisel used for metal work.

COMBINATION SQUARE—The head on this tool moves along a metal ruler to allow the user to mark 45- and 90-degree angles.

COMMON NAILS—Wire nails used for rough carpentry.

CONDUCTOR—Anything capable of carrying electricity. In home wiring, usually copper or aluminum.

CONDUIT—Lightweight metal tubing that contains and protects electrical wires.

CONTINUITY TESTER—This battery-powered tool is used to determine if electrical current can travel through a device or wiring system.

COPING SAW—A special saw for making ornate and curved cuts.

COUNTERSINK—The sinking of the head of fasteners, screws, or nails, even with or below the surface.

CRIPPLE—A short stud that is installed above a door or window.

CUPPING—A wood warp that causes boards to curl up at the edges.

CUT NAILS—Flat flooring nails.

DADO—A square groove cut in a board, usually across the grain.

DOOR SWEEP—A weatherstrip item that is attached to the bottom of an exterior door to prevent air infiltration between the threshold and the door.

DRYWALL—This is a wallboard made of gypsum covered on both sides with heavy paper. Also called Sheetrock, gypsum board, and sometimes some unprintable terms.

DUCT TAPE—This is a tape used by do-it-yourselfers for hundreds of things, none of which should be on ductwork.

DUPLEX NAILS—These two-headed nails are for the purpose of the secure but temporary joining of wood members.

EASEMENT—A legal way for utility companies and municipalities to use a small portion of your property for such things as utility poles, sewers, and the servicing thereof.

EAVES—The bottom of the roof edge that sticks out beyond the wall.

EFFLORESCENCE—An ugly whitish powder caused by salts that are leached up to the surface of masonry work.

ELECTRICIAN'S TAPE—A waterproof tape used to protect and insulate bare electrical wires.

ENTRY BOX—A box that houses fuses or circuit breakers and is where the electricity enters the house.

EPOXY—This two-component resin is used in both adhesives and paints. Both yield a very strong bond. Just be sure to follow all directions as to mixing, drying, and setting times for best results.

EXPANSION JOINT—A flexible material is needed between two adjacent surfaces because they tend to expand and contract. The expansion joint allows this to happen without damage. A prime example would be where a concrete patio is poured right against a house.

FASCIA BOARD—A flat horizontal strip of lumber fastened to the end of rafters to hide and protect them.

FAUX FINISH—Any of several techniques of painting such as sponge painting, rolling, ragging, combing, and other unique methods of finishing,

FEMALE—Any mating piece into which the other part can be inserted. (For example, a nut with internal threads is female and the bolt with external threads that goes into it is male.)

FENCE—No, not the one that keeps the neighbor kids out of your back yard. This fence is an adjustable guide against which a power tool is moved to cut a straight line.

FILE CARD—This tool is used for cleaning the teeth on files. A suede shoe brush does just about as well.

FILES—These tools are used for shaping and smoothing wood and metal.

FINISHES—The topcoat that protects the piece of wood or metal. This can include paint, lacquer, shellac, varnish, polyurethane, or any of several other compounds.

FINISHING NAILS—Small headed nails that are driven below the surface with a nail set. They can be hidden with a dab of wood putty or other such compound.

FIRE STOP—Also called "fire blocking." Since the space between studs is open, there could be drafts that could cause a fire to spread. These spaces can be closed with the addition of fire stops during construction.

FIREBRICK—Special brick that resist extreme heat and are thus used to line the walls of a fireplace.

FLASHING—Strips and pieces of either metal or composition used to seal or divert water at points where the roof and another building material come together.

FLUE—A pipe, chimney, or other channel whereby smoke and combustion gases are carried to the outside.

FOOTING—A base, usually concrete, that carries and spreads the load of a masonry wall.

FRAMING—The skeleton of the structure, usually 2 x 4 lumber.

FROST LINE—The depth below ground at which freezing occurs. This varies with the local climate.

FURRING—Strips of wood that are secured to a wall to provide a nailing surface for a new facing such as paneling.

FUSE BOX—See ENTRY BOX.

GABLE—The triangular area formed when two slopes of a roof meet at a peak.

GALVANIZING—The process of coating iron or steel with zinc to prevent rusting.

GATE VALVE—A positive action valve that regulates the flow of water to either fully open of fully closed.

GFCI—Ground Fault Circuit Interrupter. A safety device that instantly shuts off current if even the smallest leakage occurs.

GLAZING—The installation of glass.

GLOBE VALVE—An adjustable valve that lets you control the rate of flow of water.

GLUE GUN—See HOT MELT GLUE GUN.

GRADE—No, not the kind you get when you take a test. This is the slope of the earth around your home.

GRAIN—This is the pattern of a piece of wood as made by the annual growth rings.

GROUND—A safety measure that takes advantage of the fact that electricity seeks the shortest route to the earth.

GROUT—A thin mortar that fills the joints between tiles.

GYPSUM BOARD—See DRYWALL.

HACKSAW—A saw for cutting metal.

HARDBOARD—A man-made fiber board composed of wood waste materials, often called Masonite, a popular brand of the stuff.

HEADER—A support member over a door or window, usually made from two boards sandwiched together.

HEX NUT—A six-sided nut.

HIP ROOF—A downward sloping roof section that comes from the ridge to each outside corner of the house.

HONE—A stone for sharpening tools

HOSE CLAMP—A nifty little gadget used to hold an automobile hose in place. Over the school year, we'll find other handy uses for this device.

HOT MELT GLUE GUN—An electric gun that melts glue that can be triggered out on the work. Newer models are cordless.

INCANDESCENT BULBS—The conventional type household light bulbs.

INSULATION—Any of several materials used to retard heat flow and thus help keep the home cool in the summer and warm in the winter.

JACK STUD—No, this is not a pick-up artist named Jack. These are framing members used on both sides of a door or window to support a header.

JAMB—The top and sides of the opening for a door or window.

JIGSAW—Usually a bench tool that has a skinny blade that cuts intricate curves and designs.

JOINT COMPOUND—The tape used to hide joints between sheets of Sheetrock. For how the tape is used, see Taping and Bedding.

JOISTS—Large horizontal timbers used to support floors and ceilings.

KILOWATT-HOUR—The watt is the rate at which electrical energy is consumed. A kilowatt is one thousand watts. The kilowatt-hour is the base unit for measuring consumption.

LAMINATE—Materials in which two or more layers are bonded together.

LEVEL—A tool that shows whether a surface is horizontally level or vertically plumb.

LOCKING GRIP PLIERS—Also know as Vise Grips. The initial gripping is done by squeezing with the hand. Additional gripping power is done by turning a knurled knob at the base of one handle. The hold is released with a touch of the release lever.

LOW VOLTAGE LIGHTING—A system using a transformer to step down voltage, often employed for outdoor lighting

MALE—See FEMALE.

MALLET—A hammer with a wooden, plastic, or rubber head.

MASKING TAPE—Tape used to protect areas where you don't want paint to go.

MITER—Beveled cuts, often at the ends of butted joints.

MITER BOX—A tool that guides a saw into cuts of 45 degrees, plus other angles.

MITER CLAMP—Also called a corner clamp. Used to hold pieces forming a mitered corner together while adhesive sets up.

MORTAR—A bonding mix for holding brick or stone work together. Commonly made of cement, lime, sand, and water.

MORTISE—An inset chiseled out of wood to accept another piece, such as a hinge.

NAIL SET—This small tool drives the nail head below the surface.

NEC—National Electrical Code. Safety guidelines for electrical wiring.

NEWEL POST—The main posts in the start and finish of a stairway.

NIPPLE—No giggling, class. This is a small steel pipe. Like the short pipe that comes out of the wall for the tub spout to attach to.

OC—On Center.

ORBITAL SANDER—A power sander with a rotary motion to give a finer finish.

ORBITAL SAWS—Besides the back and forth motion, this power saw has a rotary motion for faster cutting.

PACKING NUT—The nut under a faucet handle that keeps the "innards" inside.

PENNY—A term denoting the size of nails and designated by "d", which makes no sense but if we told you what it all means, we'd have to kill you.

PHILLIPS SCREWDRIVERS—No, it's not the tool belonging to somebody named Phillip. It is a tool with a crossing tip for screws that mate for a sounder fit.

PIER—A masonry footing used as part of some foundation systems.

PILOT HOLE—A starting hole for fasteners.

PILOT LIGHT—A small permanent flame that ignites when a gas furnace, water heater, or range call for heat.

PIPE JOINT COMPOUND—A putty-like substance used on threaded joints in plumbing for less likely leaks. Thanks to Teflon tape, this messy product has lost favor.

PLANE—A smoothing tool.

PLENUM—The chamber above the furnace from which heat ducts branch off.

PLIERS—A gripping tool.

PLUMB—Absolute true vertical.

PLUMBER'S AUGER—Also known as Plumber's Snake.

PLUMBER'S FRIEND—The plunger that handles drain clogs.

POINT—See TUCKPOINTING on page 207.

PRIMER—The sealer coat of paint.

PUNCH LIST—The homeowner's list of things that need to be taken care in a new or remodeled home.

PUTTY KNIFE—It is not actually a knife but a tool for applying various compounds.

PVC—Polyvinyl Chloride. The plastic pipe used for a variety of cold-water plumbing installations.

RAFTERS—The support framing for a roof.

RETAINING WALL—A wall built to prevent erosion of a sloping area.

RISER—The vertical piece between steps on a stairway.

ROUGHING IN—In construction, this is the period when plumbing and electrical components that will soon be covered up are put in place.

RUN—A length of electrical wiring or conduit.

R-VALUE—The R stands for resistance to heat transfer in insulation. The higher the R-value, the better the insulation.

SASH—The movable section of a window.

SCREED—A long board for the first smoothing of newly poured concrete.

SHEATHING—The outside material attached to studs and rafters.

SHIM—A thin material placed between two surfaces to bring them into level or plumb.

SHOE MOLD—The small molding piece that conceals the gap between the floor and the baseboard. It looks much like a quarter round.

SHORT CIRCUIT—An electrical problem brought about when hot and neutral wires touch.

SIDING—Any material used to cover the exterior walls of a structure.

SLIP JOINT PLIERS—The most common pliers that have a pivot rivet that slips into two or more positions for a better grip.

SNIPS—Metal trimming shears.

SOCKET SET—Wrenches with a drive handle that accept various sizes of sockets.

SOFFIT—The underside covering of the eaves overhang, a stairway, or an arch.

SOIL PIPE—A drain pipe from a house to the sewer system.

SOLE PLATE—The bottom horizontal member of a stud wall partition.

SPAN—The horizontal distance between structural supports

SPLINE—A flexible rubber-like material used to hold screening in a metal frame. Also a skinny piece of wood used for stronger joints.

STACK—The vertical drain line in a home's plumbing system.

STORY POLE—A pole with marks to help in making each course of bricks the right height without measuring.

STRIKE—The metal plate on a door frame that accepts the bolt of the doorknob.

STRINGER—The long heavy-duty zig-zag timber that supports a stairway.

STUDS—The vertical framing member of a wall system

TAPING BEDDING—The process of applying drywall tape over joints between gypsum board sections.

THERMOCOUPLE—A safety device that lets a gas valve know that the pilot light is lit.

THRESHOLD—The plate at the bottom of an exterior door.

TIMBER—What you yell when felling a tree! Also heavy duty lumber that is at least 5 inches in its smallest dimension

TOENAIL—Attaching boards by driving nails at an angle.

TOILET AUGER—A snake used is unclog a toilet.

TOP PLATE—The horizontal piece at the top of a stud wall.

TRAP—The u-shaped part of a drain that holds water to prevent sewer gas from entering the house.

UL—Underwriter's Laboratory. An independent testing organization that establishes minimum standards for primarily electrical devices.

UNDERLAYMENT—The material laid over the subfloor.

VALLEY—The place on a roof where two sloping surfaces come together.

VAPOR BARRIER—A membrane that prevents the passage of moisture.

VOLT—A measure of the pressure of electrical current.

WARPING—Distortion that occurs as a defect in lumber.

WATER CLOSET—An outdated polite term for toilet.

WATT—A measure of the rate at which electricity is consumed.

WIRE NUTS—Plastic connectors used in electrical wiring.

About the Authors

Al Carrell has been writing the syndicated column "Super Handyman" for more than three decades. He is also the host of a home repair show that has run in the Dallas/Fort Worth area for fifteen years, currently on KAAM. He cofounded and is regularly featured on *Your New House*, a nationally syndicated television show that runs in 150 markets. He has also appeared on *NBC Today*, *Good Morning America*, *Home Matters*, and *Our Home*. He has written seven books on home repair, including the best-selling *The Super Handyman's Encyclopedia of Home Repair Hints*, which was a *Popular Science* book club selection. He lives in the Dallas area.

Kelly Carrell has been assisting her father in writing the "Super Handyman" column for fifteen years and is the cohost of the home repair call-in radio show. She has appeared with her father on several television feature spots, including a segment on *Your New Home*, and has been both a cohost and a guest on several local radio shows. At home, she is the ultimate do-it-yourselfer and is known as the Super Handymom. She lives in the Dallas area.